THE ECONOMICS OF MANAGING LIBRARY SERVICE

THE ECONOMICS OF MANAGING LIBRARY SERVICE

Bruce P. Schauer

Drawings by Nolan Anderson

AMERICAN LIBRARY ASSOCIATION
Chicago and London 1986

Designed by Charles Bozett

Composed by Impressions, Inc.
   in Times Roman on a
   Penta-driven Autologic
   APS-μ5 Phototypesetting system

Printed on 50-pound Warren's 1854,
   a pH-neutral stock, by the
   University of Chicago
   Printing Department

Bound in B-grade Holliston linen cloth
   by Zonne Bookbinders

Library of Congress Cataloging-in-Publication Data

Schauer, Bruce P.
   The economics of managing library service.

   Includes index.
   1. Library finance. 2. Library science—Economic aspects. 3. Library administration—Economic aspects. 4. Microeconomics. I. Title.
   Z683.S33   1986   025.1′1   86-14186
   ISBN 0-8389-0453-X

Copyright © 1986 by the American Library Association. All rights reserved except those which may be granted by Sections 107 and 108 of the Copyright Revision Act of 1976.
Printed in the United States of America.

CONTENTS

FIGURES	vii
TABLES	ix
PREFACE	xi

I MICROECONOMIC THEORY

1. Microeconomics and Library Market Analysis	3
2. Consumer Preferences	20
3. Individual and Market Demand for Library Services	48
4. Library Production	79
5. Supply of Library Services	107
6. Equilibrium Analysis	134

II APPLICATIONS AND EXTENSION OF MICROECONOMIC THEORY

7. Quantitative Methods	153
8. Production Decisions	163
9. Information Economics	196
10. Cost-Benefit Analysis	215
11. Public Libraries: Community Finance	236

INDEX 273

FIGURES

1. Consumer's Budget Line   23
2. Effect of a Change in Price   25
3. Change in Income   26
4. Indifference Curve   30
5. Intersecting Indifference Curves   31
6. Indifference Curves   33
7. Equilibrium of the Consumer   35
8. Corner Equilibrium   37
9. Composite-Good Approach   37
10. Library Budget Allocation   38
11. Time and Money Constraints   40
12. Learning Curves   44
13. Impact of Learning on Budget Lines   45
14. Income-Consumption Curve   50
15. Engel Curves   51
16. Subsidies   52
17. Consumer's Demand Curve   54
18. Income and Substitution Effects   57
19. Substitute Library Commodities   60
20. Market Demand   62
21. Geometry of Elasticity   67
22. Price Elasticity and Price-Consumption Curves   67
23. Budget Line and Demand for Reading   74
24. Library Output   87
25. Average and Marginal Product Curves   89
26. Three Stages of Library Production   91

viii   Figures

27. Library Production   94
28. Library Isoquants   94
29. Marginal Rate of Substitution   97
30. Returns to Scale   100
31. Economies of Scale and Total Product Curves   101
32. Short-Run Total Cost Curves   111
33. Total Product and Total Variable-Cost Curves   112
34. Average Cost Curves   114
35. Average and Marginal Cost   115
36. Optimal Input Combinations   117
37. Long-Run Total Costs   119
38. Short- and Long-Run Cost Curves   121
39. Economies of Scale   123
40. Input Price Change   125
41. Short-Run Benefit Maximization   127
42. Long-Run Equilibrium   129
43. Long-Run Adjustment Process   130
44. Equilibrium   135
45. Technological Innovation   138
46. Direct vs. Indirect Delivery Method   139
47. Allocation Process   141
48. Long-Run Supply and Constant Costs   142
49. Seasonal Variations in Demand   144
50. Information Search   146
51. Consumer Demand for Information Search   146
52. Path to Equilibrium   148
53. Addition of Nonmutually Exclusive Events   158
54. Conditional Probability   160
55. Breakeven Chart   164
56. Standard Deviation   168
57. Regression Diagram   174
58. Correlation   179
59. Inventory Control Model   184
60. Operation in First 5 Minutes   191
61. Operation in Second 5 Minutes   191
62. Operation in Third 5 Minutes   191
63. Operation in Fourth 5 Minutes   191
64. Final State   192
65. Library Construction Tree Diagram   203
66. Acquisition System Decision Tree   207
67. EVSI for Cataloging Vendor Decision   211
68. Optimal Level of Information Service Output   239
69. Peak-Load Pricing   260

TABLES

1. Market Options   23
2. Library Output   87
3. Average and Marginal Product   88
4. Library Production Function   93
5. Total Cost Schedules   111
6. Stock Level Calculation Table   170
7. Circulation History   176
8. Circulation, Shelflist, Acquisitions   181
9. Reference Desk Activity   190
10. Probabilities of Reference Activities   191
11. Network Payoff Table   198
12. Minimum Payoff   199
13. Maximum Payoff   200
14. The Hurwicz Payoff Table   200
15. Minimax Regret Criterion   201
16. Survey Results   203
17. Probabilities of Completion Time   204
18. Payoff Table for Library Machinery   209
19. Choice with Perfect Information   209
20. Opportunity-Loss Table   210
21. Project Costs and Benefits   218
22. Alternative Circulation Costs   227
23. Net Gain in User Effort   228
24. Alternative Circulation Costs   228
25. Library Location Benefits   231
26. Benefit Evaluation for Library Location   232

PREFACE

Economics concerns itself with the ways in which scarce resources are allocated to achieve an objective. Scarcity is a fact which faces individuals, organizations, and governments alike. Limits on resources imply the need to make choices between having more of one thing and less of another. Microeconomics, in turn, provides us with a useful theoretical basis for analyzing choices. In particular, given objectives, it assists us in formulating techniques for determining the tradeoffs between alternative means for achieving desired ends. While economics does not supply us with the tools to answer some of the questions which arise in the production of library services, such as how to resolve a conflict between gains in efficiency and changes in income distribution, it does provide us with a method for analyzing the impact of a course of action on our objectives.

Unlike private firms, libraries lack useful output measures and prices for evaluating activities. However, the nature of the problem confronting information managers is analogous to that of the private firm, namely, to maximize the effectiveness of limited resources. Information producers are engaged in a multitude of activities, including the supply of facilities, open hours, journals, books, videos, staff, meeting rooms, reference services, circulation services, programs, and storage. To provide these services, the library combines inputs. An information manager must choose not only the quantity, quality and combination of outputs to supply, but also the quantity and mix of inputs to produce the output. For example, within a given facility the choice of where, or even whether, to store an item may affect access and, consequently, use (output); the number of staff may limit the number of open hours; and so on. Hence, there is a tradeoff between storage and access, between quantity of staff and number of open hours, and between alternative input combinations and output.

To evaluate our options, we must first acquire an understanding of consumers and producers. Microeconomics supplies us with a useful theory of consumer behavior and also of the nature of production, thereby permitting us to predict what may occur to use as we alter the input mix. Further, it details the way in which a balance can be achieved between conflicting objectives. Basically, we will analyze choices based on the added cost and added benefit of alternative courses of action.

As we have stated, information managers cannot adequately address policy decisions without an understanding of how consumers make decisions, of how production will be affected by altering the input mix, and of how the library is currently used. While microeconomics suggests decision guidelines, it doesn't supply us with all of the tools needed to analyze use and production data. Therefore, in the second half of the book we will extend microeconomic analysis and draw upon operations research and statistics, both of which rely on mathematical techniques. We will provide an introduction to some of the most important elements of quantitative decision models. In this manner, we intend to build a bridge between the economic theory presented in the first part of the text and the policy decisions that confront information managers.

Completion of this text would not have been possible without the support of the King County Library System, which granted me a six-month sabbatical. I extend a special thank-you also to Jana Varlejs, who recommended me to this project; to Michael Levin, who read the drafts and provided useful comments and criticisms; to Nolan Anderson, for illustrating the text; to my cats, Walter and Harold, for keeping me company while I prepared the manuscript; and to Anne Janisse, my best friend and partner, for keeping me in good humor these past four years.

I Microeconomic Theory

1

MICROECONOMICS AND LIBRARY MARKET ANALYSIS

THE ECONOMICS OF MANAGING LIBRARY SERVICE examines microeconomics and its application to library management problems. Its emphasis, however, will be on theoretical analysis, rather than investigation of existing library services. A theoretical approach has been chosen since it will allow for a more general application of economic analysis to information management. It permits us to make sense of complex situations. Moreover, for the purposes of explanation and prediction, a simple study of facts or historical circumstances will not suffice. Instead, we rely on theories to illustrate how events or facts are related to one another.

This book is written so that it will be of use to students and librarians with little mathematical background, as well as those with some interest in mathematics. With this in mind, the text is divided into two parts. Part 1 presents the central theoretical apparatus of microeconomics. This serves as a foundation for analyzing the behavior of libraries and their users. The second portion of the text begins with an introductory chapter that includes a discussion of the elements of probability theory and then goes on to practical applications of probability theory and economic reasoning.

Microeconomics is concerned with the allocation of limited resources among competing uses to fulfill human wants. Economic models, based on information relating causal factors to one another, can be used to predict alternative outcomes of policy decisions. Hence, the models presented in this text provide a valuable framework for examining library service production: selection of materials, loan policy, reference policy, and investment in resources for growth. In this chapter we will introduce a few key economic concepts, discuss the role of models, and provide an outline of this text. Subsequent chapters will include theory, applications, and problems for the reader to analyze.

Economists analyze the influence of economic variables—wages and prices—on group behavior. Individual decision-making units are studied in order to establish a logical relationship between individual behavior and that of the group. Specifically, economic theory is composed of propositions which are utilized to interpret economic behavior. The tools of analysis are based on the formulation of hypotheses and the deduction of predictions from them. Economic theory can be divided into micro, macro, static, and dynamic. Within the context of markets for goods and services, microeconomics is concerned with the mechanics of individual behavior. Macroeconomics, on the other hand, examines the behavior of economic aggregates, including the study of money, employment levels, and gross national product (GNP).

Static theory eliminates the time element; its objective is to determine the direction in which economic forces move in response to changes in other variables. In static analysis the focus of attention is on a particular aspect of analysis; other things will remain constant. For example, if we want to investigate the effect of a change in a library's loan period on use, we assume that there is no change in the supply of library materials. This is a simplifying mechanism which helps us to understand problems. Static theory does not attempt to establish connections between various conditions at points in time or how long such adjustments take.

The economic theory presented in this text is static analysis; it builds relationships between economic variables as they are at a moment in time. Although nothing else is considered, other things are going on at the same time. Nevertheless, we hold the latter constant and focus our attention on one aspect at a time, so as to understand the problem easily and clearly. (In contrast, dynamic models are specifically concerned with the time factor. Dynamic theory investigates the time required for adjustments to change and the conditions which lead to economic stability or instability over time.)

Economic theory provides the librarian a basis for understanding and analyzing events related to the consumption and production of library services. We will be concerned with the explanation and prediction of observed phenomena: What determines prices of library outputs? What affects the consumption choices of consumers?

Microeconomics encompasses the study of factors which influence these choices and the way in which these decisions merge to influence the workings of markets for goods and services. Prices, determined by the forces of markets, play an essential role in the decisions of economic entities. Price is a measure of value and can be expressed in terms of dollars, time, or other cost–related terms. In the context of the market for library services, the price the library pays for materials it uses to produce library services can be expressed in terms of dollars. The price consumers pay for library output can be expressed in terms of the time required to acquire the service. Demand theory furnishes a framework for understanding how price affects the quantity which consumers will demand. The theory of supply gives us the tools with which to analyze the role of price on quantity produced.

With an appreciation of supply and demand, librarians will be able to examine the economic impact of legal, technical, and other societal trends which affect the demand-and-supply relationships of information services. Specifically, microeconomic theories are useful in examining library costs, consumer demand, the "price" of library materials, the effect of technology on cost functions, production techniques, acquisition and weeding policies, fees, marketing, service evaluation, and other library-management concerns. In addition, based on economic theory, we will develop techniques which enable library managers to alter the library's operating environment to attain desired objectives. The combined effect of these capabilities should enable us to increase the benefits of library services to the library user and the taxpayer.

Library Decisions as Economic Problems

Libraries, as producers of information services, can be looked at in terms of the theory of markets, which includes the demand for and the supply of goods and services. We will examine library consumers in terms of demand theory, and its services in terms of supply theory. A library manager's central problem, evaluating choices within the context of limited resources, is analogous to the problems faced by all economic entities. Managers must select items which they will use to produce a particular array of library services whereas consumers must choose which items to purchase from a bundle of market commodities. Each market player is concerned with how to allocate his or her limited income. The principles of microeconomics are applicable to the understanding of the problem of choice. More generally, they are concerned with studying human behavior as a relationship between ends and scarce means. Economics does not suggest the end, only how to achieve the end with the minimum expenditure of effort.

A library must allocate resources among competing uses and must combine and process these resources to produce the level and composition of output which meet its objectives. In particular, public libraries are engaged in the production of information activities, including circulation, reference services, in-house use of materials, and programming. The production of each service involves the use of inputs: books, magazines, records, software, indexes, personnel, equipment, and facilities. Each input contains a quality dimension: (a) information—accuracy, intelligibility, timeliness, format, organization; (b) personnel—skills and knowledge; (c) facilities and equipment—design and location; and a quantity dimension—number of items, equipment, hours, etc.

Given a limited budget, library managers must make choices among outputs, which in turn involves selecting the level and composition of inputs needed to produce output. The nature of a library's problem is similar to that faced by consumers, firms, and other economic organizations: given scarcity, choose those resources and production techniques which maximize objectives. Microeconomics provides a method for analyzing the problem of choice and leads us to the formulation of resource-allocation techniques. Our aim is to identify a method for analyzing the tradeoffs involved in choosing among objectives, to determine the costs and benefits of utilizing resources, and to select the technique which maximizes our objective.

An example of a method of describing library activities in terms of supply/demand concepts highlights the value of creating an economic analog of library transactions. Libraries which are involved in interlibrary loan activities can be viewed as trading partners. Within this context, we can discuss the problems inherent in trade between two persons, countries, agencies, etc. The advantage of this methodology—the theory of exchange to analyze the interlibrary loan—is that it highlights the costs/benefits in transactions between two independent economic entities.

We conclude this section by observing that the problem of the library can be described as the efficient distribution of scarce resources among competing demands over time. This problem parallels that of all other economic entities, and is the focus of microeconomic analysis.

Definition of Economics

Economics is a useful tool for examining the dynamics of the organization, behavior, and operation of economic decision-making units. It has been defined as the scientific study of the method by which scarce resources are allocated among alternative ends to satisfy human wants. In general, it is concerned with the production, allocation, valuation, and consumption of goods and services. Usually, the study of economics is divided into two components: micro and macro. Microeconomics examines the behavior of individual economic units—the consumer, firm, etc.—whereas macroeconomics is concerned with the behavior of aggregated economic variables—levels of employment, GNP, international trade, etc. Microeconomics is the study of the organization of productive resources for the benefit of human wants.

Human wants are satisfied by goods, services, and experiences. Generally, wants are met by the service a good can render. That is, we want the enjoyment of reading a book, not necessarily the object itself. Although wants are not always met in the marketplace, microeconomics is concerned with the way in which the price system handles the allocation of scarce resources to satisfy wants. The model of the price system deals with how relative prices—the relation between prices—are determined. Price theory has several analytical categories: demand theory, supply theory, market organization, distribution of resources, general equilibrium, and welfare economics.

Demand-and-supply theory is concerned with what determines the price and quantity of goods and services sold in the market. The theory of demand addresses the question of how consumers make choices between work and leisure, between consumption and investment, and between goods and services for the purpose of satisfying wants. Supply theory examines the ways in which producers organize the factors of production to yield the output from which it derives its income. The way in which markets are organized—perfect competition, monopoly, etc.—has an effect on the price and quantity observed in input and output markets. Economists have developed models for a variety of forms of market organization: oligopoly, duopoly, and imperfect competition. Use of these models relies upon an understanding of the principles and mechanics developed in the perfectly competitive market model. Therefore, we will build an understanding of price theory by concentrating on perfect competition.

Distribution theory is concerned with what determines the prices and incomes of the factors of production, such as capital and labor. Stated differently, it is the analysis of how all that is produced in a country is shared by the constituents of society. If we view factors of production as goods and services, then the principles of demand-and-supply theory can be extended to cover factor markets.

We will analyze economic problems by using partial equilibrium analysis. This technique concentrates on the market for a single good or service, whereas general equilibrium examines the process by which all markets achieve equilibrium, the point at which supply equals demand, simultaneously. In contrast to those components of economic theory which are concerned with describing events, welfare economics utlizes price theory as a tool for evaluating economic efficiency and social welfare.

The focus of the first part of the text will be on demand and supply theory; in Part 2 we will concentrate on techniques for evaluating and improving economic efficiency.

Theory of Consumer Behavior and Demand

Consumption theory is concerned with understanding the process by which individuals allocate resources to satisfy human wants. While a person's desire for a particular good during a given time period is not insatiable, human wants, in the aggregate, are unlimited. *Resources* are objects or services used to produce goods which can be used to satisfy wants. Economic resources are scarce and command a nonzero price. There are goods and services for which no direct price is charged, but an indirect price is paid by the individual or the community for their use. (This special category of goods and services will be discussed in Chapter 11.) A good or resource which is not desired or which does not require effort or sacrifice to obtain is not an economic good. If it is not scarce, no economic problem exists, since all wants can be satisfied.

Given the condition of limited resources, consumers are forced to choose among alternatives. Since one cannot have all the goods and services desired, choice involves sacrificing one thing for another. Choices are constrained by costs, and *costs* are measured by what one gives up, exchanges, to acquire what is desired. The economic resource used in the process of obtaining wants is income, I. Income is often treated as money income. Price—a measure of sacrifice or value—and income are usually measured in terms of dollars per unit of good. The only purpose of money in the economic model is as a unit of account. We can substitute any commodity for money as a unit of account—time, or other goods and services.

To summarize, an economic resource is an object or service that is desired and scarce. Scarcity implies that, to obtain a want, something else must be sacrificed.

In the standard approach to the theory of consumer choice, preferences are represented by a utility function. *Utility* represents the value-in-use of a commodity or service. It is a subjective indication of the power of an object or experience to yield satisfaction. Utility is a relative concept. Changes in tastes, seasons, age, or fashion may affect the utility of a good or service. Thus, it may not only vary from individual to individual but also for an individual over time. Finally, utility is only used in reference to consumer goods, and not producer goods. A book may have utility for the person who uses it, but the machinery used to produce books does not yield satisfaction to the supplier. Use of the machine in production is guided by the profit motive and not by personal satisfaction.

Briefly, a *function* describes the relationship between one or more variables. A utility function provides information about the individual's willingness to exchange one good for another in a given market bundle. Another way of looking at this exchange is to note that the amount of goods, Y, that a consumer requires to compensate for the lost utility of a unit of X indicates the value, or price, of X.

The model of consumer choice that we will be investigating assumes that the consumer has a given income and treats the prices of goods and services as given. Based on this information, the consumer chooses a market basket which maximizes utility, subject to the constraint that the total expenditure on the goods and services purchased does not exceed income. The solution to the consumer's constrained maximization problem, the choice which yields maximum utility, depends upon the prices of goods and services and the amount of income. Thus, a library service consumer will be constrained by his or her income (time and/or money) and the prices (time and/or money) of library services and other items in the consumption bundle. The utility-maximizing quantity of library service is dependent upon relative prices and income.

Economists define the relationship between the quantity demanded of a good and prices and income as the demand function. We will show that the demand function exhibits an inverse relationship between the quantity demanded of a good and the price of a good when relative prices and income are held constant. That is, as the price of library services decreases, the quantity demanded will increase. This relationship between the quantity demanded of a good and its price is known as the *law of demand*. We can use this general relationship to analyze "library consumption" decisions and to predict the outcomes of changes in incomes and relative prices on the choices of library consumers.

Theory of the Firm

The firm is an economic entity that employs and combines inputs to produce goods and services which are sold to consumers. Resources that are used to produce an economic product are defined as *inputs*. Inputs have a variety of uses in the production process. Alternative uses may be limited in the short run. For example, human capital may have to be retrained to be of value in a new production setting, a machine may have to be refitted, the production process may have to be reorganized, etc., and this takes time. The longer the period of time under study, the more flexible resources are considered to be.

The classical economic division of resources has been land, labor, and capital. Although each category contains numerous types of resources, this device is a convenient shorthand for defining classes of resources. *Land* is generally understood to mean natural resources; *labor* is expressed as human effort; and *capital* includes buildings, equipment, inventories, etc. A fourth category has been added to some schema, and is usually considered to be a component of labor: entrepreneurship. *Entrepreneurship* is defined as the mental effort required in the production, marketing, and distribution of goods and services.

Libraries combine people, equipment, inventory, and buildings to produce information goods and services. Thus, information goods and services are economic resources; they take time to gather and process for use. This process involves a variety of knowledge-intensive activities, from the organization of materials to in-depth reference services. Other productive activities of the library include document delivery via interlibrary loan, circulation services, cultural activities, and warehousing/curatorial services.

In microeconomic theory, the analytical device used to represent the technological process by which firms transform inputs into outputs is known as a *production* function. *Technology* is defined by economists as the bank of knowledge concerning the production process. This includes knowledge of the principles of physical and social phenomena and their application to the agricultural, industrial, and service sectors of the economy. Technology sets the limit on the quantity and mix of goods and services that can be produced from a given amount of inputs. A production function, in the form of a table, a graph, or an equation, expresses the relationship between the different combinations of inputs per period of time and the maximum quantity of output that can be produced per period of time. In essence, the production function summarizes the technological constraints facing the firm. Examination of the economic theory of production functions will supply useful insights into library operations.

Typically, in the production of outputs the firm can substitute inputs, so that a number of input combinations will produce a given output. Given limited resources, the problem facing the firm is to choose that combination of inputs which yields the desired output at the least total cost. Firms, constrained by the prices of inputs and the current state of technology, face a problem analytically similar to that of the consumer's maximization problem. Just as the consumer maximizes utility for a given budget, the firm faces the problem of maximizing output for a given level of cost. The primary difference is that the firm and the consumer have fundamentally different objectives. Consumers seek to achieve a level of satisfaction while firms attempt to achieve maximum profit.

Likewise, the problem facing library managers is to maximize output for a given level of cost. Unlike firms, which use price to guide final output, the library manager must employ a surrogate indicator of value. That value may be guided by library use or some weighted measure of use.

In the theory of the firm we find that, for a given output and given input prices, we can derive the input combination which produces that output at the lowest total cost. The relationship between output and the cost of producing that output is known as the *total-cost* function. For each level of output, the total-cost function depicts the production cost when the least-cost, or optimal, mix of inputs is chosen. If we assume that the firm chooses output levels to maximize profits, and if the firm is a "price taker" (i.e., it does not influence prices) in the output market, then the amount the firm will supply at any given commodity price can be derived from the total-cost function. The association between commodity price and the quantity supplied by the firm is defined as the *supply function* of the firm. Determining an industry supply schedule depends upon the nature of the product and type of industry. Thus, the study of the library as a firm involves an understanding of production function, as well as the relationship between output level and cost and between price and output level.

Organization of Markets

Markets for goods and services involve the interplay of the economic agents involved in the production, sale, or purchase of a particular commodity or service. They refer to the linking of the demand for and supply of an economic good. For example, the fact that the price of serials is rising faster than the price of monographs reflects the workings of those markets. The impact of automated circulation systems depends upon how the affected markets—supply of and demand for circulation-related services—respond. Relatively lower prices for paperbacks have influenced the demand for hardback editions. As you see, to understand the economics of library services we must study the workings of markets.

To analyze markets, we will focus on factors which influence the decisions of individuals and firms. Initially, we concentrate on the impact that price has on buyers and sellers. Both economic agents of demand (consumers) and supply (firms) take prices as given—"price takers." By combining these two segments of the market we are able to determine both the quantity and price of goods and services in the marketplace. The mechanism that illustrates the interplay of buyers and sellers is usually described in terms of demand-and-supply curves. *Demand* is the relationship between price and quantity demanded; *supply* represents the association between price and quantity supplied.

Market demand-and-supply curves represent the aggregation of consumers and firms, respectively. The interaction between supply and demand determines the quantity which will be supplied and purchased at the market price. Both sides of the market are affected by economic forces, including preferences, technology, weather, and the prices of related goods. Thus, supply-and-demand analysis provides a powerful tool for analyzing the effects of changes in economic variables related to the quantity consumers demand and firms supply of a particular good or service and the price at which exchanges occur.

Partial vs. General Equilibrium Analysis

Partial equilibrium analysis is concerned with the way in which price and quantity are determined in a single market. According to the microeconomic model we will develop, price and quantity are determined by supply-and-demand curves, which are derived under the assumption that the prices of other goods and services are constant. In other words, each market is viewed as independent of other markets—or as if changes in one market do not cause significant changes in price in other markets. While this approach is valuable in the study of a wide variety of theoretical and practical problems, its basic assumption may not always apply. Thus, changes in one market *may* affect the price and quantity in other markets. General equilibrium analysis broadens the scope of microeconomic theory by taking into account the interrelationships between prices.

Both partial and general equilibrium analysis are valuable analytical devices. Partial equilibrium analysis would be adequate where the price of a commodity which is not related to library services changes, but when prices in other markets have a significant impact on the prices of library services, we would use general equilibrium analysis. For example, if the price of transportation has a significant effect on the supply and/or demand of library services, a general equilibrium analysis would give a clearer picture of the ramification of a change in the price of fuel on the price of information services.

Positive and Normative Analysis

In economics, we draw a distinction between the study of how things are and how they ought to be. The component of price theory that describes the consequences of events which have an effect on markets is known as *positive* analysis. In contrast, price theory can be used as a normative device for evaluating desirability, or the economic welfare effect. Normative economics is concerned with the goods and services that ought to be produced, how production should be organized, and how factors of production and income should be distributed among the members of society (including those not yet born). Deciding whether particular economic arrangements are better than others requires a criterion for determining what is best. Any such criterion, or value judgment, is based on the social perspective of the evaluator rather than on models or theories.

To make a statement concerning the net impact of a policy in terms of its desirability involves both positive analysis, to determine objective outcomes, and a subjective value judgment. Consider a change in library materials circulation policy, in which patrons will no longer be allowed to request particular materials. To determine the desirability of this policy, we evaluate its impact in terms of (a) how it affects the use of these materials, and which user groups will benefit and which will lose benefits? (b) how much does use change and how many people gain or are harmed? and (c) does the benefit outweigh the cost?

The first two steps involve identifying the qualitative and quantitative nature of the consequences of the new policy. These steps describe objective, testable outcomes of policy and lie within the realm of positive analysis. Note that the determination of objective outcomes relies on propositions which can be tested on the internal logic of the analysis and on the basis of empirical evidence. Microeconomic analysis, a form of positive analysis, is based on the standard rules of logic and evidence that are useful in ascertaining the truth or falsity of statements.

On balance, to decide the normative consequences of policy requires judgments which cannot be tested by fact or logic. That is, notions of desirability rely upon definitions which cannot be supplied by scientific technique or analysis. Nonetheless, economists have developed a welfare criterion, based on positive analysis, for evaluating economic welfare. Positive analysis assists us in determining the likely outcomes of policy, and welfare criteria, based on a few generally accepted principles of appraisal, are utilized to render judgments on the desirability of policy.

Welfare criteria are based on appraisal principles that are useful in making judgments of an economic system. Normative economics has developed three such principles. The first principle is that an economy is to be judged on the basis of the private and public goods and services it produces and consumes over time. Goods and services produced, an indication of wealth, are not studied for their own sake but because they are capable of promoting human welfare. Economics views wealth as the means and welfare as the end. *Wealth* is expressed in terms of goods and services, while *welfare* refers to net satisfaction. Economists use the value of output as a way of comparing economic alternatives. Thus, the first principle is used to analyze the question of whether or not, given resource limits, society can improve upon the existing market bundle, thereby increasing the well-being of society.

The second principle suggests that an individual is the only judge of how a particular market basket affects his or her sense of well-being. Some societies place limits on principle 2—usually on children and the mentally handicapped and on the effects of certain activities: speech, religion. Finally, statements concerning the desirability of economic events are dependent upon individual appraisals of individual welfare, rather than an evaluation based on a group concept of what society ought to be.

Perhaps the most often used welfare criterion for normative appraisals of the economy is the Pareto optimality criterion. Pareto optimality (or economic efficiency) is defined in terms of the well-being of people. An "efficient" outcome is one that makes people as well off as possible. The criterion suggests that an efficient distribution of goods exists when no possible reallocation of resources will make one better off without making one or more economic units worse off. Roughly speaking, economists use the Pareto principle to analyze and evaluate the process of exchange. For instance, if in one equilibrium, A, no one is worse off than in another, B, but at least one economic agent is better off in A than in B, then the particular assignment of economic resources, production, and distribution of goods and services in A is judged to be superior.

The Pareto principle cannot be used to evaluate the redistribution of resources (this applies to the configuration of resources between all such economically feasible states). In other words, the Pareto criterion does not allow us to compare two states in which one or more economic agents gain at the expense of others, nor does it allow us to compare the social outcomes which lie on a curve representing the limit on economically feasible welfare outcomes. Yet, if a change must be made on grounds other than efficiency, the Pareto principle indicates that efficient points are generally preferred over inefficient points.

For instance, assume points A and E are efficient points, but at point A, Person 1 is wealthy while Person 2 is very poor. Now assume that a move to point D, an inefficient point, or to point E would make Person 2 equally better off at the expense of Person 1. We cannot use the Pareto principle to compare points A and E, but we can state that if we must make a change on grounds other than efficiency, in this instance point E is clearly preferred to point D.

We must be careful, however, not to conclude that any efficient point is better than any inefficient point, for to do so would ignore the change in the distribution of satisfaction. While economists may seek to prove that one scenario is more efficient than another, there are other goals besides efficiency. Nonetheless, there will usually be an efficient point that makes two parties better off than an inefficient point.

The notion of compensating losers helps us address comparisons between states where one party benefits and another loses. This concept of potential for compensation is used in cost-benefit analysis, but in reality, policy rarely involves actual compensation. Evaluating movements along the social production function curve relies upon welfare theories that lie beyond the scope of this text. As it concerns library services, the Pareto optimality criterion is useful in evaluating those resource, production, and distribution configurations which can be compared within the bounds set in the preceding paragraphs.

Economic Models

The basic methodology used to conduct economic analysis is similar to that used to conduct other types of scientific analysis: formulation of models. *Models* are abstractions, or simplifications, of a real system. Models can be represented by tables, diagrams, or systems of equations. The process of model building involves making a number of assumptions about a system. Based on these assumptions, predictions can be deduced. Assumptions serve the purpose of simplifying and abstracting from reality; they permit the economist to generalize. Since we cannot consider all the complex factors which affect outcomes, we seek to examine only the important factors. Hence, we will be making assumptions that reveal the essential causal relationships between economic forces.

One may ask how generalizations or theories are established in a field of study which cannot conduct experiments. Economists construct a model of the real world, repressing features deemed not to be essential while emphasizing others. We abstract, simplify, and isolate to create order. Finally, based on a process of logical deduction, we make predictions which are tested by comparing observable events against what the theory predicts. Testable predictions serve to validate or invalidate a hypothesis. If a hypothesis yields predictions which are repeatedly borne out by observable outcomes, we accept it. Thus, one would test our assumptions about the behavior of consumers by comparing predictions of the hypothesis with observations from the real world.

The value of a hypothesis depends in part on how accurate a prediction we require. Of course, a model which predicts with a high degree of accuracy is highly useful. Other tests of a model's predictions include testing the logical consistency of assumptions and whether or not the predictions flow from the logic of the assumptions. We can also evaluate the merits of a model on the basis of the generality of its applications. For example, a model which predicts a particular individual's choices would have less value than one which attempts to predict the choices of the behavior of a large group of individuals. While the latter model, which ignores a number of details, is less precise than the former, it has a greater number of applications. The validity of its applications can be tested by fact, empirical evidence, or logic.

To summarize, economists build models so as to simulate real working systems. Due to the complexity of real systems, models are used to simplify, for the purpose of understanding and predicting. The value of a model lies in within the generality and accuracy of its predictions, both of which can be tested by scientific analysis.

Economists use models to test economic theories, to make forecasts, to simulate economic events, and to evaluate the impact of economic policy. Theoretical models reflect an economist's notion of how, given particular assumptions, economic entities will behave. Behavioral assumptions are usually based on the principles of maximization and equilibrium. A system of equations may be set up to define the model. Equations illustrate the relationships between two or more factors, such as input and output, economic payment and productivity, and profits and revenue and cost. Input-output relationships usually express scientific or engineering relationships; behavioral assumptions are related to economic rewards, and indicate how economic decisions are made; and the profit relationship is based on a definition. These relationships can be expressed in a static or a dynamic model. The interrelated components of static models are all dated at the same point in time, whereas a dynamic model interrelates economic magnitudes over time.

Plan of Study

As we have suggested, the economist's paradigm provides a way of looking at the world. Given scarcity, individual economic agents are assumed to follow certain guidelines in an attempt to maximize their well-being. Consumers base decisions upon income, prices, and preferences. Underlying the choices of producers are input prices, input productivity, and the price of output. Markets, acting to allocate resources, link the two activities in such a way as to make their behavior mutually consistent. Microeconomics examines the ways in which choices are made by individuals operating within the context of scarcity. We use theory to explain and predict the behavior of people, households, and firms as a response to changes in income, tastes, technology, and prices. In addition, economists are interested in the means by which resources can be traded or combined to produce satisfaction.

To accomplish this objective, the text is divided into two parts; and Part 1 is concerned with developing an understanding of positive economic theory. Based on the condition of scarcity, our intention is to develop and describe the principles that lead to the maximization of utility and output and the minimization of costs. Part 2 extends the theory presented in Part 1 to develop techniques for managing information services.

Chapter 2 presents a simple model of consumer preferences. The discussion enables us to understand the process of choice and to predict how much of various goods and services a consumer is likely to purchase. Our model focuses on two of the most common factors which influence consumer behavior: the objective ability of the consumer to obtain goods and services, determined by the consumer's income and the prices of goods and services, and the consumer's preferences concerning the relative desirability of various levels and combinations of goods and services. For the sake of simplicity, we initially concern ourselves with income and prices measured in dollars. Since most libraries do not charge for their services, later in Chapter 2 we will incorporate the notion of time as a measure of cost. We will relate this concept of cost to consumer choice in the library and between library services and other goods. To build a model of consumer behavior, we introduce the concepts of utility, indifference curves, marginal rate of substitution or exchange, and the budget line. In addition to being useful for analyzing and predicting the behavior of consumers, the model of consumer tastes will assist us in understanding the forces underlying markets.

Chapter 3 builds upon the methodology developed in Chapter 2—to study how consumers respond to changes in income and to prices, and the means by which goods and services can be exchanged and combined to maximize utility. Based on reactions to changes in income and prices, we derive an individual's demand curve for library services. Some of the major concepts presented in this chapter include the income and price consumption curves, elasticity, substitution and income effects, and normal and inferior goods. These concepts are useful in understanding how individuals respond to changes in their income and the price of library services, and form the basis of marketing theories.

Chapter 4 describes the firm in terms of its technology. We will begin to develop the analysis of the factors which determine the level and mix of goods and services a firm will offer for sale. To begin, we examine the physical relationship between inputs and output. The productivity of inputs determines how much output can be produced, while input prices limit the amount of particular inputs a firm can employ. In the process of developing a model of the firm, we will discuss the motivation of the firm, and provide methods for representing input productivity, the law of diminishing marginal returns, and returns to scale.

Chapter 5 presents a framework for examining how a firm chooses an optimal input combination and the nature of production costs. In particular, we will define production costs; we will also examine the factors which affect costs and how costs vary with the level of output produced. In Chapter 6, the theories of supply and demand are combined to complete our model of markets. We look at markets to investigate the workings of the price system. Prices signal the individual economic agents of the market as to the cost and value of goods and services. Given prices, each side of the market, acting within the context of scarcity, strives to maximize some measure of well-being: utility, community benefit, profit. It is in this chapter that we will show how price is determined in the market and how changes in the factors which affect demand and supply alter the market price and quantity. We will show how these results can be used to shed light on library-management issues.

As an introduction to Part 2, Chapter 7 will sketch the basic concepts of probability. Chapter 8 will cover breakeven analysis and its applicability to collection development and information storage options. In addition, we will extend probability theory to several models of inventory control and waiting lines. In Chapter 9, we explore methods for making decisions under uncertainty. Estimates of risk can be obtained from prior knowledge, experimentation, or consultation. Our investigation of this topic will lead us to formulate several rules and techniques for making decisions under uncertainty. Applications include the purchase of alternative acquisition systems and estimating the value of a consultant's advice.

Chapter 10 presents the elements of cost-benefit analysis as applied to library investment decisions. While the costs of a library may be relatively easy to identify and measure, the benefits are not. We will examine techniques for establishing the benefits of library service and the issues that surround various types of benefits. In Chapter 11, we will discuss public library finance—more specifically, the rationale for financing library services vis-à-vis taxes, direct user charges, or some combination of the two methods, as well as the implications of the way in which they are funded. We will also review pricing theory and its application to information services.

Summary

Economics is concerned with the allocation of scarce resources among competing uses over time. In particular, it is concerned with the use of these resources in production and with the level, composition, and distribution of goods and services to the members of society. These activities are directed toward the satisfaction of human wants. Economic resources are used to satisfy human wants; and to obtain the use of a resource requires sacrifice. Microeconomics examines individual economic units to understand how their combined decisions, coordinated through market interactions, affect society. The methodology used to study the behavior of complex economic phenomena involves the building of models. Models are composed of a set of propositions from which conclusions are derived. Abstract theories and models neglect certain variables and relationships while emphasizing considerations that are presumed to have an important effect on the phenomena that models are designed to predict. Important tests of a model's value include its ability to help explain or predict the behavior of the phenomena under investigation, the range of behavior to which it can be applied, and its adherence to the rules of logic.

The individual, the firm, and the economic system are all faced with the problem of allocating scarce resources among competing ends. We will examine the library as though it were a firm supplying resources in response to demand. The library employs inputs to produce a wide variety of information services, and input choices involve setting the level and quality of the resource to be employed. Library managers select the number and types of personnel, books, records, software, and equipment—even the number of branches, their location, and number of open hours, as well as checkout periods, and renewal and fine policy. Facing a constraint (limited budget) on the ability to employ economic resources, the library manager must make choices about the number and types of inputs to purchase and the range of information activities the library intends to perform. Each library must choose which services it will provide, how it will provide them, and in what quantity. Choice within the context of scarcity involves tradeoffs—costs and benefits—between two or more economic magnitudes. A library can operate with few branches or many, long or short hours, more or fewer personnel, and more or fewer books. And within each location, similar choices must be made. Microeconomics, concerned with the problem of choice, suggests rules and procedures that aid librarians in understanding their markets and utilizing resources efficiently.

Exercises

1. Relate the tasks of an economic entity to a library.
2. Describe the difference between a statement, such as 10 percent of the library's users are children, and a model which attempts to predict use patterns on the basis of economic variables.

3. If you were modeling an interlibrary loan system, which variables would you devote most of your attention to?
4. Assume that the library is going to purchase computer terminals for the cataloging department. List some of the variables you would examine prior to purchase.
5. What is the difference between positive analysis and normative analysis?
6. If a good or service is not being used, does this suggest that it isn't scarce?
7. Which is more useful, a model which predicts why a particular library consumer chooses mysteries or a model which predicts what causes a group of individuals to use more or less library service?
8. How is price established in the market for a particular library service?
9. What determines how much of a particular commodity a consumer can purchase?
10. Explain the role of markets.

Suggested Reading

Alcahin, Armen, and William Allen. *Exchange and Production: Competition, Coordination and Control.* 2nd ed. Belmont, Calif: Wadsworth, 1977.

Cohen, M., and E. Nagel. *An Introduction to Logic and Scientific Method.* New York: Harcourt Brace, 1934.

Friedman, Milton. "The Methodology of Positive Economics." In *Readings in Microeconomics,* ed. William Breit and Harold Hochman. New York: Holt, Rinehart & Winston, 1971.

Marshall, Alfred. *Principles of Economics.* London: Macmillan, 1920.

2

CONSUMER PREFERENCES

The consumer preference model developed in this chapter supplies a foundation for predicting the quantities of information services a consumer may select. The basic model, developed for a single consumer, serves as a building block for understanding the behavior of groups of consumers. We will discuss how the interaction of preferences, prices, and incomes affects consumer choice. Using these concepts, we will construct a consumer budget-allocation model. Income and prices represent the objective ability of the consumer to obtain goods and services; preferences, the subjective component of our model, indicate the relative desirability of goods and services. Consumers, who seek information to achieve some personal objective, judge the value of information on its ability to contribute to their utility. The problem facing the consumer is to allocate a limited income among a variety of priced goods and services in such a way as to maximize some measure of well-being. Economic theory furnishes us with an analytical structure for investigating the process of consumer choice within the framework of subjective evaluations known as *benefits* and objective limits known as *costs*. Information managers can employ consumer theory as an input to policy decisions.

Although library services are not directly priced, the basis for selecting particular library services is analogous to choosing other products. Initially, for the sake of simplicity, price will be expressed in terms of money. Later in the chapter, we will extend the model of consumer choice to incorporate the notion of time, instead of dollars, as the measure of price. Our goal is to build a model which helps us to predict how much of various information goods and services a consumer will purchase.

Ultimately, information managers are interested in meeting the current and anticipated demands of consumers in their service area. Consumer preference theory provides a prelude to analyzing the demand for library services. Why do people come to the library? What affects this choice? And, once in the library, how do consumers choose library materials? In information markets, a varied clientele visits the library with a wide range of information wants. These wants, the subjective component of our model, are based on factors which may vary with age, education, income, and other preference-related variables. The objective ability to translate information wants into goods and services depends upon the prices of information services, income, and the prices of other goods. Together, wants and objective ability determine how consumers behave in libraries. Hence, an understanding of the mechanics of consumer choice can assist information managers in policy decisions.

The medium of exchange in the library marketplace is time not money. In some instances, library personnel are asked for guidance in finding information; in other exchanges the consumer utilizes indexes provided by the library; some consumers simply browse; and some consumers employ a combination of these information-seeking activities. In each of these situations time is used to acquire a particular information want.

On what basis do consumers choose to use one of these information-gathering techniques? How much of any of these activities is based on prior knowledge of the services of a library and how much is determined by the nature of a given library market's trade environment? (By *trade environment* we mean the amount of information the library provides the consumer: indexes, types of catalogs, signs, graphic instruction [pamphlets], method of library organization, and number and type of staff.) In other words, how do libraries simulate traditional price markets? What types of signals do they provide the consumer—how is the choice process facilitated? Through catalogs, signs, lists, reviews, annotations? Once a consumer has chosen an information-gathering technique how does he or she choose the information itself? Depending upon the nature of the information, do they choose by author, review, friend, publication date, cover, number of illustrations, readability, or availability? Although it is not necessary to know exactly how each consumer chooses information, it is of more than passing value to understand how particular classes of information are sought and found. Our model will provide us with techniques for analyzing these questions and thereby yield clues to their answers.

In the next few sections we will construct a model for representing the way in which preferences affect the choice process. The model, developed for a single consumer, will serve as the foundation for analyzing the behavior of groups of consumers. Therefore, we center our discussion around common factors which influence consumer choices. Our model of consumer preference consists of two primary aspects, objective ability and subjective evaluations by the consumer. Income and price, the objective component, place limits on consumption options. The final choice is dependent upon this limit and a

22   Microeconomic Theory

subjective evaluation of one's options. To build the model of choice, we introduce and develop concepts which allow us to represent these two factors.

By the end of this chapter, you should be able to employ these tools to gain some insights into the mechanics of choice and ways in which we can think of our constituency and our library resources.

Budget Lines

The first step in building a model of consumer choice will be to represent the objective constraint. Then, to highlight the mechanism of constrained choice, we will focus our attention on a two-goods situation. To simplify the analysis, we assume that the consumer must allocate all income to these two goods. Given that the consumer must allocate all income on two goods, information services (l) and shelter (s) we can express this case as

$$I = PlQl + PsQs \qquad \text{Eq. 2.1}$$

where I is income, PlQl is the price times quantity of information service units, and PsQs is defined in the same manner for shelter. Algebraically, when I, Pl, and Ps are constants, this equation defines a straight line. Then, if we solve the equation for Qs, we have

$$Qs = (I/Ps) - (Pl/Ps)(Ql) \qquad \text{Eq. 2.2}$$

The X and Y intercepts of this line are found by dividing income by the price of the good represented on the respective axis of the graph. An intercept indicates the amount the consumer could buy of either good if all the consumer's income was allocated on one good. The slope of this line is determined by the prices of the two commodities and is the coefficient of Ql or minus the ratio of prices, $-Pl/Ps$.

The line we have constructed is known as the *budget line*. A budget represents a constraint against which the consumer must make decisions; it identifies the boundary of opportunities available to a consumer. Our hypothetical consumer has the option of choosing any market basket on or inside the options (budget) line. Points inside the line involve income expenditures less than the consumer's income, and any point outside the budget line requires outlays larger than the consumer's income. In essence, an options line identifies the limits of scarcity for our consumer and forces choices among possible alternatives.

As we have indicated, income and the prices of goods and services limit economic choices. A study of a hypothetical consumer who has a weekly income of $240 that can be used to purchase information services and shelter will serve as a useful point to begin our discussion of budget lines. Let us assume that the price of a unit of information service, Pl, is $4 and that the

Table 1
MARKET OPTIONS

Options	Shelter	Information Services
A	30	0
B	25	10
C	20	20
D	15	30
E	10	40
F	5	50
G	0	60

price of a unit of shelter, Ps, is $8. Table 1 lists alternative market options that can be purchased by our consumer. Baskets A and G represent market options which involve spending all of one's income on a given product. The other market baskets in Table 1 are alternative market options which cost $240.

Another technique for presenting the data in Table 1 is shown in Figure 1, where the vertical axis represents quantity of shelter and the horizontal axis indicates the quantity of information services. Line AG connects the market options which are available to the consumer, given income, and is the budget

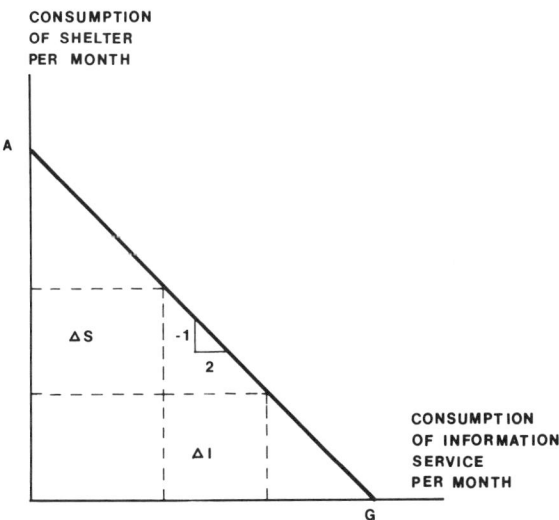

FIG. 1. Consumer's Budget Line

line. Based on the assumption that fractional units may be purchased/selected (assumption of continuous divisibility), we draw the budget line as a continuous line rather than a number of points, such as A,D,G. At first glance, this may seem to be an unreasonable assumption. Can you purchase one-quarter of a novel, one-half of a movie? The answer lies in viewing consumption as the average consumption of a good per unit of time—that is, one-half a novel per week is the same as one novel every two weeks.

To illustrate the importance of the price-ratio concept, we use the notion of tradeoffs. The slope of the budget line equals the rate of change in the straight line, or the amount of information service units the consumer must sacrifice to purchase one more unit of shelter. Given that the price of library service is $4 per unit and the price of shelter is $8 per unit, our consumer must exchange one-half unit of shelter for an additional unit of information service. Hence, we say that the slope of the line, determined by prices, indicates the relative cost of each good. In this case, the slope of the budget line, minus the ratio of the prices, or $-1/2$, tells us that shelter costs twice as much as information service.

So far, we have examined the objective constraint on the consumer's problem of choice. The extent to which consumers are able to purchase library services depends on a number of factors, including their income and prices. We used an information service and a noninformation service to highlight the process of allocating income, given prices. This example can be extended to two types of information services (materials, search strategies, etc.), and in the course of this text we will discuss these types of consumer allocation decisions. In the next section, we will illustrate the impact of changes in income and prices on the consumer's options.

Changes in Prices and Income

The level of income and relative prices determine a given budget line. Thus, changes in income or prices will cause the budget line to shift. The next two sections will introduce the effect of price and income changes on budget lines. A detailed discussion of the impact of income and price changes on consumer behavior can be found in Chapter 3.

PRICE CHANGES   Assume that the price of one library service, bookmobile service units, increases while income and the price of books-by-mail service units are held constant; and let the initial budget line be AF. As shown in Figure 2, the effect of an increase in the price of bookmobile service units causes the budget line to shift from AF to A'F. Recall that the vertical and horizontal intercepts are derived by dividing income by the price of the respective library service. Thus, when income remains constant and the price of one good goes up, while the other stays the same, one intercept will decrease

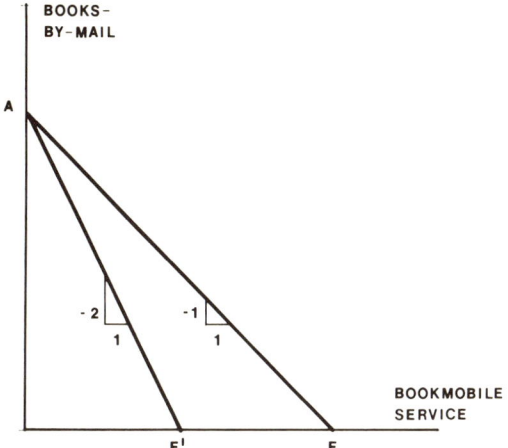

FIG. 2. Effect of a Change in Price

and the other stays constant. Observe that the vertical intercept has remained constant while the horizontal intercept has decreased. The inward movement of the options line reflects the fact that when income and the book-by-mail price are held constant, our consumer is further constrained by the increase in the relative price of bookmobile service.

From our previous discussion of budget lines we know that the slope measures relative prices. Thus, the new slope reveals that the price of one of the services has become more expensive in terms of the other service. For example, assume that our initial budget line, AF, had a slope of $-1/1$, $-P(BMS)/P(BBM)$, which illustrates the fact that books-by-mail has a price equal to bookmobile service. Given the recent price change, the new slope, $-2/1$, indicates that the relative price of bookmobile service is now twice that of books-by-mail. Note that if both prices should change in the same direction by the same proportions, the slope of the budget line will not be affected. For example, if, during a period of inflation, wages and prices change at the same rate, then the entire budget line would stay the same.

To summarize, changes in prices affect either the X or Y intercept and alter the slope of the budget line. We depict this change by shifting the budget line on the axis where the price has been changed. An increase in price, shown as a "shifting in" of the budget line, indicates fewer choices. Price decreases allow for greater choice, and are shown as a "shifting out" of the budget line. Since budget lines represent the limit that prices and income place on consumers, they are a powerful device for examining the impact of changes in price on the objective ability of consumers to make choices.

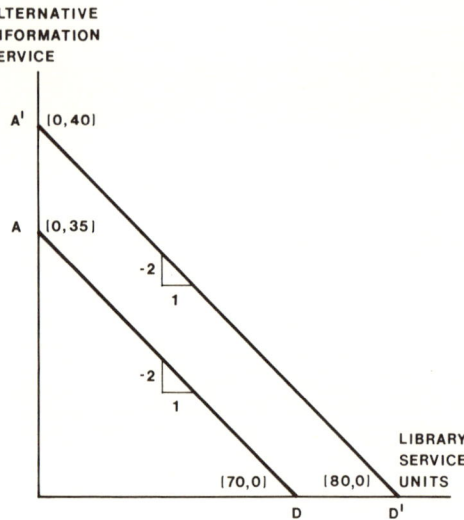

Fig. 3. Change in Income

INCOME CHANGES Budget line AD in Figure 3 is drawn for an income of $280/week, a price of $4 per library service unit, and $8/unit of an alternative information service. Increasing the consumer's income to $320/week, while keeping prices constant, results in a new budget, line A'D'. The new budget line shows the maximum amount of each service that the consumer can purchase. Observe that the change in income has caused a parallel shift in the budget line. This occurs because prices have remained constant while income has increased. In other words, the ratio of prices, the slope, has remained constant, but changes in income give us new horizontal and vertical intercepts. In this example, since income has increased, our consumer can obtain more of both goods, but the rate at which one good can be exchanged for another has not been altered.

The usefulness of this model for analyzing the impact of income changes on library services may not be obvious. Since libraries do not charge money prices, how does a change in income affect choice? If consumer income increases, how do we diagram the effect on libraries? For the moment, we simply note that as income increases, our consumer is able to purchase more library service units by means of higher taxes or increased leisure time. Regardless of the actual outcome, this model illustrates a method for analyzing changes in the income of consumers.

Now that we have shown how income and prices form the constraint on the consumer's ability to purchase goods and services, we are ready to examine the next element of our model, preferences. Having accomplished this, we will then be able to bring the two sides of the constrained choice equation, objective ability and subjective willingness to exchange, together and find its solution.

Consumer Preferences

Casual observation of library-service consumers shows that there are wide differences between their preferences for these services. To represent this diversity and still account for the importance of tastes on choice, economists have developed some basic propositions concerning human behavior. They identify characteristics that are thought to be shared by a majority of people, but these characteristics are not used to explain why a person holds certain beliefs or tastes.

Economics does not have an acceptable theory of how tastes are formed or why they change. Instead, economists take preferences as given; they then build a model which seeks to illustrate the influence of consumer preferences on the consumer's constrained resource allocation problem. Recall that assumptions serve to simplify and abstract from reality. By assuming constancy, we are able to represent the way in which a particular factor exercises its influence on choices. For example, in the library market we observe regular patterns of use associated with time of day and types of materials. When we assume that preferences are constant, we are able to analyze the effect of other factors on these patterns, such as changes in staffing, open hours, loan period, duplication policy, and method of delivery, independent of any change in tastes. Of course, tastes can change, and if we recognize such an occurrence we will be able to incorporate this into our analysis.

To construct a model of consumer tastes, economists have developed three basic axioms about the nature of consumers' preferences. The first axiom assumes that one can evaluate a variety of market options and rank them in order of preference. Consumers will prefer market option X over option Y, option Y over option X, or be indifferent between the two. For instance, a library user may prefer mysteries over romances, or may find romances and mysteries equally satisfactory—the latter indicating indifference between two types of services.

The second assumption is that the ranking of market options is logically consistent, or *transitive*. For example, a consumer who prefers library services to watching television, and watching television to shopping, will logically prefer library services to shopping. While not all individuals' preferences are transitive, it helps to keep in mind that we are constructing a general model about consumer behavior which seeks to represent the diversity of tastes. Therefore, it seems plausible to assume that preferences are transitive.

Another common trait of consumers is that they generally prefer more of a good if that choice does not imply less of any other good. Hence, library market option A, 10 open hours per weekday and 4 full-time staff each day, would be preferred to a library market option of 10 open hours and 3 full-time staff per day. In addition, we assume that by adding a certain amount of open hours to the second market option, we are able to make the consumer indifferent between the two. The "more is preferred to less" concept only holds for those commodities and services that are perceived as "good," rather than "bad" or "neutral." The model is versatile enough to incorporate "bad" and "neutral" commodities. These types of commodities/services will be treated in other sections and chapters of the text; for the moment, we assume that more (note that an increase in quality also implies more) is preferred to less.

Athough not all people exhibit the consumption traits associated with the behavioral assumptions we have examined, these assumptions appear to be reasonable and applicable to most consumption decisions. The purpose of these assumptions is to help us build a model of general consumer behavior. And, as we shall see, they provide us with a basis for examining how preferences affect the choices of consumers.

Utility

People come to the library to achieve some objective. The extent to which information services serve wants or preferences indicates the relative value or satisfaction yielded. This subjective evaluation of information is what the consumer will use as the criterion against which cost, measured in terms of price, will be weighed. *Utility* is the term that economists employ to represent the sense of well-being or satisfaction a consumer derives from a particular market bundle, a combination of goods and services, that might be consumed. It is a variable or concept whose relative magnitude shows the level or direction of preference. The sense of well-being that an information consumer derives from library services may be tied to school grades, health, income, relaxation, learning, etc.

Since human wants are unlimited but time and money are not, the consumer must make choices between alternatives. When operating in a scarce environment, choices are directed toward some end. To demonstrate preferences in actual choices, economists assume that rationality leads consumers to maximize utility. Thus, time and money will be allocated in a fashion which permits maximum satisfaction. The market option which maximizes utility is selected within the framework of preferences and constrained by prices and income.

At one time, economists treated utility as quantitatively measurable in a cardinal sense, where the difference between two measurements (such as length and temperature) is numerically significant. For example, the difference between 100 pages and 50 pages, or between 15 feet and 5 feet, is numerically significant, and relative comparisons can be made on the basis of these figures. To indicate that there is no single way of measuring or scaling utility, we emphasize the term *relative*.

The utility associated with a particular market basket is known as *total* utility. *Marginal* utility indicates the additional (or rate of change) satisfaction received from an additional unit of a commodity, all other factors constant. Changes in other factors, such as income, preferences, or level of other commodities, will affect the rate at which utility changes. Economists assume that as a person consumes more and more of a particular good there is a decline, beyond some point, in the extra satisfaction a consumer derives from the last unit of the commodity consumed. This hypothesis is known as the *law of diminishing marginal utility*. The idea of marginal utility has some evidential basis. Generally, the more income a person has, the more he or she saves toward future consumption; as successive units of food or water are consumed, the less hungry or thirsty we become. Also, each good has a limited number of uses to which it can be put. With additional units of a good, we begin to move down the scale of importance and total utility increases in smaller increments.

Up to this point we have been discussing utility in a cardinal sense, but we can also rank utilities ordinally. An ordinal ranking of preferences merely indicates the relative ranking of objects, without regard to a significant numerical scale. In this instance, a consumer simply lists the options available in order of satisfaction derived. The most preferred alternative yields the highest level of satisfaction, but in ordinal ranking we need not specify, in a numerically significant manner, the difference between options. The model which assumes cardinal utility is a special case of the model in which consumers rank their preferences ordinally. Mathematically, the consumer's optimum in the ordinal model of consumer preferences is the equivalent of the cardinal model.

While both approaches yield the same optimal solution, the ordinal utility method has several advantages. The consumer only has to be able to rank market options in order of preference, rather than having to tell how much more preferred one option is over another. The ordinal utility model permits us to more clearly depict the effect of economic factors on the process of choosing the utility-maximizing basket. Finally, the ordinal utility approach provides us with an easier method for deriving the consumer's demand curve.

Indifference Curves

Given the assumption of ordinally measurable utility, the basic device for illustrating the ordering of various market options is an *indifference curve*. It is the analytical device used to plot points of equal satisfaction—utility. One method for making two consumption options equal is by adding a given amount of one option to the basket until both are viewed as equal. For example, if one library option has 5 units of hours and 3 units of reference service and the other has 5 units of hours and 1 unit of reference, we could make the options equal in utility by adding units of hours to the second basket.

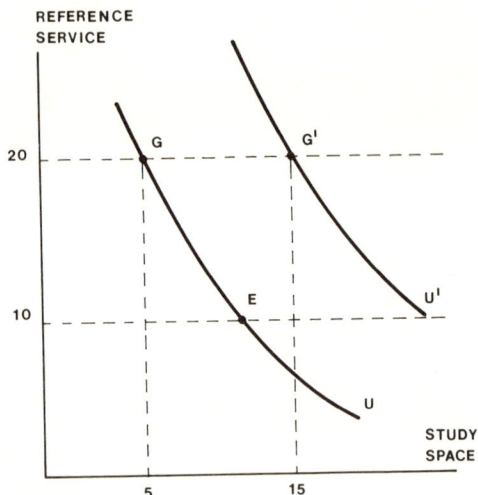

Fig. 4. Indifference Curve

Indifference curves have three characteristics: they are negatively sloped; those which are higher than others represent greater levels of satisfaction; and they cannot intersect. The sign of the slope of indifference curves can be deduced from our assumption that more is preferred to less. In Figure 4, the consumer is attempting to rank combinations of reference service and study space. If our consumer were to have more of one library option and the same amount of the other option, he or she would be better off. However, the consumer will no longer be on the same indifference curve. For example, let us start out at point G on indifference curve U, and assume we keep the amount of reference service constant. As we increase the amount of study space, the consumer obtains greater satisfaction, but we would no longer be on the original indifference curve. Instead, we would move towards point G' on indifference curve U'. Since our definition of an indifference curve is that the consumer be indifferent between two library market options, our library user must choose a market option which has less reference service and more study space. The only way this can be accomplished is to remain on the same indifference curve, where all market baskets are equally valued. Since market baskets that are equally satisfactory must contain more of one good and less of the other, the indifference curve must be negatively sloped.

For any two information services a consumer has many indifference curves, which make up what is known as an *indifference map* (it depicts the consumer's tastes). From our discussion of the slope of an indifference curve, we note that any point which lies above a given preference curve will be preferred. This is

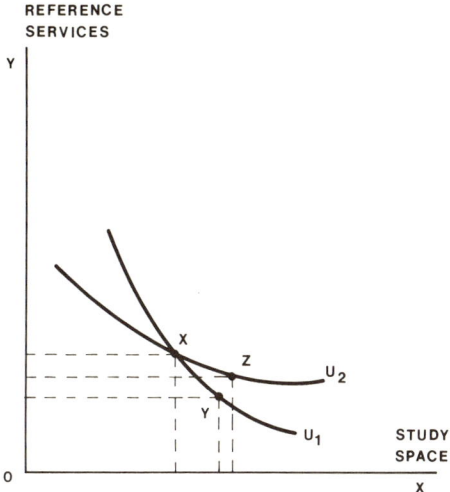

FIG. 5. Intersecting Indifference Curves

the same as stating that higher indifference curves represent a preferred position. Points which lie below a given indifference curve, options which contain less of one or both services, yield lower levels of satisfaction. The consumer's preference map is ranked ordinally as we move away from the origin, from most preferred to least preferred. Although we cannot state how much better off a consumer is between any two indifference curves, it is sufficient that our analysis be able to distinguish between relative states of preference.

Finally, intersecting indifference curves contradict the rule of transitivity and the generally accepted notion that more is preferred to less. In Figure 5 we have two utility curves, U1 and U2, which intersect at point X. Point X lies on the same indifference curve as Y and Z, which implies that X is equal to Y and X is equal to Z. Under the rule of transitivity, Y must be equal to Z. However, point Z represents a library service option that has more of both services than Y. Given our definitions of indifference curves, this would mean that Z would be equal to Y and preferred to Y, at the same time. Thus, the fact that indifference curves cannot intersect is logically consistent with the rule of transitivity.

Marginal Rate of Substitution

In the indifference curve model, economists employ the concept of *marginal rates of substitution,* MRS, to explain the curvature of indifference curves and to measure the willingness of a consumer to exchange one item for another.

The marginal rate of substitution indicates the rate at which a consumer is willing to exchange one library service for another and maintain the same level of satisfaction. It is equal to -1 times the slope (the rate of change between two points on the curve) of the indifference curve.

Convex indifference curves imply that the MRS declines as we move down the curve. Basically, this means that as more and more of one good is consumed along an indifference curve, a consumer becomes less willing to give up another good to obtain more of the first good. To illustrate this point, note that at point G in Figure 4 the consumer has a large quantity of library reference service and a small quantity of library study space. It seems reasonable to assume that the consumer's MRS between study space and reference service would be lower—less willing to exchange study space for reference service—at point E than at point G (the notion of convexity only holds for two "goods"). At point G, reference service is relatively plentiful. Hence, the consumer will most likely place a higher subjective value on study space, implying a willingness to give up a larger amount of reference service to obtain an additional unit of study space. In essence, the MRS between study space and reference space is higher at point G. The important point to remember is that the assumption of a declining MRS is directly linked to the notion that relative amounts of a good affect the consumer's subjective evaluations. We must also point out that the concept of declining MRS applies to a given indifference curve, and not to a movement from one curve to another; a higher indifference curve is not necessarily flatter. This is simply another way of stating that if a consumer has more study space and the same amount of reference service— point G' on indifference curve U'—the MRS would not have to be flatter at this point.

Apart from convexity, the characteristics of indifference curves are logical implications of the postulates of consumer preferences. The notion of convex indifference curves cannot be logically deduced from our assumptions concerning consumer preferences. The concept of convexity is based upon the notion of diminishing marginal utility. Due to the fact that the rate of increase in total utility diminishes as more of a product is consumed, the more a consumer has of a good (already plentiful) the less willing he or she is to exchange some other commodity for the first commodity. In other words, we assume that the MRS depends on the initial distribution of library service that is held by the consumer. If our consumer had 20 units of reference service, one would expect the MRS at this point would be different from a market option which only had 10 units of reference service. Basically, we assume that the more of one service a library user has, the less value will be placed on another unit of this service. Given tastes, the MRS between two goods varies, depending on the quantity of services that the consumer has available at a given point in time.

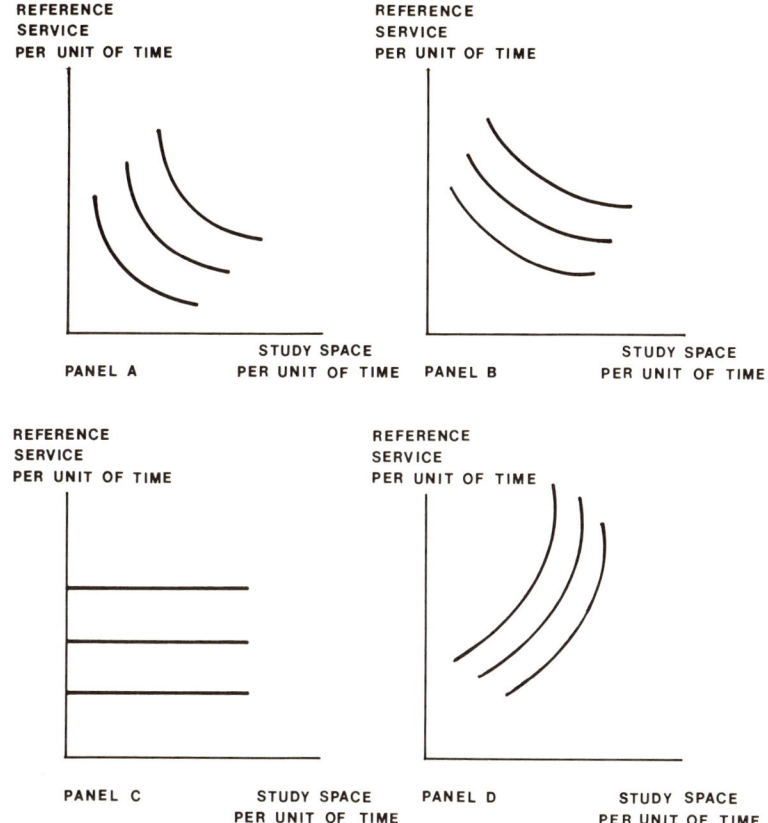

FIG. 6. Indifference Curves

Each library consumer has a different indifference map, which is indicated by the shape of their indifference curves. In Figure 6, there are four different indifference curves—steep, relatively flat, flat, and sloping upward. For a consumer with the steep curves, in panel A, the MRS of study space for reference service is higher than for the consumer in panel B. The consumer in panel C is indifferent toward reference service and in panel D we have a consumer who finds reference services a nuisance. Patrons probably would define a given level of distraction as a "bad." If we define a "bad" as having less of that "good," we would retain the principle that more is preferred to less. One way of incorporating the notion of undesirability, or satiation, is to draw an indifference curve which slopes down, but at some point—a threshold to be avoided—starts to slope up.

34   Microeconomic Theory

As you can see, indifference maps provide a useful framework for representing and analyzing the preferences of consumers. Information managers can employ this device to analyze the effect of different policies on the choices consumers make. Indifference maps, like the ones in Figure 6, can be used to investigate the repercussions of policy changes on groups of consumers with similar preferences.

Preferences can change, but during the course of analysis we assume that they are constant. This limitation does not inhibit our ability to analyze change. Economists take the preferences of consumers as given and then illustrate the effect of a change on resource allocation as a change in slope of the indifference curves. Major adjustments in consumption patterns are usually associated with altered supply conditions, such as the introduction of new technology. Examples of the effect of technology on the price of the information services are automated circulation, paperbacks, and audio cassette players.

For example, in the library market we may notice that the consumers are selecting more audio cassettes. We could hypothesize that this represents a change in preference for the packaging of music or spoken recordings. Another way of looking at what is occurring is to examine this change in terms of the price (or quality) of tape recorders and other leisure-related goods and services. Upon closer examination, we may discover that the tastes of our library consumer haven't been altered radically but that the price change has been the primary determinant of choice. Both explanations are adequate to explain the increase in use of audio cassettes at the library, but only one of the explanations is based on a model which predicts this change on the basis of a readily observable change—prices. Some adjustments in consumption patterns are associated with changes in age, education, and income—lifestyles—but since we are unable to devise a theory which explains how preferences change, we have developed a model which allows us to illustrate differences in tastes as well as changes in tastes. Thus, with this tool and additional information we would be able to show how these factors affect the choices of consumers.

The nature of indifference curves is based upon our original assumptions concerning rational consumers. Given the general characteristics of indifference curves, we will be able to derive the optimum market option. In order to understand how this occurs, we introduced the notion of marginal rate of substitution. This concept allowed us to show the rate at which consumers are willing to exchange one good for another. Now that we have discussed the limits on choice and how consumer preferences affect choices, we are ready to combine the two major elements of the theory of consumer choice. We will examine how the consumer arrives at the market option which maximizes utility.

The Consumer's Equilibrium Choice

To demonstrate actual choices, we must bring together the budget line and the indifference map of a consumer. The consumer is said to be in equilibrium

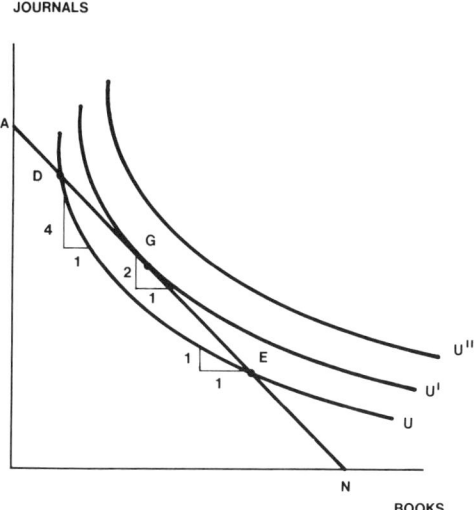

Fig. 7. Equilibrium of the Consumer

when he or she obtains maximum satisfaction within the objective limits set by prices and income. The budget line represents the boundary of choice; and our consumer can move along it but not beyond it. Therefore, the problem is to choose a point on the budget line which yields the highest level of utility.

Let us assume that a consumer is trying to choose between the use of books and the use of journals. The budget line, AN, represents the ratio at which the consumer is currently able to exchange books for journals, or $-Pb/Pj$. Indifference curves represent the MRSbj, or the rate at which our consumer is willing to exchange books for journals. Other library choices which consumers make are when to arrive at the library vs. when to complete other activities, staff use or indexes, books-by-mail or bookmobile service, etc., and we can use the indifference-curve approach to examine choices between these services.

The consumer's equilibrium occurs at point G, which lies on the highest obtainable indifference curve in Figure 7. Point G is selected because it is the library option which provides the greatest satisfaction, given income and prices. Library market options on indifference curves which are to the right of U' are beyond the reach of our consumer. Those options which lie below U' are assumed to be affordable, but provide less satisfaction than options on U'. Note that, given convexity, the optimum choice occurs at the point of tangency between the budget line and the indifference curve, where the slopes of the indifference curve and the budget line are equal: MRSbj = Pb/Pj. This point represents the balancing of the consumer's subjective evaluations with the objective market cost.

Next, let us discuss in greater detail why our library consumer chose market option G instead of other options on the same budget line. In Figure 7, point D lies on U, a lower indifference curve which intersects the consumer's budget line. At this point the MRSbj is expressed as a willingness to exchange 4 units of journals for 1 more unit of books. But the prevailing price ratio (slope of the budget line) suggests that the consumer only needs to give up 2 units of journals to gain an additional unit of books.

Recall that the MRS illustrates the consumer's subjective marginal benefit of exchange, and marginal benefit measures the additional benefit to be gained from an extra unit of a good. At point D in our example, the marginal benefit of another unit of books is 4 units of journals. The objective cost, or price ratio, a measure of the added or marginal cost of acquiring another unit of books, is 2 units of journals. At point D, the consumer's marginal benefit of 1 more unit of books in terms of journals is greater than the marginal cost of 1 more unit of books, and he or she will be better off by consuming more books. In the process of consuming more books, our consumer moves to a higher indifference curve and achieves a higher level of satisfaction.

Given the indifference map in Figure 7, at all points along the budget line, other than point G, our consumer will gain exchange between the two library services. For example, if the consumer were to choose a point below G, he or she could attain a higher level of satisfaction by consuming (purchasing) fewer library books and more journals. Note that at point E the consumer stands to gain from trading books for journals—the MRS is less than the price ratio. At point E, a unit of books is only worth 1 unit of journals to the consumer; however, it costs 2 units of journals. For this reason, the consumer will find greater satisfaction in an exchange which moves the person toward point G. Movements along the budget line in the direction of the optimal point cause the consumer to reach a higher level of utility, and at the optimal point the marginal benefit of books in terms of journals is equal to its marginal cost.

Up to this point, we have been observing choice between two library services, and we have concluded that the optimum consumption choice occurs at the point of tangency, where MRS equals the price ratio. If we were examining a library market opportunity set with three services, we would have to draw a three-dimensional preference map. Whenever more than three choices are considered, the opportunity space becomes increasingly difficult to illustrate. With the realization that a typical consumer is faced with a diversity of library services, we observe that most people consume only positive quantities of a limited number of library services. We may assume that, for most library patrons, this occurs because of a lack of knowledge about the service or its usefulness and limits on time.

In cases where a zero amount is purchased, we can employ the convex preference curve (as shown in Figure 8) to show that the most preferred position would occur at the corner of the budget line. Another way of examining consumer choice in a multidimensional market is to use expenditures on all other

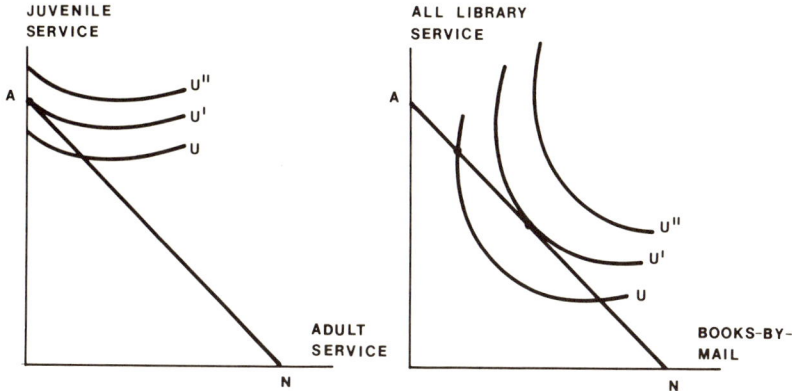

FIG. 8. Corner Equilibrium   FIG. 9. Composite-Good Approach

commodities as a composite good and place this amount on one of the axes (Figure 9). In order for the composite-goods approach to be valid, we must assume that all prices remain constant, and this assumption permits us to treat all other goods as a single good. In other words, if the prices of other goods are allowed to vary, expenditures on other commodities would not be a reliable indicator of the quantity of other goods our consumer could purchase. A composite-goods approach to consumer choice is theoretically appealing when government budget allocation between library services and all other government services is analyzed. For information managers, this approach might prove useful in structuring a consumer questionnaire or in the budget process, for looking at the effect of one service on the quality/quantity (level of satisfaction) of overall library services.

The model of consumer choice rests upon several key assumptions concerning consumer behavior, the nature of preferences, prices and income. We introduced the concepts of budget lines, utility and indifference curves to help us model preferences and constraints on choices. Budget lines incorporate the objective element, and indifference curves depict the subjective evaluations of consumers. Bringing the two sides of the equation together allowed us to show how and why a rational consumer will select the market option which leaves him or her with the greatest level of satisfaction.

Application: Library Materials

In this section we will examine choice between two types of library materials, videos and books. (However, the analysis can be extended to investigate choices

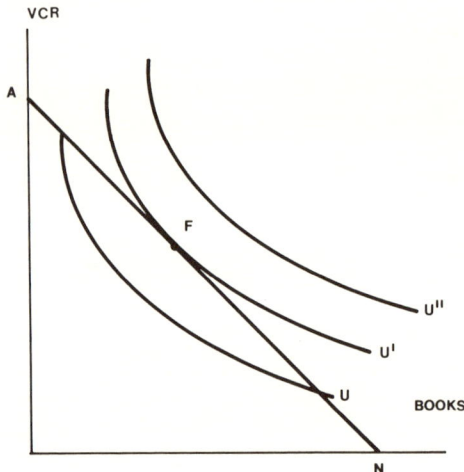

Fig. 10. Library Budget Allocation

between any two library options, such as catalog use and browsing.) We shall assume that the consumer has access to a video cassette recorder/player (VCR) outside the library. In addition, we assume that our consumer has an indifference map that shows the scale of preferences for various combinations of these two goods; that income, prices, and preferences remain constant; that all income will be allocated between these two goods; and that the consumer acts rationally.

To illustrate the value of the indifference-curve model, we view the consumer's problem in terms of allocating limited income between videos and books. Visualize a series of indifference curves which reveal combinations of additional videos and books that add to the consumer's utility. We know from our model that the greater the information/entertainment gain, the higher the indifference curve. Each point on any indifference curve contributes the same amount of utility. Our next step is to superimpose a budget, represented by line AN in Figure 10, on the consumer. Upon inspection, one finds that the optimum combination of videos and books occurs at point F. At this point the consumer has allocated his or budget in a manner which produces the highest obtainable level of satisfaction.

Being able to solve the consumer's problem may appear to be easy, but its importance should not be overlooked. The analytical apparatus we employed permits us to investigate the changes in the library's goods and services, as well as changes in other markets on the consumption of information services. We have developed a system for evaluating the objectives of consumers, namely, the budget line and indifference curves. With this structure, we are able to predict how consumers will allocate their limited income.

People come to the library to find, use, and borrow services. To use the library, a consumer may be required to have a user's card. In addition, consumers must use their time to find and select items, or wait for others to assist them in their choice. The library may supply information-choice aids through a combination of personnel and capital. How the consumer uses the library depends upon a number of complex factors, such as age, education, preferences, income, prices of other goods and services, and the price of library services. It is to the latter that we turn our attention, in the next section.

Time: The Library Patron's Budget Constraint

Earlier, in the discussion of the price of library service, we suggested that time, as a constraint on the consumer's choice, would supply us with a useful way of investigating the limits on a consumer's ability to purchase library services. We will examine a time model of consumer choice so that the reader may apply its reasoning to specific library problems.[1]

In the standard approach to economic theory we assume that the consumer is involved with consumption and production activities. Production activities involve the sale of one's resources (time, talent) to firms in order to generate income with which to purchase (consume) goods and services. Consumers attempt to maximize utility they can obtain from goods and services, subject to income and price constraints. We can express this notion mathematically as

$$\max_{x_1,\ldots,x_n} U(x_1, x_2, \ldots, x_n) \qquad \text{Eq. 2.3}$$

subject to the constraint

$$I = p_1 x_1 + p_2 x_2 + \ldots + p_n x_n \qquad \text{Eq. 2.4}$$

where U is utility; $x_1, \ldots, x_n$ represents the quantities of goods 1 to n, $p_1, \ldots, p_n$ represents the prices of goods 1 to n, and I represents money income. Changes in the market option which yield maximum utility can be explained by changes in income, prices, and tastes. In the traditional approach to consumption theory we restrict our attention to market transactions which involve dollar-denominated transactions. Now we will extend this theory to incorporate the notion of time as a component of the utility-maximizing equation.

All library activities require that the consumer use time in the form of reading, using indexes and catalogs, asking questions, and travel time as an input to utility generating activities: education, production, and entertainment, to name just a few. The value of time can be approximated by its equivalent

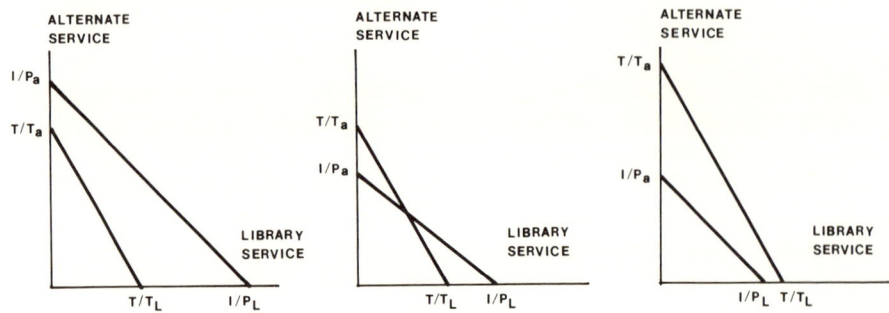

FIG. 11. Time and Money Constraints

in income sacrificed. For situations where time cannot be converted into added income, the consumer has a multiple constraint. In this instance, the consumer's options are limited by the time required to consume a library service, Tl; the time required to consume all other commodities, To; the price of library services, Pl; the price of other commodities, Po; money income, I; and consumption time, Tc, expressed as

$$(Pl)(Ql) + (Po)(Qo) = I \qquad \text{Eq. 2.5}$$

$$(Tl)(Ql) + (To)(Qo) = Tc \qquad \text{Eq. 2.6}$$

When there isn't a direct charge for library services, the income constraint isn't of direct concern. And yet, as we will show, income can affect the amount of library services a consumer purchases.

Within the context of constraints, we will examine how different time and money constraints affect choice between library and other information services. In Figure 11, consumption of library services is subject to a money-income and time constraint. The way we have drawn the budget lines suggests that library services are more expensive in terms of time, whereas, the alternative service costs more in terms of income. Hence, the time-budget line is steeper than the income-budget line. Each panel of the figure illustrates a different type of consumer: panel A shows the case where income is so large that time is the dominant constraint; panel B portrays the situation in which each constraint is binding over a certain range of options; and panel C depicts the case where income is the primary constraint.

Up to this point we have been examining the situations in which time and income are inconvertible. Generally, though, time and income *are* convertible. On the household level, time can be used to generate money income or consumption time. Time spent on consumption reduces the need and/or time to earn income. Someone who engages in income-earning activities is reducing consumption time. Since time can be sold to earn income, the two are convertible into a single constraint. (Note: The actual time spent on either activity depends upon tastes and prevailing wages.) In other words, time can be converted into goods by working or by buying. Put differently, in the consumer's production function, time and goods can be substituted for one another.

Conceptually, we are stating that time spent on consumption activities could be spent on income producing activities; the value of lost income is a measure of the value of consumption time. The implicit assumption is that the consumer has an option to work as much as he or she wishes at a given wage rate. Obvious objections to this assumption are that employment opportunities may be limited or wages may change with the number of hours worked. Yet neither of these problems is insurmountable. If opportunities to work are limited, as in the case of a low-skills student, we can revert to the case where only time is a constraint and not worry about income as a constraint on library use. If wages vary with the number of hours worked, we could use some average wage for that category of employment. The most appropriate method of dealing with this problem is to assume that full income is the amount of income a consumer would earn by allocating the maximum possible time to work.

In addition to the problem alluded to above, observe that not all consumption can be categorized as pure consumption. Some library activities are investment activities and others are leisure activities. Those library services which are related to production activities are analogous to the person who chooses to do his or her own automobile repairs, thereby lowering the need for additional income. This person, as with the person employed outside the home, is lowering consumption time and increasing income, whereas an individual who is consuming leisure activities sacrifices income time in order to increase leisure time. In both cases, time spent consuming library services is convertible into an equivalent constraint on consumption.

Economists have extended the theory of consumption to include the distinction between market goods and particular utility-relevant attributes. Commodities, comprised of goods and time, are desired for the satisfaction provided through their attributes: color, taste, comfort, entertainment, knowledge, prestige, etc. The process by which many of these utility-generating attributes are yielded involves use of the consumer's time: books plus time provide entertainment and knowledge. Thus, utility is generated by production within the household and is subject to income constraints (limits on the ability to purchase market goods) and time constraints (limits on the ability to produce attributes). In this new approach, utility can be expressed as a function of the goods, $x1$ to xn, and the time, $t1$ to tn, required to produce attributes or commodities, $A1$ to An:

$$U = U(A1, A2..., An) \qquad \text{Eq. 2.7}$$

where $A1$ is produced by combining $x1$ and $t1$, and so forth:

$$A1 = f(x1,t1); A2 = f(x2,t2); ...; An = f(xn,tn) \qquad \text{Eq. 2.8}$$

Observe that both the goods and time required to produce a good depend upon the state of technology. To maximize utility, the consumer chooses how much and which types of goods (books, journals, records, videos) and time (day, evening) to use, subject to the household production function and the constraints on resources: time and income.

In this model the consumer's decisions closely parallel those of the producer. The consumer combines inputs—time and goods—to produce output, subject to the constraint on the consumer's resources and production function. Using the concept of MRS, we know that if the value of time, relative to goods, is high the consumer will trade goods for time.

Using the two types of library use, pure consumption, and consumption that contributes to production, we observe that the cost of pure consumption is the wage foregone. As we move from pure consumption to pure production, the cost of consumption moves from the wage rate, w, to some figure less than w, because as consumption begins to contribute to production it contributes indirectly to earnings. Goods and services can be distinguished according to the relative importance of time in the full cost of a commodity and the relative importance of forgone wages.[2] The latter is dependent not only on the time required but its cost in terms of the extent to which it is used for consumption and not production. In this way, time as a factor affecting consumption choices permits us to analyze library services with respect to the amount of time required for use and the nature of use/consumption or production.

Employing a more general case than the one in Equation 2.6, we express the time constraint as

$$T = tpw + t1 + t2 + \ldots + tn \qquad \text{Eq. 2.9}$$

where T is the total time available, tpw is production time in the firm's workplace, and t1 to tn is the time spent consuming commodities A1 to An. If the individual can work any number of hours at a given wage rate, w, the total time endowment, T, is worth wT in units of money income. Thus, the income constraint can be expressed as

$$I = wT = p1x1 + p2x2 + \ldots + pnxn \qquad \text{Eq. 2.10}$$

where I is total income, p1 to pn is the price per unit of goods, and x1 to xn is the quantity of goods consumed to produce commodities A1 to An. We are now in a position to combine the income and time constraints:

$$wT = (wt1 + p1x1) + (wt2 + p2x2) + \ldots + (twn + pnxn) \qquad \text{Eq. 2.11}$$

where wt1 to wtn represents the value of time in terms of the wage rate required to produce commodities A1 to An.

In the time-allocation model, the consumer's objective is to maximize utility, subject to the constraints on resources and the production function available. Using the cardinal notion of utility, we find that this condition occurs when the marginal utility of a commodity, which consumers produce with goods and time, is equal to the marginal utility of the resources (goods and time) used to produce it. Using the indifference-curve approach, we showed that, in equilibrium, the MRS in production equals the ratio of the prices of the resources used in production. By combining time and goods into a single resource constraint, this model allows us to conduct an economic analysis of non-price market choices.

Price and Income Changes: Time-Allocation Model

In the time-allocation model, the effect of changes in time and income on a consumer's budget is the same as was suggested in the section "Budget Lines." Given prices, changes in income affect the amount of goods and services a consumer can purchase. In Chapter 3 we will study, in more detail, the impact of changes in income on the consumption of library services.

Changes in prices alter the rate at which consumers can exchange one good for another. Given income, the relative price of each good determines the amount the consumer can buy. In the library, price changes are analogous to changes in distance from the library, in open hours, and in restrictions on the ability to check-out library materials. Price changes in goods and services outside the library also affect library consumption. If we consider the wage rate as the price of time, then changes in wages will have an impact on library use. In Chapter 3, we will use the time-allocation model to examine the ways in which price changes affect library service consumption.

Application: Learning and Cost of Library Use

In this section we will examine the affect of a change in the time component of the consumer's production function. We will rely on the budget line to help us explore the way in which learning relates to the ability of a consumer to use library services. Learning curves are used to illustrate the concept of increased proficiency based on experience gained through repeating simple or complex tasks. We can measure the gains in proficiency in terms of time, accuracy, or dollar cost of performing a procedure. Typically, the time required to complete a task will be reduced at a decreasing rate and will follow a predictable pattern such as the one shown in Figure 12A. An alternative way of examining the impact of learning is to measure task proficiency, which usually increases at a decreasing rate, as depicted in Figure 12B. The opportunity gains involved with learning are dependent upon the amount of human skill required to complete the task. For example, low learning rates occur in machine-labor fabrication because the speed of the job is more dependent upon the capability of the equipment than the skill of the operator. Changes in the type of machinery will alter the rate of learning. Rather than discuss

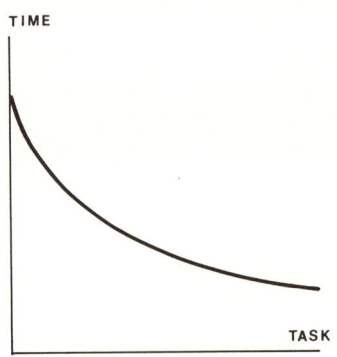 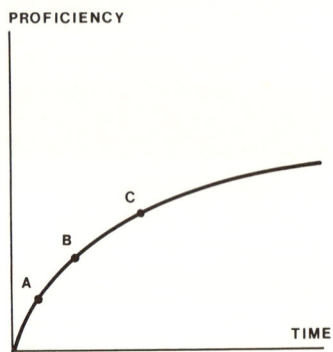

Fig. 12. Learning Curves

the technical aspects of learning curves, we will analyze the impact of learning on budget lines.

We have stated that consumers choose market options based on prices and budget limitations. According to economists, there are two types of goods: investment goods and consumption goods. Investment goods yield returns over a period of time, whereas consumption goods yield their benefits in the time period they are used. Athough most goods are a combination of these two types, let us assume that the ability to use the library is an investment activity. Now let us explore the impact of this investment on budget lines. We will restrict our attention to use of the library's catalog. Since our purpose is to illustrate the effect of learning on price or cost of library services, we will assume that the prices of all other goods remain constant.

Time spent on learning to use the catalog is time which cannot be spent on other activities. Thus, time spent learning adds to the cost of using the library. We want to examine what happens to this cost (the exchange of time spent learning) in relation to benefits. Basically, we are introducing the concept of information value and cost into the consumer-choice model. The cost of searching for library items must be added to the cost of library service. One way of reducing the cost of searching is to learn how to use the library. However, the benefits from learning depend upon the portion of income expended on library services. For the library consumer, this depends upon the relative value of time as expressed in terms of wages. Thus, the relative value of learning increases with increases in the wage rate. But as wages go up, the value of time begins to exert an opposite effect on library use. In effect, assuming a direct relationship between education level and wage suggests that, with respect to learning how to use the library, the level of education follows the law of diminishing returns. Roughly speaking, this implies that as the level of education increases, the cost of using the library decreases, up to the point at

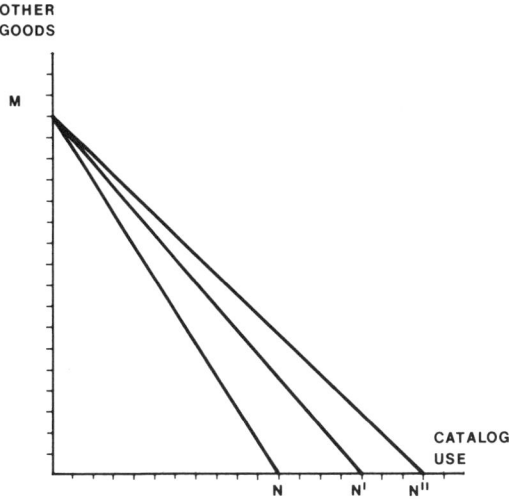

FIG. 13. Impact of Learning on Budget Lines

which the cost of time is such that alternatives to library service are less expensive.[3]

Using Figure 12B, as we move from point A to C let us analyze the influence of learning on budget lines. If we assume that point A represents time period 1, point B time period 2, and so forth, we can show the impact of learning on the cost of using the catalog. Figure 13 illustrates the effect of learning on budget lines. Note that the budget line shifts to the right from MN for point A, to MN' for point B, and to MN" for point C, which implies that a library user can use (consume) the catalog more frequently than before.

Using the concepts of learning and time, we have shown how the time-allocation model can be used to examine the effect of changes in relative prices on the consumption of library services. The time approach and the money approach to analyzing consumer choices both rely on the same technical apparatus: budget line and indifference curves. The value of these theoretical methods lies in their ability to provide important managerial input for the evaluation and analysis of information services.

Summary

Librarians are interested in consumer preference as it concerns providing services and materials in the appropriate combination and quantity. To this end, we developed a model of consumer choice which employs the consumer budget line and the indifference curve to reveal how the consumer would choose a market option from a given range of opportunities. The market opportunity set defines a range of limited opportunities as the area under the budget line. The slope of the budget line is negative because along the opportunity line, an increase in X is associated with a decrease in Y. A budget line defines the range of opportunities available to the library consumer, and this market opportunity set constitutes a portion of the available library services: each consumer has different limits on time. The ratio of prices determines the slope, and time/income and prices determine the Y-and X-axis intercepts and, therefore, the position of the budget line.

Indifference curves are graphic representations of consumer tastes. A single indifference curve is designed to depict a series of market options which the consumer finds equally satisfactory. An indifference-curve map shows curves of varying levels of utility. The slope of an indifference curve measures the rate at which a consumer is willing to exchange two goods. Upon evaluation, we concluded that the equilibrium consumer market option occurs at the point of tangency or on the highest obtainable indifference curve. At this point there is a balance between the objective and subjective elements of the consumer's constrained choice problem. In other words, the consumer's willingness to exchange is equal to his or her ability to exchange. The optimum market choice was defined as the one where the willingness to exchange goods is equal to the rate at which the consumer is able to exchange goods. Based on this knowledge, we will be able to explore consumer response to changes in economic conditions and construct the model of demand. To enable us to predict the impact of changes in library practices and policies to a greater degree of accuracy, in Chapter 3 we will explore the concept of price elasticity of demand and interrelationships of the demand for different library services.

Exercises

1. Assume that a consumer has 15 hours of leisure time per week, and that the cost of using a unit of library service is .75 of an hour and the cost of using all other leisure pursuits is .50 of an hour. Draw a budget line showing the maximum amount of each commodity that our consumer can purchase.
2. Suppose that, in library system A, users are required to use a materials location system which requires twice as much time as library system B. What do you expect will be the impact on directional questions in library system B?
3. What is a learning curve? Describe the impact of learning on budget lines.
4. Assume that we know that browsers achieve a higher rate of success than persons who use the card catalog. Describe, in terms of price, why one might expect this to occur.
5. Define marginal rate of substitution and discuss how you would use this concept to analyze the composition of the use of library services.

6. Assume that a library consumer can purchase 25 units of library services and 50 units of another service. Given that the price of library service is $5, what is the consumer's income? What is the price of the other good? Given that library services are drawn on the X-axis, determine the slope of the budget line.

References

1. Gary S. Becker, "A Theory of the Allocation of Time," *Economic Journal* 75:229 (September 1965): 493–517; Nancy V. DeWath, "Demand for Public Library Services: A Time Allocation Approach to User Fees." (Ph.D. dissertation, University of California—Berkeley, 1979); and Jack Hirshleifer, *Price Theory and Applications,* 2nd ed. (Englewood Cliffs, N.J.: Prentice-Hall, 1980), pp. 162–171.
2. DeWath, "Demand for Public Library Services," p. 113.
3. Ibid., pp. 133–138.

Suggested Reading

Browning, E. and J. Browning. *Microeconomic Theory and Applications.* Boston: Little, Brown, 1983. Chap. 2.

Reuter, V. "Using Graphic Management Tools." *Journal of Systems Management* 30:4 (April 1979): 6–17.

Wallendorf, M. "Understanding the Client as Consumer." In *Management Principles for Nonprofit Agencies and Organizations,* ed. G. Zaltman. New York: AMACOM, 1979. Pp. 256–290.

White, L. *The Public Library in the 80's: The Problems of Choice.* Lexington, Mass.: Lexington Books, 1983. Chap. 4.

3

INDIVIDUAL AND MARKET DEMAND FOR LIBRARY SERVICES

In this chapter we extend the model of consumer choice to derive individual and market demand curves. Building upon the concepts developed in Chapter 2, we examine the effect of changes in income, prices, and other circumstances on consumption choices. Then, using the consumer preference model, we will show how changes in the price of a good are used to derive an individual's demand curve for that good, and how these curves are aggregated to obtain a market demand curve.

Demand is a key instrument of analysis in microeconomics. The demand for a particular good or service is a function of the consumer's tastes, income, the price of the good, and the prices of goods which are related to it in consumption. Initially, our interest will be centered on the demand curve as it relates price to quantity, independently of other variables. Thus, demand expresses the consumer's willingness to purchase a good at various prices, all else held constant. It is a list of price and quantity relationships, for a particular good, which, when plotted on a graph, with price on the Y-axis and quantity on the X-axis, becomes a demand curve. Demand curves slope downward, indicating that higher quantities are purchased at lower prices and smaller quantities are purchased at higher prices. Economists call this inverse relationship the *law of demand*. The foundation of this law rests on consumer preference theory and empirical evidence.

For most purposes, it isn't the individual's demand or, the price-quantity relationship that is of interest; rather, it is market demand: the amount that all consumers in a given market will purchase at prevailing prices. We will show how how the individual's demand curve is linked to the market demand curve. After we explore this relationship, we discuss how the prices of related goods affect consumption and *elasticity,* the sensitivity of quantity demanded to changes in price, as well as income.

The study of demand permits us to analyze how consumers react to changes in the market. As we know, libraries do not make a direct use charge for their services. In Chapter 2 we began to develop a model which allowed us to analyze non-dollar-price market decisions. In order to use this model as a basis for economic analysis, one must have an understanding of key economic concepts and relationships. Most of these relationships are best understood through the standard dollar-price and -income approach to market analysis. Therefore, our first step in building the theory of demand will be to use dollar prices. Then we will use the time-allocation approach to investigate consumer reactions to changes in prices and income. This should help us move toward our goal of understanding how consumers choose information.

Consumption Decisions and Income Change

To isolate the effect of a change in income on consumption patterns, we assume that preferences and the prices of other goods do not change. From Chapter 2, we know that a change in income—all else held constant—affects the X and Y intercepts of the budget line without changing the slope. Put differently, changes in income, shown as a parallel shift of the budget line, do not affect the opportunity cost of a good, namely, its price along the budget line. In Figure 14 the original budget line is A'H' and the optimum market choice is represented by point F. As we increase the consumer's income, the budget line is shifted upward to the right to A"H". Just the opposite occurs when we reduce the consumer's income. In this case, starting with line A'H', a decrease in income shifts the budget line downward to the left to AH. Clearly, in both cases, the new optimum market basket depends on the consumer's preferences as depicted by the indifference curves and the level of the price ratio, Pl/Py. For the set of indifference curves in Figure 14, when the consumer's income is increased the new equilibrium occurs at point G, and when it is decreased it occurs at point E.

By connecting points E, F, and G, generated by changes in income, we have what is known as the income-consumption curve. It depicts the relationship between a change in income and the change in quantity demanded. An income-consumption curve relates levels of income to consumption patterns. This relationship between changes in income and consumption is used to help define two categories of goods, normal and inferior, and to predict consumption patterns. Figure 14 suggests that as we increase income, consumption of library service increases, and less is purchased as we decrease income. Economists define this type of good as a *normal* good.

50 Microeconomic Theory

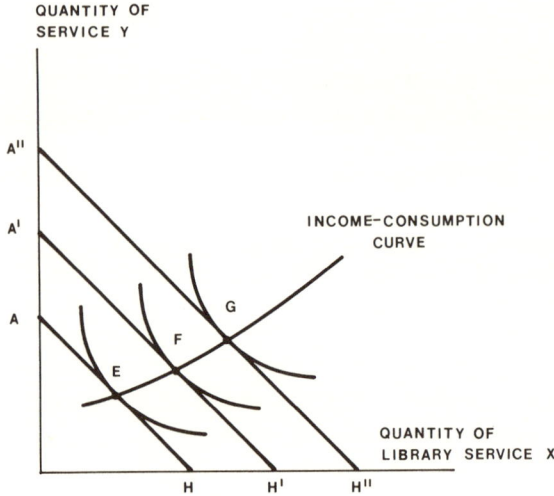

FIG. 14. Income-Consumption Curve

Not all goods and services exhibit this type of consumption pattern. For some goods, consumption decreases as income increases; and as income decreases, consumption increases. Goods of this sort are known as *inferior* goods. The distinction between an inferior good and a normal good varies between individuals. In other words, the goods themselves are not intrinsically normal or inferior; instead, the definitions refer to the response of the consumer to a change in income, and these responses depend upon their underlying preferences. Hence, while library service may be a normal good for some consumers, it may be an inferior good for others. Also, the level of income may affect the way in which a consumer reacts to changes in income. For instance, within a certain range of income a good may be normal, but as income rises it may become an inferior good. When we analyze goods in terms of the income-consumption curve, it helps to remember, we are focusing on the relationship between income and quantity demanded, not the relationship between a change in income and the percentage of income spent.

While the difference between normal and inferior goods doesn't depend on the intrinsic attributes of the item, there are certain characteristics of inferior goods which help us to distinguish between the two types of goods. Usually inferior goods belong to a class of goods which contain items of low to high quality: paperbacks/books, bus rides/transportation, Chevrolets/autos, hamburger/meat. As income increases, people are able to switch to consuming goods of higher quality. Broadly defined, goods tend to be normal goods: autos, housing, food, books, records.

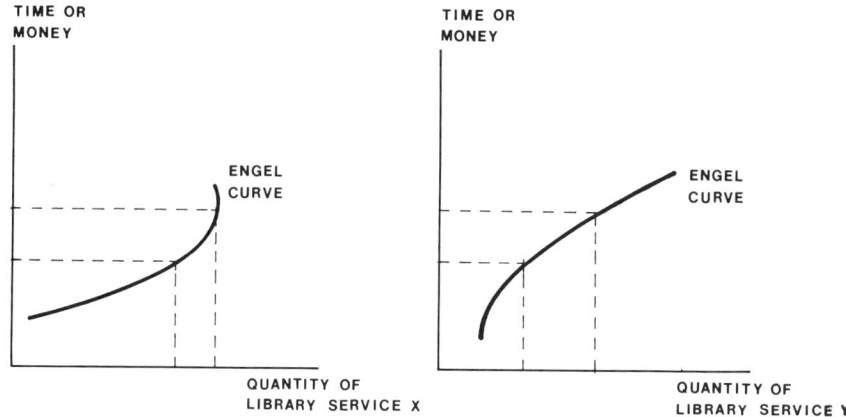

FIG. 15. Engel Curves

Economists have developed a tool, known as the Engel curve, which represents the relationship between the level of income and the equilibrium quantity purchased. We can derive an Engel curve from the income-consumption curve by plotting the quantity consumed on the X-axis and the level of income on the Y-axis. The shape of the Engel curve for a particular library service depends upon the service, preferences, and level of prices. For most goods and services, the Engel curve increases with income, but some rise more sharply with changes in income. Figure 15 shows the effect of income on the consumption of two commodities. As income goes up, the change in consumption of good X gets smaller, and at some point consumption decreases. For good Y, the change in consumption is positive over the entire range of the Engel curve, and incremental changes get larger as income rises. This occurs for those goods that aren't necessities—leisure-related goods and services. At low income, necessities have a priority over other goods and services, but as a consumer's wealth increases, added income may be devoted to other goods. How library use will be affected by income and changes in income is an interesting empirical and theoretical question which will be addressed when we discuss library consumption, using the time-allocation model.

We have used the theory of consumer equilibrium to examine the relationship between income and quantity demanded. Assuming that all other determinants of demand are held constant, we showed that, for most goods, income and consumption are directly related. As income changes, we were able to depict a series of equilibria for a consumer, each one corresponding to a different level of income, when prices and preferences are held constant. From these points we generated an income-consumption curve and the related Engel curve. These curves enable us to predict how a consumer will react to changes

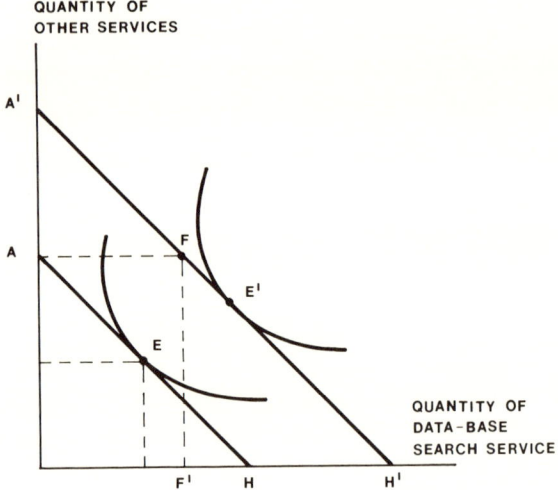

Fig. 16. Subsidies

in income. Income is just one of the factors affecting demand. After we explore the impact of a change in income on the quantity demanded of a fee-based service, we will study a consumer's reactions to a change in the price of a good.

Library Market Application: Effects of a Subsidy

It has been suggested that information vouchers/stamps could alleviate equity problems associated with fees for library services.[1] To show how the concepts presented in the previous section can be used to analyze this proposal, we will examine possible consumption changes resulting from increasing income through a voucher program provided free to individuals. Of necessity, since most libraries do not charge for their services, we are hypothesizing the impact of subsidies on library consumption and prices. The net impact of subsidies depends on the size and nature of the tax used to fund them, the amount of subsidy, prices, and the degree to which a change in income or prices affects consumption. The analysis in this example can be used by information managers who provide fee-based services with discriminatory prices—a pricing schedule which varies across consumers, such as those often found in academic library settings.

Let us assume that a library charges a fee for information searches on automated databases. In Figure 16, given that AH is the original budget line, the introduction of a database-searching subsidy, such as library stamps, has the effect of increasing income, which results in the shifting of budget line AH to A'H'. If we assume that the consumer has been given a subsidy which must be spent on information services, points above F are unobtainable; therefore, the effective budget line is AFH'. With a cash subsidy, the budget line would be A'H'. On this line the consumer is able to use the added income to purchase other goods and services. But since the subsidy we have given cannot be used to purchase other goods and services, options above point F are not available to the subsidy recipient. Even so, our consumer can have F' units of data search for "free" and still spend all income on other goods.

In Figure 16, the new optimum occurs at point E'. The consumer has chosen to spend some additional income on data search, but consumption didn't rise by the full amount of the subsidy. In essence, even though database searching is a normal good, its consumption has not increased by the full amount of the voucher; instead, the consumer has used the remainder of the subsidy to increase consumption of other goods and services. Aside from any equity or efficiency ramifications of the program, given fees for service, a subsidy program would lead to an increase in database consumption.

Price Changes and Library Service Choices

As we indicated, the consumer's central problem is to maximize utility, given scarce resources. Earlier, we found that consumers maximize utility when choosing a market option for which their willingness to exchange one good for another equals their ability to exchange these goods in the market. Stated differently, the consumer chooses the market option which is most preferred from among those that are affordable. While the use of this result may not be apparent, its value will become clear when we explore the relationship between changes in price and consumption choices.

Our interest is centered on the connection between the price of one good and the amount a consumer will purchase. This relationship is more commonly known as the *demand curve*. To isolate the impact of price on quantity demanded, we hold constant other factors that influence consumption choices. Under these conditions, changing the price of one good allows us to observe what happens to the consumption of that good. We will use the analytical structure of indifference curves and budget lines to derive a demand curve.

For the sake of simplicity, suppose that there are only two goods, reference services and circulation services. Suppose that we hold the price of circulation services, the money income of the consumer, and tastes constant, but we allow the price of reference services to vary from one level to another. Next, assume that the consumer's initial equilibrium point occurs at point A in Figure 17A, where the price of reference services is denoted by r4. As we let the price of reference services fall from r4 to r3, the budget line swings out to the right.

54   Microeconomic Theory

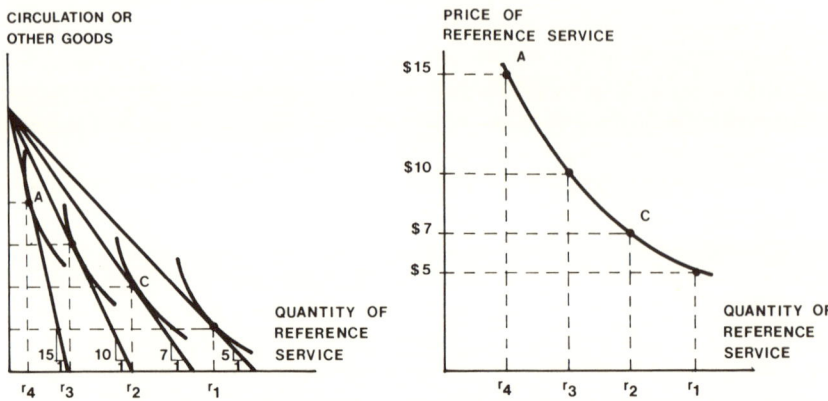

Fig. 17. Consumer's Demand Curve

Each time we lower the price of reference services, the library consumer chooses a new optimum basket, based on preferences and the new price. For each change in the price of reference services the consumer is confronted with a new budget line. We observe that as we lower the price of reference services, the consumer is able to choose a new market option on a higher indifference curve. Thus, as we lower the price of one good, while holding everything else constant, the consumer is able to increase the level of utility. For the particular set of preferences shown, the consumption of reference services increases as price is lowered. The reasons for this outcome will be explored in detail in the section Income and Substitution Effects.

We observed that, at the various possible prices that could prevail in the market for reference services, different equilibrium quantities would be purchased. The line that connects these equilibrium points is called the *price-consumption* curve, and it is from this curve that we derive the demand curve. Demand relates reference consumption to price, when other prices, income and preferences are held constant. While the price-consumption curve is not the demand curve, it conveys the same information. Essentially, to convert the price-consumption curve into a demand curve we need to plot the price-quantity relationship on the appropriate graph, where price is plotted on the Y-axis and quantity is plotted on the X-axis. Figure 17B shows the price-quantity association of reference services. It reveals the quantity of reference service that a consumer will purchase at alternative prices.

Using consumer preferences to deduce a demand curve suggests several important points. First, Figure 17A shows that as the price of a good varies, so does the ability of the consumer to reach a given level of utility. As the price of reference service is decreased, the consumer is able to reach a higher

Individual and Market Demand   55

indifference curve; and as the price is increased, the consumer's ability to reach a given indifference curve is lowered. Since the demand curve is simply another mechanism for illustrating the price-consumption relationship, a library consumer's level of satisfaction varies along the demand curve. The price of a good affects the consumer's ability to obtain library options and, consequently, the level of satisfaction.

Next, note that the demand curve is a schedule of points of possible equilibrium. Given that at each equilibrium position the price ratio equals the MRS, we can state that each point on the demand curve represents the amount of reference service which maximizes a consumer's level of utility for that price. In other words, each point on the demand curve represents the additional benefit the consumer receives from another unit of reference service. For example, at point C in Figure 17B the distance Cr_2, or \$7 per unit, is a measure of how much the additional unit of reference service is worth to the consumer. To show that this must be so, refer to Figure 17A. When the consumer's equilibrium is at point C (r_2 units of reference), MRS_{rc} is \$7 per unit of reference. Given that the MRS is a measure of what the consumer is willing to give up to obtain an additional unit of reference, it is a measure of the extra benefit a consumer receives. And since at each point on the demand curve its height is equal to the MRS, we can state that each point along the demand curve indicates the marginal benefit of the good to the consumer. Thus, the price at which a consumer purchases a given good reveals its relative value to the consumer.

We have found that the consumer, faced with the problem of choosing among limited options, will select a mix of goods and service which maximizes utility. Using the mechanism of indifference curves and budget lines, we were able to model the process of choice. Operating under the assumption that all other variables are held constant, we investigated the way in which a consumer reacts to changes in the price of one good. Proceeding in this way, we observed which market option will be chosen at possible prices. For each price, a different budget line is drawn and a new market alternative is selected. Having obtained a series of points which depict the price-consumption curve, we were able to derive the demand curve. This curve is a schedule of possible prices and the quantities that would be bought. Each price-quantity point shows the value the consumer derives from that level of consumption. (In the next section, we will examine in greater detail the effect of a change in the price of a good.)

Income and Substitution Effects

While the demand curve we derived sloped downward, this may not always be the case. In this section we will suggest a reason for assuming that the downward sloping demand curve is the norm. We will use preference theory to examine the mechanics of price changes and to show why downward-sloping demand curves are considered to be the rule and not the exception. When the price of reference service units is allowed to vary, the consumer chooses a new market option. Conceptually, the movement from the original equilibrium point to the new point can be divided into two components: the substitution effect and the income effect.

When the price of reference services decreases, there is a natural tendency to increase consumption of the now relatively cheaper good at the expense of circulation services, which are now more expensive. The individual library consumer reallocates income in favor of less costly goods and away from other goods. In essence, a substitution of one good for other goods occurs—the substitution effect. In addition to the substitution effect, a change in the price of reference service has an income effect.

First, let us define real income as the *level of satisfaction*. As a result of a fall in the price of reference service, the consumer, given income, can now purchase the same quantity of each good and still have income left over. This increase in purchasing power suggests the ability to attain a higher indifference curve. The size of the gain will be greater, the greater the role that reference service plays in a consumer's budget. Therefore, we can think of the income effect as operating along the income-consumption curve. It represents the change in quantity demanded of reference service due to a change in real income, all prices held constant. It is called the *income effect*, because the increase in purchasing power that results from a price reduction is as if income had risen while prices remain constant. As the power to acquire goods increases because of this force, the consumer must decide how to spread it over different goods and services.

Refer back to Figures 14 and 17A; and notice that when we increase income or decrease price, the consumer is able to reach equilibrium on a higher indifference curve. Thus, price decreases exhibit a similar effect as income increases; they augment real purchasing power. Yet, there is a significant difference between the outcome of these two changes in economic conditions. When price has been decreased, the new equilibrium occurs on a higher indifference curve but at a point where the slope is lower than on the original indifference curve. The consumer has moved down the indifference curve to a point where the lower-priced good is consumed in greater quantities. But as we change income, the consumer moves to a point on a higher indifference curve, where the slope is the same as it was on the original indifference curve. Understanding the difference between these two effects will help us to explain why demand curves have a negative slope.

Figure 18 illustrates a method for separating the two effects, income and substitution. The consumer's original budget line is QR and the optimum market option is E. If we lower the price of reference service units so that the new budget line is QR', our new optimum will be at point E'. The increase in

Individual and Market Demand 57

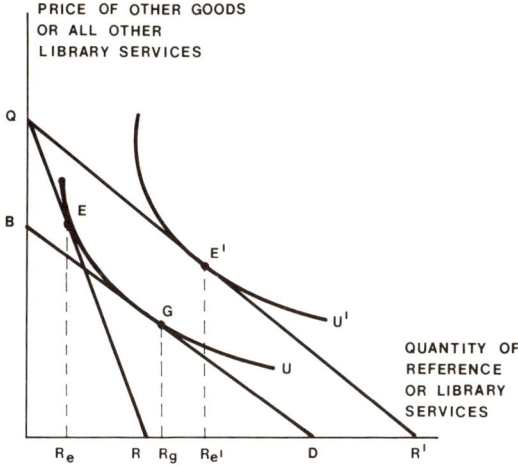

FIG. 18. Income and Substitution Effects

reference service used, from Re to Re′, resulting from a price decrease, illustrates the total effect of a price reduction on reference use.

The substitution effect reveals, independent of any change in income or well-being, how a change in relative prices affects consumption. To isolate the substitution effect, we keep the consumer on the original indifference curve, while at the same time allowing reference service consumption to occur at the lower price. We accomplish this by drawing the new budget line to reflect the lower price while, at the same time, reducing income so that it is possible to attain the original indifference curve. Our new budget line, BD, would be parallel to budget line QR′, reflecting the lower price, but tangent to the original indifference curve, U, indicating a lower income. The new equilibrium point, G, represents the hypothetical market option a consumer would select if income were reduced just enough to leave satisfaction equal to the original option but with the price ratio changed.

The substitution effect is shown as the movement from point E on the original budget line to point G on the hypothetical budget line. Lowering the price of reference service, while holding income constant, has induced the library consumer to increase consumption of reference service from Re to Rg and to reduce the consumption of circulation services. We have moved down the indifference curve to a point where the MRS is lower; consequently, the increase in consumption of reference services. Put differently, the substitution effect is the change in the quantity demanded of reference service due to a price change, when the level of satisfaction is held constant.

Next, let us consider the income effect, shown by the movement from point G on the original indifference curve to point E′ on indifference curve U′. This movement does not involve a change in price; the price ratios on budget line BD and QR′ are equal. Thus, the income effect illustrates the effect of a change in the quantity demanded of reference service due entirely to a change in income, all other prices held constant. Increasing income, while holding price constant, has induced the consumer to increase consumption of reference service from Rg to Re′. In contrast to the substitution effect, the income effect of a lower price permits the consumer to attain a higher sense of well-being.

The purpose of this analysis has been to allow us to suggest a reason for believing that the demand curve will slope downward, or that the law of demand is valid. The substitution effect of a price change always involves the inverse relationship between price and quantity. This result is directly related to the fact that indifference curves have a negative slope. However, the income effect is not predictable solely on the basis of theory. For normal goods, the income effect conforms to the law of demand. In this case, both the consumption and income and substitution effects involve greater consumption when the price of reference service is lower. Thus, for normal goods, the demand curve will slope downward.

In the case of inferior goods, the income effect works in the opposite direction: when the price is reduced, consumption decreases. The reason is that a price reduction leads to an increase in real income, and this implies less consumption of an inferior good. The net result of the income and substitution effects depends upon which of the two is larger. Ordinarily, the substitution effect is strong enough to offset the income effect of an inferior good. The reason we expect the substitution effect to be quite strong stems from the fact that most inferior goods belong to a category of goods with similar characteristics but varying quality. Because, for example, library services belong to a general class of services known as information and entertainment services, a price reduction in library services would lead to a large substitution effect away from goods with similar attributes.

Cases where the income effect is the larger of the two are extremely rare. Why? Note that the larger the fraction of income that is spent on a good, the larger will be the income effect. If we lower the price of reference service by 15 percent the benefits will be greater for persons who spend a large portion of their income on libraries. Since few goods account for a large portion of a consumer's income, the income effect resulting from a price reduction is usually quite small. This would be especially true for the narrowly defined group of goods known as inferior goods. Consequently, even for most inferior goods we expect the demand curve to be downward sloping.

Individual Demand

Up to this point, we have shown that the consumer's underlying preferences and the price of the good in question, all else constant, determine the consumer's demand curve. In addition, we examined the impact of changes in income and the price of a good on its level of consumption. We found that, for most goods, as income rose or price decreased, so did the level of consumption. But we must be careful to distinguish between these two changes. Recall that we are building a model to represent the way in which each variable, taken separately, influences the quantity consumed. A demand curve is intended to separate the effect of price on quantity purchased. Prices of other goods, income, and tastes must be kept constant because they can affect the consumption of a particular good. While we could have constructed curves which relate the consumption of good X to the price of some other good Y, economists have found it more useful to relate quantity demanded to its own price. Changes in its price are then shown as movement along the price-quantity curve. Variations in income, preferences, or the prices of other goods result in a shifting of the entire demand curve.

The demand curve is a replotting of the price-consumption curve. Since a change in the income of an individual causes the price-consumption curve to shift, the demand curve shifts too. Another way of illustrating this point is to note that in Figure 14 each point on the income-consumption curve depicts an equilibrium market option, when price is constant. Replotting these points on a price-quantity graph reveals that, as income changes, the demand curve shifts in the same direction as the change in income: to the right when income increases and to the left when income decreases. Similarly, a change in preferences will cause a shift of the demand curve in the direction of the change in preferences: an increase in desirability, reflected in an outward movement of the demand curve, and the reverse for a decrease in desirability.

A change in the price of other goods alters the ability of the consumer to purchase market options. The way in which the demand curve is affected depends not only on the direction of the price change but also on the relationship of that good to other items. (The nature of how items are related to one another will be examined in the next section.) It is important to remember that when the price of a good changes, the quantity demanded also changes, and this is shown as a movement along the demand curve. In contrast, when income, preferences, or the prices of other goods change, consumption quantities change because of a shift in the entire demand curve. Hereafter, when we speak of quantity demanded we are referring to a point on a particular demand schedule, and when we refer to demand we are indicating an entire demand schedule.

Complements and Substitutes

Demand curves are analytic devices for examining the effect of price on quantity while holding other factors constant. We have held these factors constant since they affect the consumption of a particular good. In effect, a fuller statement of the demand for a particular good would, at minimum, include

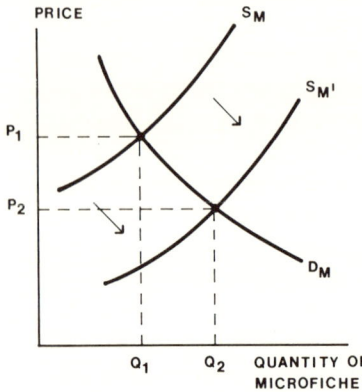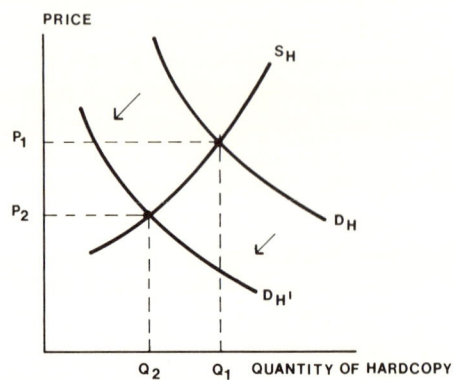

Fig. 19. Substitute Library Commodities

the prices of other goods. In the previous section, we showed that a change in preferences or income causes the demand curve to shift. Now we will draw attention to the influence of a change in the prices of closely related goods.

Economists have classified closely related goods into complements and substitutes. Goods which tend to be *consumed together* are considered complements; and their consumption tends to rise and fall together. One could state that complements enhance the value of each other (e.g., gasoline and automobiles, records and phonographs). Examples of complementary information services include periodical indexes and serials (internally or by interlibrary loan), films and projectors, and video cassette recorders and video cassettes. For example, if the price of indexes falls, the demand for serials will increase; likewise, if the price of video cassette recorders falls, the demand for video cassettes will increase. The demand of one item moves in tandem with that of the other, so that a price reduction of video cassette recorders leads to shifting of the demand curve for video cassettes.

On the other hand, substitute goods are defined as *pairs of goods with similar attributes,* so that they can replace one another in consumption. Thus, a reduction in the price of one would lead to a decrease in demand for the other good. Microfiche and hardcopy, and printed indexes and electronic databases, are library market examples of substitutes. For example, if there is a price reduction for current serials on microfiche, we might expect to see a reduction in the demand for the hardcopy. The size of the reduction in demand depends on how closely serials on microfiche substitute for hardcopy, which in turn depends upon storage requirements, market acceptance, and level of theft.

Figure 19 illustrates the impact of a change in the market condition of serials on hardcopy and on microfiche. For the moment, we will concentrate on the solid lines, with Dm and Sm representing the demand and supply of serials of microfiche, respectively. Similarly, Dh is the demand curve for orginal hardcopy and Sh is the supply of orginal hardcopy. Equilibrium exists in both markets. P1 and Q1 denote the initial market price and quantity.

Now let us assume that there has been a reduction in the price of serials on microfiche. Such a decrease might stem from a decrease in the cost of inputs required to produce them or from a technological improvement. This is shown as a shifting of the supply curve to the right, so that, at all quantities, the price of serials on microfiche will be lower. We wish to find the effects of a change in the supply of microfiche on the price and quantity traded of both microfiche and hardcopy. To isolate the effect of this change, we hold the demand curve for microfiche and the supply curve for hardcopy constant. Given the shift in the supply of microfiche, the price of microfiche falls while the quantity demanded increases. As microfiche becomes cheaper, consumers substitute microfiche for hardcopy in their consumption of serials. In the process, consumers have reevaluated their willingness to purchase serials on hardcopy, which is shown as a drop in demand. Observe that the end result is a lower price for both goods, but the quantity of microfiche demanded and supplied has increased while the quantity of hardcopy has decreased.

Market Demand

We have shown how to deduce a consumer's demand curve from his or her indifference map; why, in general, it will slope downward; and what causes it to shift. As we pointed out earlier, economists examine the behavior of the individual so as to make predictions about group behavior. In the case of market demand, we note that it is comprised of many individual demand curves. Individual demand curves illustrate the relationship between price and quantity for a single consumer; market demand shows this relationship for a large number of consumers. Thus, market demand rests on the same propositions as does the individual's demand. And in both cases, demand operates under the assumption that income, preferences, and the prices of other goods are held constant.

To derive a market demand curve for library services, let us assume that there are only four consumers of library services, each willing to consume a different quantity of library service at alternative prices. Each individual will have a different demand curve, indicating the person's willingness to purchase library services at possible market prices. At P3, for example, Individual A will use 5 units of library service, Individual B will use 10 units, Individual C will use 15, and Individual D will use 20 units. The combined purchases of these consumers, at price P3 and 50 units, identifies one point on the demand curve. The passage from individual demand to market or aggregate demand

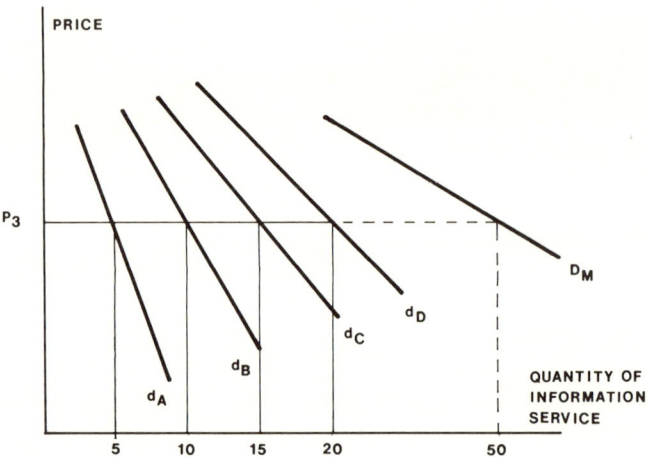

Fig. 20. Market Demand

function simply involves the summation of the quantities that would be purchased by all consumers together at various prices. An implicit assumption of this construction is that the same prices are being charged to every individual in the marketplace. When this is not the case, a market demand curve cannot be constructed.

Geometrically, our market demand curve is the horizontal summation, over quantity, of all individual demand curves. The demand for library services in Figure 20 shows how much would be bought at the various prices that could prevail in the market during a given period of time. A fundamental characteristic of both individual and market demand is that as price falls, the quantity demanded rises; and conversely, when price rises, the corresponding quantity falls. For market demand, the reasons for this inverse relationship rest on the same propositions as for the individual demand. In addition, the lowering of price brings new buyers into the market. As a result, the market demand curve usually has a flatter slope than the individual demand curve. As price falls, the increase in quantity demanded will be greater than the increase for the individual. Even so, the proportionate change (the subject of the section Time and Library Consumption) need not be any greater for the market demand than it is for the individual demand.

Determinants of Market Demand

Markets are affected by more than one variable at a time. However, a demand curve concentrates on the effect that changes in the price of a good have on quantity demanded, while all other factors are held constant. Changes in the other variables cause the demand curve to shift. Thus, when we examine a determinant of demand we will continue to operate under the assumed constancy of the other determinants of demand. An understanding of how each variable affects demand, independently of the others, permits us to analyze more complex situations, in which several variables are changing.

The theory of consumer equilibrium permits us to derive the individual's demand curve. Since the market demand is comprised of many individual demand curves, we can link their behavior together. Recall that a shift in preferences is expressed as a change in the MRS of one good for another. Increased desire for one service leads to an increase in its consumption at all possible prices, leading to a movement of the entire demand function. Similarly, changes in the objective determinants of consumption—namely, price and income—cause the demand curve to change shape or position. If each consumer's demand curve changes shape or position, so must the market demand curve. On the other hand, the shape or position of a few individuals' curves will not have a major impact on market demand. In addition, if the population increases there will be more individual demand curves. Market demand is a horizontal summation of these curves. Thus, as we add more persons to a market, more will be bought at each possible price, implying a shift in the demand curve.

The demand for library services is affected by factors similar to those that affect other goods and services. In general, the factors that cause shifts in the demand curve are:

Preferences (t). The tastes of library users—their feelings about the desirability of library services—are likely to change over time. If education becomes an important part of consumers' lifestyles, we may assume that demand for library services will increase. In contrast, an increased interest in "romance" shifts the demand for certain types of library materials—Harlequins, sagas, etc.

Income (Y). As real income rises, people generally consume more professional services; demand shifts to the right.

Expectations (E). If potential library users/clients expect a certain level of service and are "denied" that level of service, they will probably not be repeat users.

Population (G). Witness the baby boom of the 1950s and the surge in demand for children's services in libraries and, later, in academic libraries.

Seasons (S). Most librarians who work in public-service–related functions can readily identify the effect a certain season has on overall library use and on certain components of the library's information services.

Technology (T). Advances in electronics affect the price, product mix, and processing of information.

Price of related goods (Pr). If the prices of other information services drop relative to library services, the demand for library services decreases. Conversely, if relative prices of serials, paperbacks, etc. rise, we would expect to see a shift to the right of the library service demand schedule.

Another factor which influences demand, transaction costs (Ct), merits special attention. While exchange is at the center of microeconomics, the process itself involves costs. Any economy, regardless of how it integrates the activities of consumption and production, would involve the physical transfer of goods and services. Costs associated with the physical transfer of goods and services are not attributed to the organization society uses to facilitate exchange and, therefore, fall under the economic category of production costs, whereas the social process of exchange may involve costs which are a direct result of the particular method used to achieve trading. Hence, costs such as those of information, contracts and policing add to the cost of exchange. As a result, the equilibrium quantity demanded will be less than in a costless exchange. In the market economy, money is a device which reduces the cost of trading. Library cards, especially in conjunction with automated circulation systems, serve a similar purpose. As media of exchange, they lower the cost of collecting, storing, and evaluating information for transactions.

Before an exchange is made, individuals often gather information about the service they intend to purchase. Many times people call the library, prior to using services, to find out if the library handles particular items. Other times they intend to gather information concerning the quality, types of services, and policies of the library. The cost of search is attached to the price of the service. The more time spent searching for the best price and service, the less time will be avilable for other activities. In terms of opportunity cost, the larger the information cost the the lower the gain from a transaction. However, the amount of time one devotes to search is dependent upon the proportion of income spent on a good. More time will be spent on searching for a "good price" for a new car than for a new book. But the *gain* from searching is greater, too.

Contractual costs arise from carrying out an exchange, and are not reflected in the sale price. Waiting in lines and completing forms are examples of contractual costs. Policing costs involve expenses which are sometimes necessary to enforce a contract. Libraries often use fines as a method of enforcing loan policies; and personal belongings may be checked for stolen materials.

When we analyze demand, it is important to keep in mind the distinction between quantity demanded and demand. The demand curve is a list or schedule of prices drawn under certain parametric conditions. If one of these conditions should change, we have a different quantity-price-relationship at each possible price. Hence, the distinction between quantity demanded and demand defines the difference between moving along an existing demand curve as price changes and a shifting of the entire function.

Individual and Market Demand 65

To recap this important point, note that a movement along the demand curve occurs in response to a change in the price of the good, when all else is constant. In contrast, a shift in demand takes place when a change in income, preferences, transaction costs, etc. affects the quantity demanded at each potential price. This holds for both the individual and market curves. To distinquish between movements of the demand curve, we indicate an increase in demand by an outward shift (movement to the right) of the entire demand curve. Conversely, a decrease in demand refers to an inward shift (movement to the left) of the entire demand curve.

Price Elasticity of Demand

Granted that the demand curve for items or services offered by a library is negatively sloped, the degree to which a change in price affects quantity demanded varies between commodities and services. A small decrease in the price of one library service may lead to a large increase in quantity demanded for another, or it may lead to a small increase. Economists have developed a concept for measuring the responsiveness of quantity demanded to changes in price, namely, *price elasticity*.

When discussing elasticity, we generally refer to three degrees: elastic, inelastic, and unit elastic. If the price elasticity is greater than 1, the demand curve is said to be elastic. When price elasticity is greater than 1, the percentage response of quantity demanded is greater than the percentage change in price. For example, with respect to the library's loan period, this would imply that quantity demanded is highly responsive to changes in loan periods. A price elasticity of less than 1 occurs when the percentage change in quantity is less than the percentage change in price, indicating that quantity demanded is relatively unresponsive to price. Unitary elasticity, a price elasticity of 1, refers to the case where a 1 percent rise in price will lead to a 1 percent reduction in quantity demanded.

All of this can be summarized by a simple mathematical method. At first glance, the slope appears to be a reliable indicator of price elasticity. However, this is not the case. If we were to alter the units of measurement, the slope of the demand curve would change, even though the relationship between price and quantity hadn't. For example, if the time needed to consume a unit of library service falls by 6 minutes and the quantity demanded increases by 60, the slope is $-1/10$. If we were to quote library prices in terms of hours instead of minutes, the slope would be $((-1/10) / (60))$, or $-1/600$. Even though the slope has changed, the nature of the response has not. The same holds true if one changes the units in which quantity demanded is expressed. Hence, mathematically speaking, we cannot use slope to estimate elasticity. We can surmount this problem by using percentage changes rather than absolute changes in price and quantity. An unambiguous measure of price elasticity is defined

66   Microeconomic Theory

as the percentage change in quantity demanded in response to a percentage change in price:

$$Ed = -\frac{\text{Percentage change in quantity demanded}}{\text{Percentage change in price}} \qquad \text{Eq. 3.1}$$

where Ed is the price elasticity of demand, and a percentage is defined as the change in value, divided by the initial value, mutiplied by 100. Since the demand curve has a negative slope, price elasticity will be a negative number. By convention, economists usually place a minus sign in front of the formula to change it to a positive number. Another way of writing the formula is

$$Ed = (\Delta Q/Q) / (\Delta P/P) = ((\Delta Q) / (\Delta P)) (P/Q) \qquad \text{Eq. 3.2}$$

Actually, the elasticity formula is composed of a constant and a variable: the inverse of the slope multiplied by price/quantity. Since the slope of a straight line is constant, so is its inverse, 1/slope. From this it follows that elasticity varies only with changes in price and quantity. For convenience, this relationship is sometimes determined by the demand curve's slope, a steeper curve being more inelastic than a flat one. While this convention may be useful, it is important to keep in mind that elasticity varies over the entire demand curve. On a linear demand curve, we can estimate elasticity by converting the terms of the price elasticity equation to its demand equivalent distances along the line. Generally, elasticity rises as you move up the demand curve.

Figure 21 illustrates this point about elasticity in simple geometric relationships, so that we can interpret the terms in the formula for elasticity as distances along the demand schedule. The slope is constant for both small and large changes in price. Thus, at the midpoint, B, its inverse can be evaluated in terms of AB, the change in quantity, and AC, the change in price. The term P equals OA and the term Q equals AB. Substituting these values in Equation 3.2 gives us

$$Ed = (AB/AC)(OA/AB) = OA/AC \qquad \text{Eq. 3.3}$$

At the midpoint, these two terms will be equal and elasticity will be unitary. At prices below this point, the elasticity is less than 1. At point J, the elasticity, OJ/JC, is less than 1. And points above the midpoint will have an elasticity greater than 1. Given that the elasticity equation contains a constant, 1/slope, and a variable, P/Q, as we move up the demand curve, Px becomes larger and X becomes smaller, elasticity moves from zero toward infinity.

We can also link elasticity to the price-consumption curve. To derive the price-consumption curve, we varied the price of one good and connected the resulting equilibrium points. Each of these points indicates what happens to the consumption of the good whose price has changed. In Figure 22, which shows three price-consumption relationships, panel A depicts a situation in

Individual and Market Demand 67

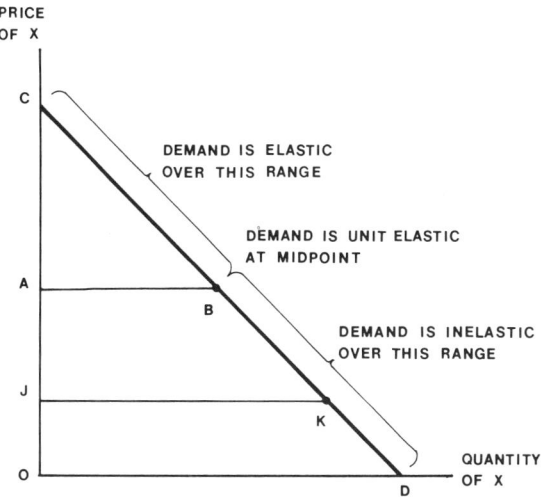

FIG. 21. Geometry of Elasticity

which a price decrease leads the consumer to allocate additional income to library consumption. Proof that this occurs can be found by observing that as the price decreases, the amount not spent on library services decreases from O1 to O2, implying that total expenditure for library services has increased. Similar reasoning can show that panel B depicts inelastic demand, and panel C illustrates the case of unitary elasticity. Typically, the slope varies along the price-consumption curve, sloping downward at high prices and upward at low prices, confirming that elasticity increases as we move up the demand curve.

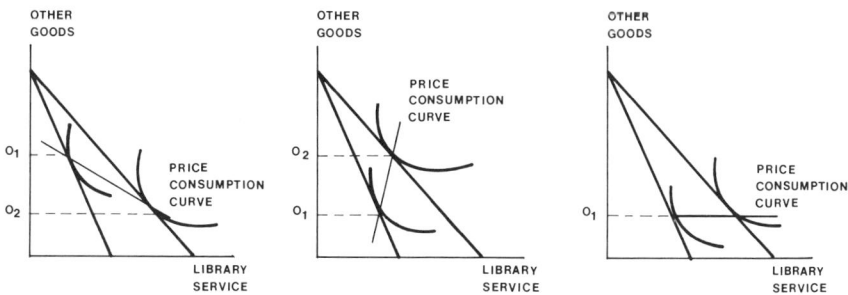

FIG. 22. Price Elasticity and Price-Consumption Curves

Factors Affecting Price Elasticity

Aside from preferences, there are three major factors which affect the price elasticity of demand: substitutablity, time, and the fraction of income devoted to consumption of a good. The first, and principal, determinant of price elasticity is the availability and "closeness" of substitutes. If a commodity has good substitutes, then the amount demanded will be sensitive to price, and its elasticity of demand would be high. This implies that price changes will cause consumers to turn to close substitutes. For example, an increase in the price of print versions of news might lead consumers to switch to more television viewing, radio, and other forms of news. Conversely, a price reduction will lead consumers to increase consumption of newspapers. The same type of relationship may exist between some of the library's services and between the library and alternative information services. If a commodity doesn't have close subsitutes, consumers will be slower to alter their consumption patterns.

The extent to which a commodity has close substitutes depends on how narrowly it has been defined. Generally, a specifically defined good has more close substitutes and its demand is more elastic. Linking this idea to the library, we find that the demand for a particular type of fiction would be more elastic than the demand for all fiction. Also, the demand for in-print materials would be more elastic than the demand for out-of-print materials.

A second determinant of price elasticity is the time period to which a demand curve pertains. The longer the time period, the easier it is for consumers to adjust to a change in price. Part of the reason the passage ot time affects elasticity is that it takes time for consumers to learn about changes in price. More important is the fact that it takes time to adjust consumption patterns. Consider a price increase in gasoline. At first, consumers will cut back on consumption of gasoline by driving less, but as time passes, consumers will find alternative means for decreasing gasoline consumption. As it concerns the library, this may mean an increase in phone calls, a decrease in number of visits, an increase in the number of items taken out per visit, and an increase in quantity demanded of library services offered by mail.

A third factor affecting price elasticity is the importance of the service in the individual's budget. For example, assume that there are two types of library users: Library User A, who, on a regular basis, borrows a large quantity of journal articles, and Library User B, who, on an irregular basis, borrows a small number of journal articles. Assuming that both consumers are purchasing (using) current materials, we could assert that the elasticity of demand for library services of Library User A is higher than that for Library User B. However, the importance of this link has not been proven. The link between number of substitutes and time is stronger, implying that if Library User A borrows a large number of articles from a small number of journals, elasticity would be high. Over time, given a price increase, User A will substitute direct or other lending services for library use. On the other hand, if User B was borrowing a limited number of articles from a diverse number of journals, the number of substitutes would probably be limited. Demand would be inelastic; library use would be less sensitive to changes in price. The key factor would be the number of substitutes.

Income Elasticity of Demand

Price is not the only factor that determines quantity demanded; therefore, we can define an elasticity measure for the responsiveness of other determinants of demand. Another important factor we discussed was the level of income. Income elasticity measures the responsiveness of consumption of a good to a change in income. In the section Consumption Decisions and Income Change, we saw that Engel curves express the relationship between income—prices held constant—and the amount of a good demanded. We can define the responsiveness of the quantity demanded to changes in income as income elasticity of demand:

$$E_i = (\Delta Q/Q) / (\Delta I/I) \qquad \text{Eq. 3.4}$$

where delta Q is the change in quantity consumed, Q is the original quantity, delta I is the change in income, and I is the original income. Income elasticity varies between goods, and in part depends upon the level of a person's income. The sign of the income elasticity distinguishes between normal and inferior goods. Recall that an inferior good is one whose consumption falls with increases in income; the opposite holds true for normal goods. A positive income elasticity means that consumption rises with income; therefore, the good must be normal. Conversely, when the income elasticity is negative, consumption of the good falls as income rises, and the good will be inferior.

Cross Elasticity

From the discussion of substitutes and complements, we know that a demand curve is affected by the prices of other goods. Cross elasticity is defined as the percentage change in the consumption of a good divided by the percentage change in the price of a different good. Between two library services, reference and circulation, the cross elasticity is defined as the relative change in the quantity of reference resulting from a change in the price of circulation, or cross elasticity of demand for reference, R, with respect to the price of circulation, C:

$$E_c = (\Delta Q_r/Q_r) / (\Delta P_c/P_c) \qquad \text{Eq. 3.5}$$

Cross elasticity is a quantitative measure of the relationship between the consumption of one good and the price of another. As such, it measures the strength of the complementary or substitute relationship between two goods. Whether two services are classified as substitutes or complements depends upon the sign of the cross elasticity. A positive sign indicates that the two items are substitutes whereas a negative sign indicates that the two items are complements. For example, an increase in the price of record players, when the price of records stays constant, will tend to decrease the quantity of records demanded. In this case, the cross elasticity is negative, indicating that the two items are complements. Although two goods may be substitutes or complements, the relationship of a price change in one item to the quantity demanded of the other item may not be equal. In other words, record consumption may be less sensitive to changes in the price of record players than record player consumption would be to the price of record players. Thus, the sign of cross elasticity would be the same but the numerical value could be different.

Time and Library Service Consumption

The model presented so far has suggested that the decisions of consumers are guided by prices, income, and preferences. The time-allocation model of consumer choice is concerned with how consumers allocate time among competing ends[2]—in particular, how the relative costs of various activities affect the ways in which consumers allocate time between work and consumption, as well as consumption time among commodities. Thus, choices are affected by relative prices, the consumer's production function, and income.

In Chapter 2 we pointed out that there is a continuum between pure consumption and pure production. Therefore, the value, or cost, of library use depends upon where it falls on the scale of pure consumption to pure production. The cost of consumption which indirectly contributes to earnings is less than the full wage rate. In other words, the cost of library use is more when it is pure consumption than when it is for production. Library time, when used as an input to increase skills, knowledge, or to enhance earning power, can be classified as production. Note that neither library services nor materials are inherently related to production or consumption. The uses to which information may be put are not determined by the materials or by the users. The use to which an individual puts a library service varies over time and the uses of a service vary over time and individuals. Nonetheless, the time allocation model permits one to examine how different types of people react to changes in price and income. That is, how these changes affect the nature of library consumption patterns over time and across the population.

The time-allocation approach provides us with a mechanism for analyzing library consumption decisions. An advantage of this model is that it allows us to examine library use based on a user's allocation between production and consumption—choices being constrained by prices, wages, and preferences.

First, let us examine some of the basic elements of time prices as they relate to library use. Then we will study the impact of changes in price, production function, and income.

Elements of the Time Price

Previously, we suggested that when time is used for consumption instead of production, it can be priced according to the sacrifice, or wages forgone. The amount of time required to consume library services is dependent upon the consumer's production function and upon the policies and operations of libraries. In this section, our examination of the consumer's production function will be limited to the types of time required to consume library services. The actual time required depends, in part, upon the consumer's education and age.

The demand for a good whose cost is monetary depends on preferences, income, and prices. Similarly, the demand for a service whose cost is nonmonetary depends on the consumer's willingness to pay, prices, and income. In the case of the library, the mechanism which constrains use, its cost, is time. A portion of this time is involved in completing library transactions—namely, filling out forms such as library card registration, paying fines, waiting in line, and learning about the types of services the library offers and its policies, such as loan period and hours. These costs add to the price of library service and are independent of the commodity to be produced.[3] Travel costs are a function of the distance to the library. Information search in the library and the time spent using library materials are two other elements in the price of library services. Each of these components of library price will have an impact on the quantity demanded of library service.

The time needed to use the library can be separated into travel, wait, and use time.[4] Travel time is determined by the distance from the library and available alternatives, including phone services, items by mail, and bookmobiles. Wait time is determined, in part, by service hours, circulation policy, binding and other collection maintenance policies, number and quality of staff, and composition and quantity of materials. The cost of waiting in the library—queue time, travel time, and use time—is based on the value of a consumer's time. The cost of time spent waiting outside the library (delay time) for the library to deliver an item is dependent upon the value of the information (dependent upon user and/or type of information), as it decays over time. Use time is dependent on the availability and quality of staff, quantity and quality of search aids, and the consumer's ability to use location devices and library materials.

To summarize, use time is a function of the commodity to be produced, the productivity of the user, and the nature of the library resources. Queue, delay, and travel time are a function of the library.

Changes in Price: Wages

Since the price of library service is determined by the amount of time required to use it, its price is affected by the value of time, or the wage rate; the ability of the library user; availability and closeness of substitutes; and library operations and policy. First, let us examine the impact of an increase in the wage rate, the price of time, on consumption of library services.[5]

After an increase in the wage rate, the price of time has risen. Time-intensive commodities (goods plus time) have become more expensive than goods-intensive commodities. Put differently, as the wage rate increases, the price of goods becomes relatively less expensive than the consumer's time. From our previous discussion of price, we know that a change in price is accompanied by a substitution effect and an income effect. The consumer shifts from time-intensive commodities to goods-intensive commodities. Also, the consumer will substitute goods for time in the production of commodities. Why might this occur? To maximize utility, the consumer chooses that combination of inputs (goods and time) that yields the highest level of output, commodities. As the price of one input rises, to produce the same level of utility at the same price (time plus goods), an individual will have to switch from the relatively more expensive input, time, to the relatively less expensive input, goods.

Based on the substitution effect, as the cost of time increases, work or production time increases. Thus, the quantity demanded for library service should decrease with an increase in wage rate. However, the income effect makes it possible to consume more of all commodities, the consumption of which tends to decrease production or work time. As with other goods, the income effect probably dominates over a certain range of income and prices, indicating that as the wage rate goes up, library use would increase—up to the point at which it became an inferior good or up to the point at which information items purchased at alternative sources were relatively less expensive.[6]

To summarize, the effect of a change in the wage rate on the use of a particular library service depends upon the elasticity of demand and the ability of the user to substitute, in the production of information and knowledge, both in the library and elsewhere.

Other Factors Influencing the Time Price of Library Use

The decision to use a particular good is based, in part, on preferences between production and consumption activities, that is, their production function and the relative costs of alternatives. For example, to produce entertainment, consumers may use their time, plus video recorders, television, books, theaters, parks, and other recreation products. Food consumption may be accomplished by combining shopping time with preparation time, or by dining out. Time is a necessary ingredient in consuming many goods and services. Aside from quality, what distinguishes them is the amount of time used to yield utility. As wages increase, consumers seek to substitute *away* from time-intensive goods and services. Thus, dining out, using prepared foods, or employing such cooking techniques as microwave ovens will increase as the wage rate increases.

Library use is an input into the production of a variety of commodities, including education, recreation, health, business, law, etc. Use of the library is dependent not only on the amount of time devoted to consumption and to production but also upon the level of information required to complete an activity and the availability of close substitutes. As the price of time increases, the consumer will seek out substitutes for library service, will attempt to reduce the time required to use the library, or will reduce the consumption of information. To the extent that library use is for production, the impact of the increase in the wage rate is mitigated, and use of the library for production may increase.

Substitutes for library services include the purchasing, instead of borrowing, of library materials. The user can switch to less time-intensive services, such as from reading to viewing movie adaptations of books and to radio or television broadcasting of news reports. Another response to an increase in wages is to increase the productivity of library time: use of goods library-intensive services such as computer searches and photocopying, use of library materials and staff during uncongested times, and use of the library when the opportunity cost of time is low.[7] Finally, information can be input into the decision process of consumers. The consumer can choose to do with less information in the production of decisions. The result of an increase in the price of information, as with other consumption decisions, depends upon the consumer's willingness to substitute other goods for information, MRS, and on the objective ability to substitute one good for another, expressed by the price ratio and the production function.

To summarize, changes in the full price, time, and money of various commodites; the means by which commodities are produced; and income and tastes will cause shifts in "library consumption" patterns. The full price of library services is dependent upon the policies and operations of the library, the nature and value of use, the ability to use facilities, and the number of close substitutes. Thus, changes in library policy, such as number and quality of staff, number and types of materials, loan period, and so on, affect the price of library use. Using the library for production mitigates the extent to which time is valued at the wage rate. In addition, the value of use is determined not only by the current use but by its value to the user over time. The ability to use the library is dependent upon the age and education of the user. Time spent in the library is just one way to obtain information or recreation services. Thus, the extent to which other services can be substituted for library services has an affect on library use.

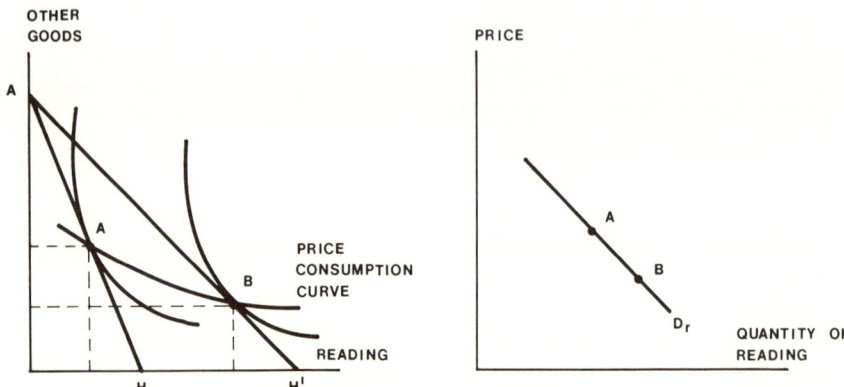

Fig. 23. Budget Line and Demand for Reading

Application: Have You Heard a Good Book Lately?

The study of budget lines and indifference curves, two of the most useful tools in microeconomics, can illuminate real behavior in markets. They can be applied, for example, to changes in technology which affect the consumption of particular goods and services. Recall that the opportunity cost of a good is the amount of other things one has to sacrifice to acquire a unit of the good you are purchasing, expressed as the price along the budget line. Books take a certain amount of time to read; television, cooking, driving to work, and so on also involve the use of one's time. What is the price of other goods in terms of reading? Clearly, this depends upon the amount of time one uses to consume other goods and services in terms of the time used to read. Let us assume that it takes a hypothetical person 15 hours to read an average-length book, whereas the cost of some other good, X, takes, on average, 3 hours. The price of other goods, X, in terms of reading, R, can be expressed as

$$\text{(hours/X)} / \text{(hours/R)} = 3/15 = 1/3 \text{ unit X per novel} \quad \text{Eq. 3.6}$$

Now let us assume that a new product, books on tape, is introduced, allowing a person to combine activities which previously restricted his or her ability to read, such as driving to work, jogging, bicycling, or walking, with reading. Since most books on tape are abridgments or condensed adaptations of the original work, books on tape are not perfect substitutes for reading the original. But, roughly speaking, books on tape serve as a close substitute for the original, and they allow one to reduce the amount of time one must give up to consume books or ideas. In Figure 23A, the budget line, AH, drawn for a given number of hours, shows by its slope the rate at which a consumer forgoes other goods to read, prior to the introduction of books on tape. After the introduction of books on tape, the new budget line is AH′. Although at first this may be mildly confusing, we are simply suggesting that books on tape allow the consumer to combine reading with other tasks to more efficiently produce a commodity such as entertainment or education. The opportunity cost of reading, its price in terms of time used to consume other goods and services, has become relatively lower. On a more mundane level, the slope of the budget line has decreased. Finally, notice that by using the indifference map in Figure 23A we are able to derive two points on our consumer's demand curve for reading, as illustrated in Figure 23B. And due to the drop in the price of consuming information, the quantity demanded increases.

Summary

The central theme of this chapter has been to analyze how consumers react to changes in market conditions. Utility theory provided us with the analytical structure needed to accomplish this end. First, we considered a change in income, expressed as a parallel shifting of the budget line, holding all else constant. In response to a change in income, we identified two possible consumption patterns: consumption of a good may rise with increases in income, or it may go down. The former exhibits the attribute of a normal good and the latter an inferior good.

Just as the consumer's reactions to changes in income are based on the theory of consumer equilibrium, reactions to changes in price are based on the indifference-curve analysis of choice. Under the assumed constancy of the other determinants of demand, by varying price we were able to generate a series of price-quantity equilibria. The relationship between the price of a good and the quantity consumed is known as the demand curve. To illustrate why demand curves have a negative slope, we examined the two components of a change in price, namely, the substitution and income effects. For most goods, both the income effect and substitution effect imply greater consumption at a lower price; therefore, the demand curve must slope downward. To gauge the responsiveness of quantity demanded to changes in price, we discussed the concept of price elasticity. Price elasticity, defined as the percentage change in quantity divided by the percentage change in price, depends upon the number of close substitutes, the time period, and the fraction of income devoted to the good. Demand is elastic when this ratio exceeds 1; price inelastic when the coefficient of the ratio is less than 1; and when it is equal to 1, demand is unit elastic.

The time-allocation model of consumer choice provides us with additional insights into library use. Proceeding in a manner similar to that used to derive a demand curve, we showed how this model can be used to analyze changes in market conditions. We identified the elements and determinants of the price of library service. Price is dependent not only on wage rate, but on the library's policies and operations, as well as the use to which the service is put and the ability of the consumer. The time-allocation model, by treating library use as a form of production, assists us in detecting the determinants of the quantity demanded of library services and serves as an introduction to the theory of the firm.

Exercises

1. Use preference analysis to show which types of library employees might be better off if medical benefits were placed in a medical reserve account and monies not used were refunded to the employee.
2. Examine the effects of either a gas-price increase or rationing of gas on library use. If you assume that there is a books-by-mail service, show how the market for in-house service would be affected by the gas-price changes.
3. Compare the costs to a user of an electronic catalog and a fiche/manual catalog (consider time).
4. If we think of lifestyles as methods for economizing on choice, then would this aid in predicting library use patterns? Why do mystery readers choose mysteries, and would we expect them to continue to read such material? Think of patterns of change—student, worker, retirement—as aids in predicting information requirements on the basis of lifestyles and/or age-based information requirements.
5. Assume that the price (time) of information falls and that the elasticity of demand with respect to price and income is greater than 1. Predict the expected effect on the quantity of information demanded. If fees were charged, what happens to total expenditures?
6. The cash price and time price of an information service are near zero; we impose a cash fee and the quantity demanded decreases dramatically. What can you state about the elasticity of demand with respect to cash price? Would you expect this elasticity to remain constant as we raise prices incrementally?
7. If the demand for library services increases (shift of curve) and there has been no increase in library revenues, what can you say about the time-price of library service to users? What happens to per capita cost of library service?
8. If two library systems have a use agreement and this agreement is broken (fees for "nonresidents" are set in place), what would you expect to happen to the demand curve for each library? (Note: In part, it depends on which library was experiencing the greater "nonresident" use prior to fees.)
9. Given the example above, if the nonresident users of one library system use particular services, what can you state about the elasticity of demand for these services?
10. If the income elasticity for a given library service rises up to a point and then declines, predict the quantity demanded, assuming all other factors are held constant. Would you expect the price elasticity of demand for a given service to be larger or smaller than for overall information services?

11. Does the effective price of library service change over the range of low-, middle-, and high-income users? (Note: As income rises, the value of time increases; ownership of information reduces waiting time and provides repeated-use availability.)
12. If knowledge can be substituted for labor, would you expect that, as income increases, more or less will be spent on knowledge services/products? What occurs if the price of knowledge services declines?
13. Describe, in terms of choice theory, the nature of search strategy. Note that choices are made between options and that one of the primary constraints is time. What do libraries currently provide to facilitate information choices?
14. If the demand for library services increases, what happens to the price of library services? Explain in terms of time.
15. Create a hypothesis for explaining why displays induce library patrons to check out these library materials at a higher rate than materials which aren't displayed. (Hint: Think in terms of patrons seeking information concerning item attributes.) Use your hypothesis to create other strategies for inducing library use.
16. Compare two information services, one free but self-service and the other dollar priced, in terms of the type of consumer you might expect to use the two different services. Explain the impact of learning on the cost to the consumer.

References

1. Bruce P. Schauer, "Utility and Economics of Information: A Survey of the Public Library Industry," in *Encyclopedia of Library and Information Science,* ed. Allen Kent, Harold Lancour, and Jay E. Daily (New York: Marcel Dekker, 1981), 32: 319-341; Lawrence J. White, *The Public Library in the 1980's: The Problems of Choice* (Lexington, Mass: Lexington Books, 1983), Chap. 12; and Paul G. Zurkowski, "Misconceptions about Information Are Costing the United States a Bundle," *Publishers Weekly* 216 (July 9, 1979): 37-38.

2. G. S. Becker, "A Theory of the Allocation of Time," *Economic Journal* 75:299 (September 1965): 493-517.

3. Nancy V. DeWath, "Demand for Public Library Services: A Time Allocation Approach to User Fees" (Ann Arbor: University Microfilms, 1982), p. 114.

4. Ibid., pp. 113-116.

5. Ibid., pp. 92-97.

6. Ibid., p. 131.

7. Ibid, pp. 122-127.

Suggested Reading

Baumol, W. "The Empirical Determination of Demand Relationships." Reprinted in E. Mansfield, *Microeconomics: Selected Readings.* 4th ed. New York: Norton, 1982.

Becker, G. S. *Economic Approach to Human Behavior.* Chicago: University of Chicago Press, 1976.

Berg, S. V. "An Economic Analysis of the Demand for Scientific Journals." *Journal of the American Society for Information Science* 23:1 (January–February 1972): 23–29.

Buckland, M. K. *Book Availability and the Library User.* Elmsford, N.Y.: Pergamon Press, 1975.

———, and A. Hindle. "Loan Policies, Duplication and Availability." In *Planning Library Services: Proceedings of a Reasearch Seminar* (University of Lancaster Occasional Papers, No. 3), ed. A. G. Mackenzie and I. M. Stuart. Lancaster, England: University Library, 1969. (ED 045 173)

Casper, C. A. "Estimating the Demand for Library Service: Theory and Practice." *Journal of the American Society for Information Science* 29:5 (September 1978): 232–237.

"The Impact of Economic Variables on the Demand for Library Services." In *Information Choices and Policies: Proceedings of the ASIS Annual Meeting,* 1979, 16: 41–50. White Plains, N.Y.: Knowledge Industries, 1979.

DeWath, Nancy V. "Demand for Information Services: A Time Allocation Approach to User Fees." In *Communicating Information. Proceedings of the 43rd ASIS Meeting,* 1980, 17: 51–53. White Plains, N.Y.: Knowledge Industry Publications, 1980.

Ghez, G., and G. S. Becker. *The Allocation of Time and Goods over the Life Cycle.* New York: Bureau of Economic Research, 1975.

Goddard, Haynes C. "A Study in the Theory and Measurement of Benefits and Costs in the Public Library (A Theoretical and Econometric Analysis with Special Reference to Indiana Public Libraries)." Ph.D. dissertation, Department of Economics, Indiana University, 1970.

Hanke, S. H. "Demand for Water under Dynamic Conditions." *Water Resources Research* 6:5 (October 1970): 1253–1260.

Hindle, A. A "Theoretical Note Concerning the Adaptivity of Demand for Library Documents." *Journal of Documentation* 33:4 (December 1977): 305–307.

Hirshleifer, J. *Price Theory and Applications.* 2nd ed. Englewood Cliffs, N.J.: Prentice-Hall, 1980. Pp. 162–170.

Newhouse, J. P., and A. J. Alexander. *An Economic Analysis of Public Library Services.* Lexington, Mass.: Lexington Books, 1972.

Sowell, T. *Knowledge and Decisions.* New York: Basic Books, 1980.

Van House, N. A., N. K. Roderer, and M. D. Cooper. "Librarians: A Study of Supply and Demand." *American Libraries* 14:6 (June 1983): 361–370.

4

LIBRARY PRODUCTION

In production theory, choices are viewed in terms of tradeoffs. Libraries utilize staff, and information resources such as documents, films, databases, equipment, and facilities, to produce information services. Information managers have the option of choosing how to combine these inputs: number and type of staff, documents, facilities, services hours, microfiche machines, copiers, telephones, computers, and so on. Furthermore, they price output; that is, they set policy regarding the use of output. To evaluate input decisions requires a technique for relating input to output (objectives). It is to this end that we will introduce the theory of the firm.

Information managers, constrained by technology and revenue, face a decision problem similar to that faced by the consumer—to maximize an objective subject to constraints. The firm, confronted with these constraints, attempts to select that input combination which will produce the maximum output. Hence, information managers require a framework for evaluating input choices. For instance, what level and type of resources should be devoted to reference, circulation, adult, young adult, children's, or special services? What level of help should be provided to users? How long should a loan period be? How many copies of a title should be purchased, and when? How should questions of weeding, off-site storage, microforms, number of open hours, and number and size of buildings be decided? Each of these decisions has implications for the type and quantity of output the library will produce. By observing the relationships between inputs and output we will find valuable clues for making such decisions. Economic theory suggests that, given certain constraints, there are distinct tradeoffs: more staff, fewer documents; more buildings, fewer open hours; more study space, less storage space; and more storage space, less display space.

Just as the study of market demand orginated with the individual consumer, market supply begins with the individual firm. In this chapter we shall investigate the factors that determine the level of output that a library may offer its public—specifically, the way in which output varies as we change the level of input under conditions of a fixed state of technology. Input productivity and cost are directly related. In this sense, production theory provides us with the foundation for understanding the nature of costs. The analytical structure we use to represent the process by which the library combines inputs to produce output is known as a production function. Production functions describe the relationship between inputs and outputs, given technology. They identify the minimum input combination used to produce a given level of output.

A library's production function summarizes the various combinations of inputs used to produce a given level of output at least cost. The problem facing information managers is to minimize the cost of producing a given level of output. In particular, libraries are engaged in the production of a diverse array of information services, including facility and equipment, document services, citation services, answer services, instruction services, and programming. To produce these services involves the use of inputs of varying qualities. Thus, the function of information library managers is to allocate resources among competing ends, and to combine and process these resources to produce the level and composition of output which meets its objectives.

Initially, our study of a library's production function will be centered on the form it takes in the short run. Operating under the assumed constancy of technology, we will investigate the way in which output varies as we vary the level of one input while holding the level of other inputs constant. As we shall see, once we remove this restriction, and allow for variation in the level of each input, the apparatus used to analyze the library's production possibilities parallels that which was used to depict the utility function of the consumer.

Use of the theory of the firm, and in particular the production function, provides us with a technique for investigating choices. It suggests the notion of tradeoffs among goals. In fact, it helps one evaluate and understand the terms of tradeoffs among goals, between inputs, and between inputs and outputs. Initially, our study of the library as a firm concentrates on the relationship between input level and output level. To this end, we will discuss the economic concepts of isoquants; total, average, and marginal physical product; the law of diminishing returns; and returns to scale. (In the next chapter, we will build upon production functions to identify the relationship between the level of output and cost and between price and output level.)

Library Production

In this section, we will briefly review the processes used by libraries to produce the library's output. We do not intend to describe the exact mix of library inputs; rather, we will simply provide an outline of how a library might produce information services. Our purpose is to suggest a convenient framework for using production theory for examining the production of library services. The broad elements of the library's production function are grouped according to output; to analyze them in greater detail, each component may be subdivided. The problem facing the information manager is to select that level and composition of services which meets the objectives within the limits of revenue. Production theory provides the methodology needed to examine how each input and process relates to output. As such, it is a critical element in the decision calculus of the library.

The major functions of a library include the supply of facilities; staff, equipment, and information within the library; access to documents and/or information located outside the institution; and administration. Most (if not all) of the functions are interrelated. Thus, the task of the library manager is quite complicated. Production theory will provide a framework for analyzing the way in which one input affects one output and the way in which one function affects another. Note that when we examine library output we will be discussing physical output, and not the value or benefits received from this output. Benefit evaluation, estimating the value or social price of library services, plays a role in benefit-cost analysis, but is not needed or useful for determining the relationship between choice of inputs and the level of output. Therefore, we will focus our attention on inputs and how they relate to physical outputs, such as number of items processed, cataloged, used, number of patrons served, number of citations produced, turnover rate, in-library use, etc. The output measure that is used depends upon the type of service rendered. Next, we will divide the major functions into their elements and review some library production decisions.

The provision of physical facilities includes the public amenities, such as restrooms, telephones, study areas, meeting rooms, lighting, heating, etc. These services can be supplied in one facility or in many; the building can be located near other businesses or in a less congested area. An alternative might be to provide mobile units. Thus, the library manager must decide the type, number, and size of the facilities and their location or access routes. Additional decisions involve the arrangement and size of different areas of the library: staff and consumer work space, document storage and display capabilities, service hours, type and number of furnishings, and maintenance. Each decision involves setting a level and mix of inputs. For example, the consumer work space involves deciding number and type of chairs, number and types of tables, type and amount of lighting, and so on. Maintenance of buildings involves deciding on the state of repair, type of janitorial service to employ, amount of insurance, and building temperature-control system. The input decision depends upon the prices of inputs: the library's technology (i.e., how each input relates to output), as well as the objectives of the organization.

To furnish access to staff, equipment, and documents entails the selection process and, in the case of documents, the indexing or organization of materials—as distinct from physical access via fixed or mobile sites. The library may also supply access to information through cable television, telephone, mail, and computer. The selection of materials involves deciding upon the type and quantity to be purchased. A mechanism for ordering must be set up, including the basis for selection and the timing of selection. In conjunction with this function, the purchasing of library materials includes choosing the ordering technique, choice of vendors, timing of orders, receipt of orders, and payment of bills. To facilitate the use of library materials, the library processes and maintains them; it classifies and catalogs materials, controls documents, provides equipment, purchases indexes, provides staff, and mounts promotional activities.

Processing functions involve the packaging and labeling of materials: the type of protection to provide materials, including covers, and the type of binding, as well as the labeling. Each of these decisions will have some bearing on the amount of time the library spends preparing and maintaining materials. Indeed, the information manager may decide to purchase these services from outside vendors—in which case the library may have more time to devote to other activities. It is in the organization-of-materials stage of production that libraries provide location and subject-signaling devices, used by both the consumer and the staff in order to facilitate the choice process. Within this function, information managers decide upon the system of organization; the method of producing catalogs and lists, and the related concept of quality; and the number, location, and form of the catalog. As an adjunct to the cataloging and indexing of materials, libraries can promote browsing by providing signs and other explanatory devices. Just as the decisions involved in the provision of facility affect the level of output, so do the decisions affecting the selection and indexing of materials.

To control library documents, managers must select loan, shelving, routing, and storage mechanisms. For instance, regarding the borrowing of library items, the library will have a policy pertaining to who may use the library, who may use which materials, the length of loan, renewal policy, reserve policy, and an overdue, lost, or damaged policy. In addition, the library manager will decide how and where each type or category of material shall be stored: on the premises, on shelves accessible to the public, or in back rooms. Other decisions include the system to lend and shelve materials, as well as security.

Briefly, the other services include the supply of equipment necessary to facilitate the use of library materials; the collection maintenance function; reference activities; the combining of trained personnel, catalogs and indexes, and materials to facilitate provision and location of information services; promotion services, including publications, exhibits, library-to-agency contact, and advertisements; and the administrative function—choosing and coordinating all production functions, including budget control, personnel policy, and provision of supplies.

To summarize, each of the activities used to produce information services involves the combining of inputs, including labor, capital, and land. Information managers must allocate resources among competing uses and select among alternative production techniques, as well as set the level and composition of output. For example, a library may decide to produce legal information services. Production of this service involves selecting the types of staff, information, and equipment; the quantity and quality of staff, materials, and equipment; format of information; organization of materials; delivery technique; service hours; types and location of service outlets; and response time. Each of these inputs has the potential for adding to the output of legal services. The amount of output depends upon the library's production function. In other words, in each library the addition or subtraction of one of these elements will most likely affect output in a different manner.

Not all libraries will employ the functions we have listed. Rather, the division of the library's production function into separate output (service) components is a conceptualization device used for analytical convenience. Each input/output choice may be linked to other choices, but the nature of each decision is similar: number and type of input to be employed in the production of output. For example, a library may have an objective of circulating X items per year, and this decision may have an effect on other objectives such as the rate at which it fills subject and title requests. However, the critical decision is the input/policy mix used to achieve the objective. Production functions supply information managers with an analytical structure for investigating alternative techniques for producing library services specifically, how the number and type of input employed affects the level of output. An understanding of production theory will enable us to investigate the nature of library costs.

Production Functions

A production function can be represented in a table, a graph, or a mathematical equation. It illustrates the technological constraints facing the library. Production functions range from the simple two-input, one-output case to the complex multiple input and multiple output cases. For example, a simple production function, with circulation as the library's output, would include materials and staff, whereas a more complex representation of the production function would include buildings, other forms of capital, and service hours.

In the production of a particular library service, the manager has the option of choosing the level and mix of human and nonhuman inputs. Some libraries use more of one resource than do others; some use inputs that other libraries do not use. Within each production technique there is a basic choice between one, two, or more inputs. There is also the decision to be made between production techniques. For example, a given-size staff may be used for several different levels of output by providing different levels of collection size. Conversely, any given collection size may be used for several different levels of output by varying the amount of staff. In short, there are variable proportions of these two factors of production, staff, and collection size, which may be used to produce a given level of output. As a result, library managers have the option of choosing between several combinations of input to yield a given level of output. On the other hand, for each level of output the library may incur different costs. Thus, managers not only have the option of several staff and collection sizes for any given level of output, they may also have the option of choosing levels of output which have different costs per unit of output.

To summarize, *production function* is the term used to describe the relationship in the library between alternative levels of physical inputs and the level of output resulting from that quantity. It identifies the maximum quantity of a good that can be produced per time period from a specific mix of inputs.

Let's define the library's output as A (materials circulated), resulting from a combination of factors of production L, M, and K. Mathematically, this is the equivalent of

$$A = f(L,M,K) \qquad \text{Eq. 4.1}$$

where the quantity of A produced per unit of time is a function of the quantities of input labor (L), raw materials (M), and capital (K). Librarians can vary the input mix and the choice of technique, but the above formula is assumed to represent the most efficient technique. Given a fixed state of technology, the library can vary its output by varying the level of inputs for a particular technique, by switching from one production method to another or by some combination of these alternative courses of action. However, the maximum obtainable level of output for any technique is constrained by the prevailing state of technology.

Let's suppose that two techniques are available to the library for producing output. Assume that in technique 1 if the library uses 5 units of each input, 500 units of output are produced; 10 units of each yields 1000 units, and 15 units of each yields 1500 units of ouput. Technique 2, employing 5 units of each input, yields 800 units of output; 10 units of each yields 1300 units of output, and 15 units of each input yields 1800 units of output. The library can obtain higher levels of output from any given level of input by using technique 2. The library's cost of using any given level of inputs is the same, regardless of whether it uses technique 1 or 2, but the level of output is greatest when the library produces the maximum amount of output possible, given a specific usage rate of inputs. Therefore, it seems reasonable to assume that the library would select technique 2. This is why we state that the production function represents the maximum level of output that can be achieved from a specified level of inputs.

Properties of Isoquants

The central problem of the library manager is analogous to that faced by all economic entities. Both the consumer and the firm face constraints. In the pursuit of utility, consumers choose which items to purchase while information managers select the ingredients used to produce a particular information service. And just as consumers were able to substitute one item for another, firms are able to substitute inputs in the production of output. Both entities are constrained by their income and prices. In the theory of consumer choice, the final decision was based on the intersection of the budget line and preferences. In production theory, the final decision is founded on the budget line, the firm's technology, and the price of output. Thus, each market actor is concerned with how to allocate its limited income so as to maximize some measure of well-being. In the case of the consumer, we assumed that he or she will select items so as to maximize utility; in the case of the firm, we assume the manager combines items so as to maximize output at least cost. Indeed, the similarity permits us to utilize an analytical framework with many of the same properties that we used to analyze consumer behavior.

By restricting our analysis to two inputs, we can represent a library's production function graphically, by production isoquants. An isoquant is a curve that traces all the combinations of inputs which will produce a certain level of output. Each point on an isoquant depicts the output which a particular combination of inputs will produce. A production function will have a system of such isoquants, one for each level of output. Actually, the same formal analytical apparatus treats both the utility possibilities of the consumer and the production possibilities of the library. Each point on an indifference curve shows the utility yield from a specific combination of two goods consumed; the entire curve illustrates all such combinations from which an equal utility is derived. As you may recall, the consumer's utility function is described by an indifference map. In production theory, isoquants play a role similar to the indifference curves of consumer theory.

Isoquants illustrate an important economic assumption concerning production possibilities—namely, that it is possible for a library to produce a given level of output by using a variety of input combinations. A library may be able to produce a specified level of reference service with a small number of staff and a large number of information resources, or it may combine a few information resources with a large staff. Although an isoquant portrays all the efficient combinations of input, with each combination showing the maximum obtainable output from given inputs, it does not by itself indicate the least-cost method of production. To identify this point requires that we know the cost of inputs—a topic which we will explore in Chapter 5.

We have suggested that production isoquants depict all input combinations that yield the same output, but in some situations the library may not have the option of selecting from among all such combinations. These two production possibilities are conceptual devices which pertain to two different time frames, commonly referred to as the long- and the short-run production responses, respectively.

Time and Inputs

We will be building a model of the library which represents the technological alternatives available to the firm. Let us define inputs as ingredients used in the production of library services. For example, we know that libraries use information resources, shelving, personnel, machines, and buildings in their production process. While the technological relationships between inputs and outputs vary between industries and over time, we can identify certain common relationships. The division of production responses into time periods provides us with a useful framework for investigating these relationships. To this end, economists divide production respsonses into short- and long-run possibilities.

Economists define the short run as that period of time during which it would be impractical to alter the level of some of the library's inputs; inputs are fixed. Usually this is the period of time in which the library's plant and equipment (other specialized inputs) cannot be altered without excessive (prohibitive) costs. On the other hand, variable inputs are comprised of those production inputs whose quantity it is practical to change rapidly: labor and raw materials.

The long run is defined as that period of time during which all inputs are variable. In contrast to the short run, when some input combinations are unobtainable, during the long run the entire range of production options is available to the library. The distinction between the short run and the long run isn't clearly defined by specific lengths of time. The nature of each period is dependent upon the industry and the production technique. Nonetheless, the concepts of the long and the short run are useful in emphasizing the fact that output changes will be accomplished with different types of production patterns. In the next few sections, we will be examining the library's production function in the short run. After investigating the way in which output responds to different combinations of fixed input, we will analyze the long–run production possibilities.

Library Production

Our investigation of library production begins with a situation in which we have a fixed input, the library building, and a variable input, labor, expressed in terms of hours per year. With the amount of capital held constant, we will

Table 2
LIBRARY OUTPUT—ONE VARIABLE INPUT

Labor (hrs/yr.)	Library Use (per yr.)
1,000	40,000
2,000	65,000
3,000	85,000
4,000	95,000
5,000	100,000
6,000	100,000
7,000	97,000
8,000	92,000

examine the way output varies as the library employs different quantities of labor. The effect of adding units of labor on the output of the library, while holding building size constant, is shown in Table 2.

Notice that as we add units of labor to the building, the output of the library increases. In general, there is a limit to the level of output that can be produced with one building and increasing units of labor. This occurs between 5000 and 6000 hours per year of labor. After 5000 labor hours per year, adding additional units of labor contributes nothing to library output. Employing *more* than 6000 units leads to a decrease in output. An alternative form of representing the information in Table 2 is shown graphically as Figure 24.

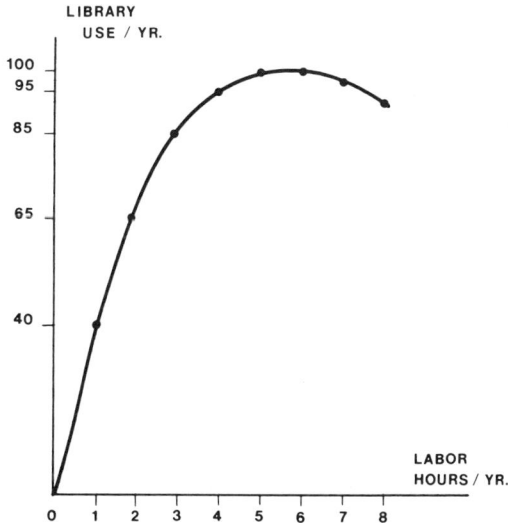

FIG. 24. Library Output

88   Microeconomic Theory

A production function provides the first step in the analysis of the library's technology. From an input-output table like Table 2, we can derive two other concepts, the average and the marginal product of labor, which will assist in understanding the production process in greater detail. The average physical product of an input is defined as the total output (product), divided by that amount of input employed to produce that level of output. The marginal product of an input is defined as the change in total output due to a 1-unit increase of the input, while holding all other inputs constant. Mathematically, average product can be obtained from the following mathematical formula:

$$APl = Q/l \qquad \text{Eq. 4.2}$$

where APl is the average product of labor and Q is the total output for a given level of labor, l. From our definition of marginal product, we can express this concept as

$$MPl = \Delta Q/\Delta l \qquad \text{Eq. 4.3}$$

Table 3 provides us with the average and marginal product for our hypothetical production function.

Total, Average, and Marginal Product Curves

Geometrically, a definite relationship exists between all average magnitudes and a marginal magnitude. The marginal magnitude exceeds average product when the latter is increasing and is less than average product when the latter is decreasing. This is based on simple mathematics. With a fixed library build-

Table 3

AVERAGE AND MARGINAL PRODUCT

Quantity of Labor (hrs/yr)	Total Output	Average Product of Labor	Marginal Product of Labor*
0	0	—	—
1,000	40,000	40.00	40
2,000	65,000	32.50	25
3,000	85,000	28.33	20
4,000	95,000	23.75	10
5,000	100,000	20.00	5
6,000	100,000	16.66	0
7,000	97,000	13.85	−3
8,000	92,000	11.50	−5

*MPl equals the change in output divided by 1,000

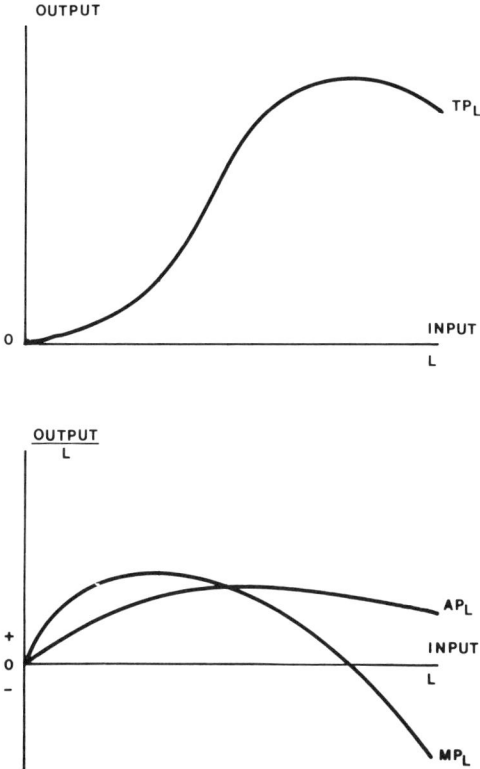

FIG. 25. Average and Marginal Product Curves

ing, when we add a unit of labor whose addition to total product is greater than the average (the marginal product of the extra person is greater than the average), the average is bound to increase. Finally, when the average is neither rising nor falling, the marginal magnitude must be equal to it. Since average product initially rises, reaches stationary point, and then declines, marginal product and average product are equal when the average product is at a maximum.

Granted these relationships between average and marginal magnitudes, there is also a relationship between the total and the marginal magnitude. In the range of positive marginal product, the total product rises. This can be intuitively appreciated: as long as an extra unit of input produces extra output, the total output increases. When marginal product is zero, the total output has reached a maximum, and when marginal product is negative, the total product curve will begin to decline. Figure 25 highlights the association between total, marginal, and average product. Mathematically, the relationship between any total, average, and marginal relationship can always be expressed in this manner. As it pertains to production theory, the significance of these connections lies in the manner in which total, average, and marginal product are related to total, average and marginal costs and the optimal level of input. The nature of the link between productivity and cost will be examined in Chapter 5.

Law of Diminishing Marginal Returns

In many practical situations, the library will be unable to alter some of its resource inputs: building, skill level of staff, and so on. We are describing the short-run production possibility, which gives rise to what is known as the law of diminishing returns. With technology and some inputs held constant, this law holds that as the amount of any one input is increased in equal increments, the resulting total output increases, per unit of input, by successively smaller amounts. Briefly, as the variable input is increased, total output increases, but the rate of increase diminishes.

Consider a library with a fixed physical plant. If we begin with just a few staff, each employee will be responsible for many tasks. Adding additional staff permits the library to specialize, making the provision of information services easier. A similar rationale applies to the situation in which the library has a fixed building and variable service hours. Starting out with 1 service hour limits the ability of the library to provide output. Regardless of how service is rendered, by adding service hours, more people can use the service; consequently, we are able to produce greater levels of output per unit of input. In the initial stages, we have too much building for the staff or service hour, but gradually, employees' tasks and service hours become redundant and their marginal product falls. Eventually, additions to the variable factor input may interfere with production, reducing total output.

When the law of diminishing returns is applied there are several points to keep in mind. First, it does not indicate when the diminishing returns become operative; it may vary from library to library and from product to product. Also, two conditions must be carefully noted: the state of technology remains unchanged, and at least one of the inputs is held constant. These two conditions apply to the short-run production possibilities of the library. Hence, the law of diminishing returns is applicable to this time period. As we shall see, varying amounts of more than 1 input, changing the library's scale of plant, gives rise to a similar law. Changes in the state of technology alter the entire production function and shift the system of production curves. These changes are a part of the long-run production responses of the library. However, for the moment, we will continue to analyze short-run possibilities.

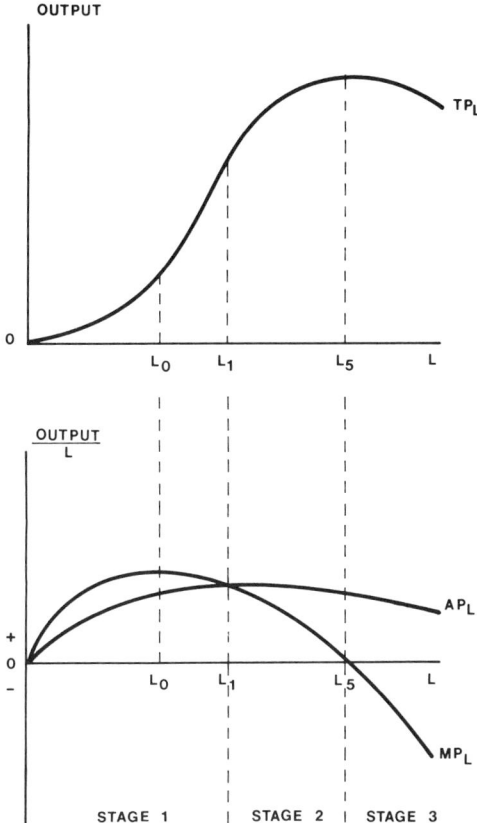

FIG. 26. Three Stages of Library Production

Application: Library Materials and Building Size

By dividing Figure 26 into three segments, we can illustrate the law of diminishing returns. In stage 1, average product is increasing, implying that successive additions to the library collection lead to proportionally greater increases in the total product. Marginal product increases, reaches a maximum at Lo items, and then falls as diminishing returns set in; average product rises and reaches a maximum at L1 items. In this initial stage of library service production, total product is rising in greater proportion than increases in input. As we move out of this stage, additions to the collection still add to total product, but at a decreasing rate. Average product is falling but marginal product is positive, implying that total product is increasing. With additional increments of input, output continues to increase, to the point at which marginal product becomes zero. Thus, in this stage of library production, increments to the variable factor input result in increases to output, but not as rapidly as in the initial stage of production. Observe that when the marginal product of library materials reaches zero, L5, the total product has reached a maximum. As we enter stage 3, additions to the library collection lead to decreases in output; marginal product becomes negative, so that even if library materials were free, it would not be worthwhile to use them in quantities in excess of L5 units, because a negative marginal product means a reduction in total output.

To help understand why this pattern of production holds up for most production situations, note that in the initial stages the amount of library materials, combined with a fixed building, is so small that the use of the building is inefficient: space is left unused. As it pertains to our earlier example of staff and building size, this implies a case of too few employees operating the library. Queues form; people, materials, and requests are not processed as efficiently as with another mix of inputs. As we expand the number of materials, more people find what they are looking for, until we reach a point where there are simply too many items in the collection. When there are too many items, the building becomes overcrowded and items cannot be located; output potential is diluted by too many items, and perhaps by older or highly specialized items. Discarding or removing items enables the collection to regain its effectiveness. For the variable-staff-size, fixed-building-size example, this implies that the expansion of staff allows for specialization of tasks and a more effective use of the building, resulting in successively greater increments to output. But eventually, too much staff leads to crowded conditions, redundant staff, and overspecialization, resulting in a decrease in output.

To conclude, we note that the law of diminishing marginal returns suggests that in the production of library services, given a fixed input and fixed technology, as we add increments of the variable input, ouput increases up to a point, then levels off, and may decline. Library managers will note that this law has implications for all library production policies: loan period, open hours, collection size, storage, equipment, and so on.

Production with Multiple Variable Inputs

As we indicated earlier, restricting the information manager's decision to two variable factors of production permits us to utilize an analytical structure analogous to the one used to examine the consumer's decision to purchase consumption goods. For the consumer, goods generate utility; for the firm, factors of production generate output. And just as indifference curves illustrate the utility alternatives facing a single consumer, isoquants depict the output

Table 4

LIBRARY PRODUCTION FUNCTION: TWO VARIABLE INPUTS

Journals	B1	B2	B3	B4
		(number of articles used)		
10	300	600	900	1200
20	800	1600	2200	3000
30	1500	4000	5500	6000
40	1900	5500	7500	8200
50	2100	7000	8500	9000

possibilities facing the single library. On any given indifference curve, the level of utility generated by a given combination of goods is equal. Similarly, any point on an isoquant shows the output produced by combining two inputs; the entire curve depicts all factor combinations capable of generating the same output. However, when we measure output, we are able to use a cardinal scale.

Let us examine the case in which the library manager has the option of varying both building size, b, and the number of journals, j. The new production function can be expressed as

$$Q = f(bi, ji) \quad i = 1 \text{ to } n \qquad \text{Eq. 4.4}$$

Table 4 presents the results of joining different combinations of building size and number of journals. From this table we can compute marginal product of an input by holding the other input constant. When 20 journals are used, the marginal product of a journal between building size 1 and building size 2 is 40 articles per year; if the building size is 3 then the marginal product of between 40 and 50 journals is 100 articles per year. In order to obtain the average product of either building size or journals, we divide the total output by the amount of building size (expressed in square footage) or the number of journals employed in the production process.

Diagramatically, we can represent the production function as a geometric surface. Figure 27 shows the output that can be produced from different combinations of two inputs, b and j.

Output, a function of input quantities of a and b, is measured by the height of the production surface OABC. Contours of equal height, shown as curves FF, GG, HH, represent isoquants. Each isoquant illustrates different input combinations, all capable of yielding an equal output. By projecting these curves onto the base plane of the three-dimensional production function, we are able to take advantage of the convenience of working in two dimensions, as illustrated in Figure 28.

Isoquants convey the same technological information as both the table and the three-dimensional surface, but in a more convenient format. In Figure 28, continuing with our example, isoquant G pertains to an output of 5500 journal

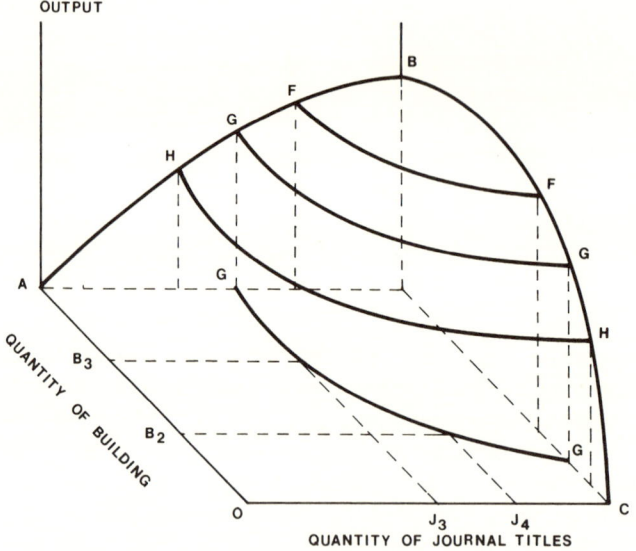

Fig. 27. Library Production

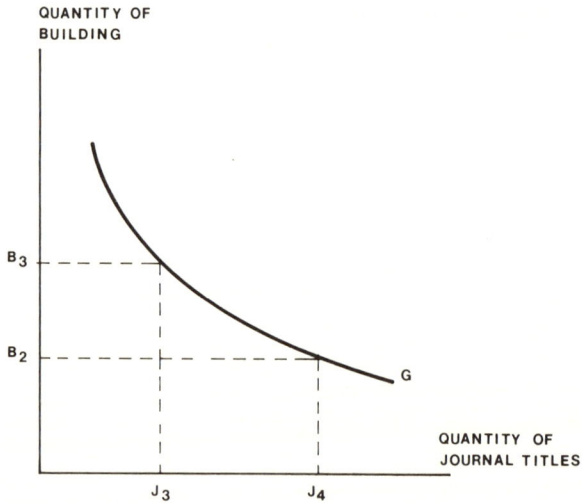

Fig. 28. Library Isoquants

articles per year, and the points on this line represent various mixes of input (B3,J3; B2,J4, ...) that can be used to produce that level of output. All these points represent efficient combinations of inputs. For example, if B1 units of building (say 1500 square feet) and J1 units of journals (50 journals) were able to produce 250 article uses per year, this combination of inputs would not be included in the production function if another, more efficient mix—1000 square feet and 50 journals—were capable of yielding an equal output.

Just as the consumer is faced with utility possibilities, the producer is faced with output possibilities. Consumers were able to combine different quantities of goods to produce a level of utility. Producers combine inputs to generate output. By restricting our attention to two factors of production, we are able to utilize an analytical device with properties similar to that of the indifference curve. Actually, the role played by isoquants in production theory is much the same as that played by indifference curves in the theory of consumer choice. Up to this point, we have shown that isoquants depict the various combinations of two ingredients of the production process, capable of yielding an equal level of output. Unlike indifference analysis, production theory permits us to attach an objective output measure to each isoquant.

Isoquants Further Considered

Like indifference curves, isoquants have three basic properties: negative slope, nonintersection, and convexity to the origin. First, observe that if both inputs are productive—that is, have positive marginal products—the isoquant must slope downward. In essence, as we increase the amount of one input, output increases (unless we reduce the level of the other input). Conversely, given a fixed rate of output, if less of one ingredient is employed, more of the other must be utilized to compensate for the loss. Since the slope of an isoquant is the ratio of the percentage change in one input to the percentage change in the other, this magnitude must be a negative number. For example, to maintain a constant level of output, a decrease in the number of open hours requires an increase in the number of library materials. This relationship holds true for any two ingredients in the library production process: staff/items, class of items A/class of items B, number of buildings/open hours, and so on.

Second, again like indifference curves, isoquants cannot intersect. The intersection of two isoquant curves would imply that one combination of inputs is capable of yielding two different maximum amounts of output. Based on our assumption that the firm uses the most efficient technique, only one level of output is consistent with a given mix of inputs. Intersecting isoquants are logically inconsistent with our basic assumption.

Finally, the rationale for convex isoquants is much the same as that which explains why indifference curves are convex to the origin. In demand theory, convex indifference curves result from the assumption of the diminishing marginal rate of the substitution of one item for another. To explain convex isoquants, production theory uses a similar concept. It represents the ability of the firm to substitute inputs for one another while holding output constant. Both assumptions are empirical generalizations and are not based on a system of logic. The marginal rate of substitution in production between input A and input B, or MRSab, is defined as the amount of input B which can be exchanged for input A without reducing the level of output. It can be expressed as minus 1 times the slope of the isoquant:

$$\text{MRSab} = - \frac{\text{change in input B}}{\text{change in input A}} \qquad \text{Eq. 4.5}$$

To show why the MRSab declines, while output is constant, let us use a simple example. Suppose that a library utilizes computer terminals and labor to produce cataloging data. If we assume a constant level of output, as the library adds units of labor, L (A in Equation 4.5), and decreases the number of computer terminals, C (B in Equation 4.5), a unit of computer terminal becomes more valuable relative to a unit of labor. It takes more and more labor to make up for the loss in productive power of the terminals; that is, it becomes increasingly difficult to substitute labor for computer terminals and maintain the same level of output. Thus, the slope of the isoquant, which equals the MRSlc, becomes smaller as we move down the curve from left to right; and the rate at which we can technically substitute labor for capital declines as more of labor is used relative to capital.

Another way of illustrating why isoquants are convex relies on the notion that the degree to which inputs can be substituted for one another is directly linked to their marginal productivities. The output rate on a given isoquant stays constant as we change the input mix. At point E in Figure 29, we require C2 units of computer terminals and L1 units of labor. We can produce the same output by reducing the number of terminals and increasing the quantity of labor—point G. Using this diagram, we can formally derive the relationship between the contribution to output due to small changes in inputs, their marginal products, and the rate at which inputs can be substituted for one another. As we shall see, this relationship is not only interesting from a theoretcial point of view, but has practical implications for the production of library services.

To derive the rate at which one input can be substituted for another while output rate is held fixed we draw a tangent to the point under consideration. In Figure 29, for example, as we move from point E to G, we have decreased the number of terminals and increased the level of labor. From this diagram, we can demonstrate that the incremental rate of substitution of computer terminals for labor is directly linked to their marginal product. If we hold labor to L1 while we increase terminals from C1 to C2, ouput increases from a lower level (say Qo), represented by the isoquant I', to the level (say Q1) corresponding to isoquant I. This change in output, (Q0 − Q1) divided by the

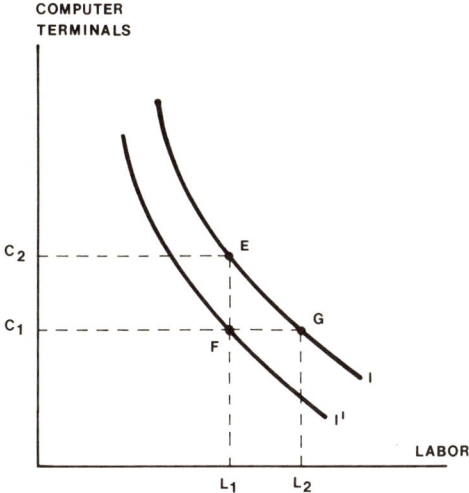

FIG. 29. Marginal Rate of Substitution

change in computer terminals, FE, represents the marginal product of computer terminals. Similarly, when we move from point F to point G we are measuring the marginal product of labor: (Q0 − Q1) / FG. Earlier, we defined the slope as the change in movement from point E to point G, or FE / FG. Thus, the ratio of the marginal product of labor to the marginal product of computer terminals, FE / FG, equals the marginal rate of substitution.

Now we are in a position to show that the marginal rate of substitution of labor for computer terminals tends to decrease as an increasing amount of labor is substituted for computer terminals. As labor is substituted for computer terminals, the marginal product of terminals falls. That is, as we increase the number of persons working in the catalog department, holding the number of terminals constant, the result is a decrease in the ability of labor to generate output. To remain on the same isoquant, we decrease the amount of computer terminals, which implies a further decrease in the marginal product of labor. A decrease in the number of computer terminals, holding labor constant, would result in a shift downward of the entire marginal product curve for labor. But at the same time, and for similar reasons, the decrease in the number of terminals leads to an increase in the marginal product of computer terminals.

Since the marginal product of labor is falling and the marginal product of computer terminals is rising, the ratio MPl/MPc, which equals the MRSlc, must be falling as labor is substituted for computer terminals. Based on the notion that the MRSlc falls as we substitute labor for computer terminals, it follows that isoquants must be convex. The slope of the isoquant which equals minus 1 times the MRS gets smaller as we move down the curve, implying that the curve is convex to the origin.

Again, the assumption of convex isoquants is an empirical one and cannot be proved or disproved on the basis of logic. However, it makes sense that when one input is abundant, it should become increasingly difficult for it to replace the relatively scarce input and continue to produce the same output. The importance of this relationship will become evident when, in the next chapter, we discuss the optimal input combination. For the moment, it is important to notice the tendency for the marginal product of one input to move in the opposite direction of the other input, when output is held constant.

Using the MRS in Production

Isoquants can be used to examine the issues that face libraries: number of locations, number of open hours, staff, items, and so on. They illustrate the different ways in which a library can combine inputs to produce a given level of output. The number of buildings and open hours affects the amount of output produced. The relative level of inputs used to produce a given level of ouput has some bearing on the marginal product of each input. The MRS provides us with information concerning the tradeoffs in different input combinations; it is a critical element in the final decision of the firm. Recall that the indifference curve and the marginal rate of substitution provided us with one element in the decision calculus of the consumer. The isoquant plays an analogous role in the decision process of the producer. To make a final decision, both economic entities have to confront their budget line, but for the moment we will concentrate on isoquants.

Let's assume that a number of different combinations of building and open hours yields the same level of output. For example, 3 buildings and 10 open hours per day or 2 buildings and 15 open hours per day may yield 2000 units of output per day. If we start with a small level of number of open hours, the marginal product of open hours relative to buildings will be high. This suggests that as we add open hours, the marginal product of open hours will rise, up to a point, faster than the marginal product of buildings. The reader will observe that this type of analysis can be extended to cover the case in which we have a third fixed factor, such as labor, and two variable factors, open hours and buildings. In this case, as we add more of either variable input, the marginal product of labor will follow the rule of diminishing returns.

The isoquant forces us to recognize that there is a tradeoff between the number of buildings and the number of open hours, between the number of items and the number of open hours. In the case of number of buildings and number of open hours, one can view the tradeoffs in terms of the consumer: a library that is open more hours provides a convenience in terms of the time of day a consumer can utilize the facility; more buildings provide a convenience in terms of the length of time or distance a consumer must travel to use the service. We can also examine the number of buildings and materials. The fewer the buildings, the greater the number of materials and the greater the variety or number of requests that can be filled. On the other hand, fewer buildings may mean added travel time for the consumer. In terms of the library's production function, each input combination, yielding the same level of output, is efficient; combinations which yield less would not be considered. But which combination or rate of substitution is preferable depends upon the price of each factor of production.

To summarize, we have shown that the law of diminishing returns applies to each factor of production taken separately. If we hold the number of open hours constant, and increase the number of buildings, there will be diminishing returns to buildings. Likewise, with the number of buildings held constant, as we add increments of open hours there will be diminishing returns to open hours. And as our previous discussion reveals, with regard to changes in relative factor proportions, the law of diminishing returns continues to hold. When both inputs are variable, as we increase the number of open hours relative to the number of buildings, diminishing returns to open hours will eventually occur. Conversely, as we increase the number of buildings in greater proportion than open hours, diminishing returns to buildings will eventually set in.

As you can see, the law of diminishing returns has implications for the degree to which inputs can be substituted for one another in the production of library services. Another essential aspect of the multivariable factor of production function is the effect of proportionate changes in the level of input, that is, changing the scale of operations. In the next section, we shall examine the effect of changes in scale on output.

Returns to Scale

Up to this point, we have discussed the production process in terms of the library's technology as represented by the production function. Production functions were described in terms of the total, marginal, and average product and the relationship that tends to hold for most production processes: the law of diminishing returns. Next we examine the relationship between changes in the scale of plant and the level of output. In particular, we will examine how output responds to proportionate changes in the mix of inputs.

A proportionate change in the level of output can lead to three distinct possibilities. A doubling of all inputs may lead to a doubling of output. In this case, production is said to be subject to constant returns to scale. On the other

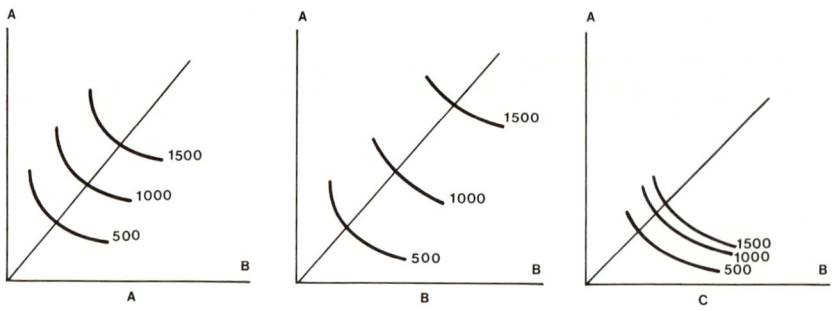

Fig. 30. Returns to Scale

hand, output may more than double. Here, production is subject to increasing returns to scale. Finally, output may increase less than in proportion to the increase in input. This is the case of decreasing returns to scale.

We can illustrate these concepts by using isoquants as well as total product curves. Figure 30 shows different isoquant maps. As we move outward from the origin on any given line, the proportion of inputs remains constant. The distance between two isoquants measures the proportionate increase in inputs required to produce a given level of input. Thus, when the distances are equal, as in panel A, the library is subject to constant returns to scale, suggesting that as the library increases the use of inputs by 30 percent, the amount of output will also increase by 30 percent. Panel B illustrates the decreasing returns situation: successive isoquants are farther apart, indicating that a 25 percent increase in the use of inputs leads to a less- than-proportionate, 15 percent, increase in output. Panel C illustrates the case in which there are increasing returns to scale.

Another way of depicting the three possible states of returns to scale is to use total product curves. Recall that a total product curve for any given input is obtained by holding the level of other inputs and the state of technology constant. Therefore, there is a family of total product curves, each one dependent upon the value to which the fixed input is set. As shown in Figure 31, output varies along a total product curve, with respect to variations in number of open hours, for each possible building size.

We can draw a line which shows how output varies with proportionate changes in use of inputs. This line indicates how output responds to changes in the scale of the library's operations. If the library is combining inputs—say staff to building size—at a ratio of 5/1, then each point on the scale expansion path would show a 5/1 ratio of inputs. The first point in the diagram, O1, indicates the level of output produced from 5 units of labor and 1 unit of building size. Expansion of both inputs to 10 and 2, respectively, results in an output corresponding to point O2; and so on.

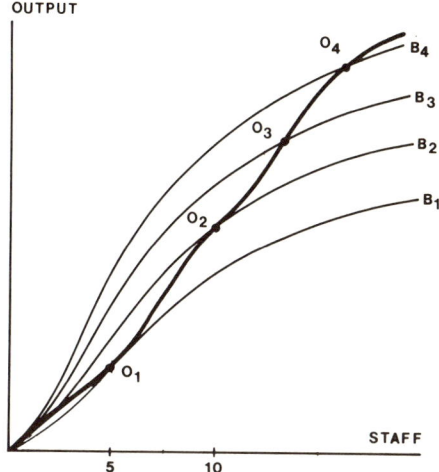

FIG. 31. Economies of Scale and Total Product Curves

Based on our earlier discussion of total product curves, we found that the nature of the marginal product of a fixed input could be detected from the shape of the total product curve. An analogous relationship exists for the scale expansion path. From the origin to point O_2, the scale expansion path is concave upward, implying increasing returns to scale (economies of scale). As we move from point O_2 to O_3, the line is straight, its slope is constant, expressing constant returns to scale. Beyond this point the line is concave downward, indicating diminishing returns to scale (diseconomies of scale).

Determinants of Returns to Scale

Economies of scale can occur for a number of reasons. Large volumes permit greater specialization of labor and machinery, or a small library may not be able to take advantage of more efficient production techniques. Some inputs are not available for use in small-scale plants; still others are not efficient when used by small operations. If a resource is indivisible, such as large-scale machinery, that resource will not be used to its best advantage at low volumes of output. Opportunities presented by the indivisibility of certain inputs lead to increasing returns to scale; larger plants will be more efficient because they can take advantage of certain inputs not available to smaller operations. At large volumes of output, economies of scale may arise, whereas random events tend to cancel each other out; furthermore, the aggregate behavior of large groups tends to be more stable. For this reason, a firm's inventory may not have to increase in proportion to its sales. Also, with large volumes of output, lower unit costs may be achieved because the costs of infrequent transactions are allocated over more units.

Greater specialization may occur as more capital and labor are used; tasks can be subdivided, allowing inputs to specialize. For example, the task of administering a firm involves gathering information and the subsequent sharing of those elements needed to operate the firm and produce output. By restricting the task, specialization allows the individual employee to acquire skills more effectively; that is, the unit cost of the information required to complete the job is lower. And when specific tasks and information are shared, the efficiency gain derived from specialization (lower information-gathering costs) leads to lower administrative costs. In other words, the economic benefit of the larger organization, specialization of function, results in a situation where a large group, working together, may produce proportionately more than smaller units.

Another determinant of economies of scale stems from certain arithmetical relationships. Specifically, the relationship between volume and area. For example, a building that measures 40 feet by 40 feet by 10 feet has a volume that is four times as great as a building that measures 20 feet by 20 feet by 10 feet, but the area of all sides of the larger building (we assume it's a box) is only twice the area of the smaller building. The larger building requires only 50 percent more materials for a 400 percent gain in volume.

As the size of the library grows, the cost of operating administrative units, such as collection development, ordering, and cataloging, may be centralized and spread over more units. Networking permits libraries to update and transmit information at lower unit costs. This gain in efficiency stems from the sharing of tasks. There is a reduction in the repetition of similar tasks, and the ability to share materials reduces materials collection costs such as storage and item maintenance. As the volume of production increases, a higher-quality product may be produced at a constant or lower unit cost. Larger libraries offer a greater diversity of services, both as it concerns the number of topics covered (breadth) and the depth of service (breadth within a topic). Thus, the quality of service may change as the scale of plant increases while unit costs remain constant or fall, indicating the possibility of increasing returns to scale. In essence, a large library or network of libraries is likely to be able to support a higher level of output per unit of input than a small library or a group of individual libraries that do not share input costs and services.

Ultimately, increases in the scale of operations may lead to decreasing returns to scale: diseconomies of scale. Larger volumes of production require more complex administrative tasks. With large organizations, coordination and control of the staff becomes difficult. Transmission of information from lower levels of the organization to upper management takes longer, and it may be distorted; decisions take increasingly longer to make and implement. Part of the problem also stems from the fact that as the firm expands, it may eventually run into a limit on the availability of inputs of equal quality. Hiring personnel of less skill results in a less-than-proportionate increase in output.

In libraries, these problems may result in materials-processing delays and, consequently, consumers wait longer for items. While networking may allow for the sharing of materials, it reduces the ability of consumers to browse the library collection; the cost of determining the value of the information is increased. Users face delays in the receipt of materials. The value of the information is reduced, as is the quality of the service. For both the consumer and the library, costs per transaction have increased in greater proportion than output. Thus, as with any organization, as the size of the library grows, the forces of economies and diseconomies of scale are at work. Large organizations afford a diversity of services, with the possible cost of too many layers of administration. Smaller libraries may be more flexible; management will be able to more easily exert its will, and fewer rigidities permit the firm to react faster to changes in market conditions. Which force will prevail must be determined empirically.

Whether or not there is a tendency for constant, or increasing, or decreasing returns to scale depends upon the nature of the firm's technology. If inputs are equally divisible and of equal quality, regardless of the scale of plant, then constant returns to scale might prevail. Generally, as an organization grows in size there are forces working toward both economies and diseconomies of scale. Which force predominates is, as we say, an empirical question which must be settled case by case.

Shifts in the Production Function

The library's production function has been described as relating input to the maximum output obtainable from each combination of inputs. A change in the state of technology will transform the entire function. Innovations such as computers and mass transit, as well as increases in the general level of education, create possibilities for the adoption of more efficient production techniques.

A technological change will shift the entire family of total product curves, as well as the scale expansion path. This type of change is to be distinguished from a change in the level of a fixed input. Recall that each product curve is drawn from the assumption of a fixed input. A change in the level of fixed input results in a shift of the product curve, whereas the scale expansion path allows for variations in all inputs. Given the assumption of fixed technology, the scale expansion curve does not shift with changes in the level of inputs.

Only when the state of technology changes do both curves shift. Technological improvements alter the level of output obtained from each combination of fixed and variable input. Not only does the output response from combining a fixed and a variable input change, so does the output obtainable from varying all factors of production. Consequently, technological change shifts the entire system of product curves, as well as isoquants and the scale expansion path. The direction of the shift depends upon the direction of the change.

Summary

The production function is the term we use to describe the relationship between alternative quantities of input per period of time and the maximum quantity of physical output per time period that results from each combination. To analyze production possibilities, we suggested that factors of production be divided into fixed and variable inputs. Corresponding to this idea, we distinguished between two types of production responses: short and long run. Short-run production responses are generally characterized by the case in which the quantities of some inputs are impractical to alter (i.e., "fixed") while others are not. In contrast, the relationship between varying all quantities of input and the amount of output corresponds to long-run output possibilities.

If some of the library's inputs are held constant, the total product which describes the relationship between the variable input and output can be derived. The technological relationship between variable input and output quantities, known as the law of diminishing returns, states that as one factor is increased while another factor is held constant, output will tend to rise at first. However, at some later point the rate of increase in total output associated with additions to the variable input will decline. The law of diminishing returns not only applies to each input taken separately, but also to the changes in relative factor proportions. Furthermore, it implies that the total, average, and marginal product curves will have the general shapes depicted in this chapter.

To investigate the case in which the library can change the rate at which it uses two inputs, we introduced isoquants. Isoquants, which are graphic representations of the library's production function, play much the same kind of role in production theory as indifference curves in consumer choice theory. Just as goods generate utility for the consumer, inputs can be regarded as capable of generating output. Indifference curves were used to illustrate all of the combinations of goods capable of yielding an equal level of utility. Isoquants are used to show the relationship between various combinations of input that result in a given level of output. Furthermore, they have the same geometric characteristics. Like indifference curves, isoquants have negative slopes and cannot intersect. And just as in consumption, the marginal rate of substitution in production, which shows the technological feasibility of exchanging one input for another, is equal to the slope of the curve.

Next, we examined changes in scale, the aspect of multi-factor production involving proportionate changes in the level of all inputs. With regard to changes in the scale of library operations, we suggested three distinct possibilities: constant, increasing, and decreasing returns to scale. Constant returns to scale holds for the case where output increases in the same proportion as the proportionate increase in inputs. Where output increases in greater proportion than increases in input, there are increasing returns to scale. Conversely, production is said to be subject to decreasing returns to scale when output increases less than the proportionate increase in inputs.

To conclude, we noted that the relationship between quantities of input and the maximum amount of output produced is altered not only by a change in the level of fixed inputs but by changes in the state of technology. The difference is that while the former involves a movement from one product curve to another, a change in technology results in a shifting of the entire system of product curves.

Exercises

1. Given a fixed public library site, add materials to the business collection. What do you expect to happen to the productivity of the added materials?
2. Consider that the library is a production plant where information services are generated. Given that the consumer is an input, what impact will an improvement in information-search technology for the consumer have on the nature of the total product curve?
3. Given a fixed site, describe a process for deciding upon the number of journal titles to offer and the length of period to store them.
4. Assume that library A has a card catalog and library B has a microfiche catalog. Assume that there is one card catalog and a fixed number of microfiche catalogs. As more users are added to the system, describe what happens to the productivity of each library's catalog.
5. A new technology, available to the library, involves the use of computers. The computer system permits the library to produce twice as much circulation services from any given computer-staff input combination. Describe what has occurred to the production function for circulation services and, in particular, to the marginal product curves.
6. Assume a library is considering employing additional staff. Would you be more concerned with the marginal or average product of labor?
7. Use the concept of a total product curve to investigate the relationship between:
   a. a fixed collection size, variable publication date, and output
   b. a fixed staff, variable training, and output
   c. a fixed level of equipment, variable maintenance, and output
   d. a fixed building size, variable study space, and output
8. Using the examples in Question 7, explain why the total product curve rises and then reaches a plateau.
9. Define an isoquant and describe its characteristics. Explain why isoquants have these characteristics.

106   Microeconomic Theory

10. Define the marginal rate of substitution and describe how it is related to marginal product.
11. Assuming that study space and video viewing space, storage space and display space, and number of topics and number of items in a topic are inputs into three different production functions, use isoquants to investigate the relationship between these inputs.
12. Use isoquants to show how different combinations of open and closed stacks (access) can be used to produce journal/article services and how different loan and collection development policies may be used to produce circulation services.
13. Given a fixed collection, explain why you think there will be a tradeoff between the level of circulation and the ability to fill title requests.

Suggested Reading

Cooper, Michael D. "The Economics of Library Size: A Preliminary Inquiry." *Library Trends* 28:1 (Summer 1979): 63–78.

Feldstein, Kathleen Foley. "The Economics of Public Libraries." Ph.D. dissertation, Massachusetts Institute of Technology, 1976. Chap. 3.

Getz, Malcolm. *Public Libraries: An Economic View*. Baltimore: Johns Hopkins University Press, 1980.

Goddard, Haynes C. "A Study in the Theory and Measurement of Benefits and Costs in the Public Library (A Theoretical and Econometric Anaylsis with Special Reference to Indiana Public Libraries)." Ph.D. dissertation, Indiana University, 1970.

Hayes, Robert M. "The Management of Library Resources: The Balance between Capital and Staff in Providing Services." *Library Research* (Summer 1979): 119–142.

McCloskey, Donald N. *The Applied Theory of Price*. New York: Macmillan, 1982. Chaps. 8 and 11.

Malchup, Fritz. "On the Meaning of the Marginal Product." In *Explorations in Economics*. New York: McGraw-Hill, 1936. Pp. 250–263.

Melcher, Daniel. "Cataloging, Processing, and Automation." *American Libraries* 2 (July–August 1971): 701–713.

Zweizig, Douglas and Eleanor Jo Rodger. *Output Measures for Public Libraries*. Chicago: American Library Association, 1982.

5

SUPPLY OF LIBRARY SERVICES

Chapter 4 dealt with the way in which the library's technology can be represented, which takes us only part of the way toward developing a method for selecting the optimal input combination. When information managers make decisions about how to produce output, not only must they decide what level and composition of inputs to use, they must also consider input costs and revenue. As a result, our next step will be to explore the nature of production costs. The relationship between input and output, which we explored in Chapter 4, has a direct bearing on the costs of library production. In fact, as we shall see, product curves and cost curves can be viewed as mirror images of one another. Finally, to complete our picture of library production, we will look at how its costs, revenue, and the price of its output—concepts not accounted for in the production function—jointly determine the optimum level of output.

In the production of output, the library may substitute one input for another; however, the benefit of substitution depends, in part, upon the relative productivity and prices of inputs. Furthermore, the library's level of income restricts its ability to employ inputs. Consequently, just as the consumer is inhibited from choosing consumption options by budget and price restrictions, the library's optimal input choice is contingent upon input costs and income. The additional factor facing the firm is the price of its output. We assume that the competitive firm takes price as given and that it can sell all the output it wants at a given price (the implications of these assumptions will be explored). Libraries do not sell their output, but the model of the firm will suggest guidelines for choosing the optimum level of output. Our aim is to provide a framework for analyzing the costs and tradeoffs involved in producing information services.

To understand costs, we first examine the concept of economic costs—what they include, factors that affect costs, and how they vary with output. Using these notions, we will develop a model which allows us to characterize the library's short- and long-run costs of production. Combining the library's production costs with its objectives permits us to determine the library's long-run scale of plant and the level of output it will choose to produce. By analyzing the tradeoffs between different levels of output, we are able to determine the rationale for selecting a given scale of plant. Regardless of its objectives, this same line of reasoning permits the information manager to analyze tradeoffs between a variety of goals and production options.

Economic Concept of Costs

Should the library choose to produce circulation services with one large outlet or with five small outlets? How should the library allocate its income among alternative combinations of staff, documents, equipment, and maintenance? To answer these questions, we must first develop a notion of *economic costs*.

Quite often, the library's costs are commonly thought of as the monetary outlays the library incurs to acquire the use of economic resources. However, this concept of economic costs is too limited for the model we are building. From our previous discussion of economic resources, we know that resources are scarce. Therefore, use of a resource to produce a particular information output limits alternative production options: staff can be used to produce administrative services, reference services, circulation services, maintenance services, and the like. Once the library has decided to employ resources for a given output, some value of alternative outputs is given up.

Economists define the cost of producing a specific output as the maximum value of these resources used in the production of alternative outputs. Notice that this definition emphasizes the fact that, by limiting choice, use of an input for a particular purpose involves tradeoffs; and to determine cost, one must consider the alternative uses—forgone opportunities—of economic resources. For example, the cost of producing circulation services is the value of the goods and services obtained from the facility, staff, documents, and equipment when they are used in alternative production possibilities. These costs, known as *opportunity costs*, and the library's production function determine the production costs of a given output.

Given the transferability of economic resources from one use to another, the full cost of production includes the monetary, or explicit, cost and the alternative-use, or implicit, cost. For example, assume that an information services owner has decided to use a facility, hire a 10-person staff, and purchase 5000 documents per year, and that the facility will be open 50 hours per week.

Suppose that the total monetary outlay for this combination of inputs is $210,000 per year and that the owner receives $250,000 revenue from sales. The store's income statement would show that revenue exceeded costs by $40,000 that year. But this figure excludes the services of the owner, as well as the return on the capital used to produce information services. These costs are considered to be the implicit costs of production.

The economic costs of a library's production is the sum of these explicit and implicit costs. *Explicit* costs are those arising from transactions between the library and other parties. They are what one usually considers as the firm's cost of operation: for payroll, materials, insurance, utilities, interest payments. Implicit costs are the costs of self-owned resources, represented by their value (or opportunity cost) in alternative uses. Although implicit costs are difficult to measure, we must consider them in evaluating production decisions.

To bring this discussion back to libraries, the implicit-cost concept suggests that the cost of resources which the library currently owns would be equal to their value in their most valuable alternative use. For example, when a librarian helps a patron find materials, the explicit cost is the salary of the librarian; the implicit cost of time spent providing directional assistance could be the value of forgone consultation services. Similarly, time spent handling requested items which are shipped from site to site could be used for in-house information services; time spent evaluating the collection could be used for developing new services. The implicit cost of a library building is the revenue the library would realize from the rent or sale of the building.

Before we consider the nature of short-run costs, we want to emphasize the importance of the alternative- or opportunity-cost concept. First, note that when we evaluate the cost of library production, all costs must be considered. For instance, when a multisite library is evaluating the cost of running a particular location, it must include not only the direct costs, such as the staff, documents, and equipment which are used at the site, but the indirect costs, such as the facility itself and centralized administrative services. In addition, the current alternative-use value of the resources must be evaluated. Thus, the value of a library building is not its historical construction cost but its current use value. Similarly, the implicit cost of a document isn't the original price but its value in current uses. The important point is that the alternative use of an economic resource can change over time; consequently, its opportunity cost will vary over time.

Finally, the notion that value is equal to a sacrificed alternative leads us to conclude that a cost is incurred even when the library acquires resources "for free." That is, the value of the time the library spends processing "free" items; volunteers need to be trained; documents need to be evaluated, placed in the collection, or discarded. In economic analysis, the library's costs of production are the sum of the explicit and implicit costs. We observed that explicit costs include the monetary payment for services of economic resources; implicit costs are associated with the use of the library's own resources and are equated with the value of their next-best alternative use.

Production Costs in the Short Run

In the short run, the library's production function relates output to the quantity of variable inputs. These inputs give rise to costs which, by definition, vary with the level of output. Furthermore, we suggested that during the short run the library cannot vary the quantity of certain inputs: plant and equipment. These resources are the library's fixed inputs, and are referred to as the library's *scale of plant*. Fixed resources result in fixed costs. The distinction between fixed and variable inputs provides the basis for our investigation of short-run production costs. Our first task will be to introduce the terminology, and then we will examine how costs vary with output.

Let's suppose that a library is involved in the production of acquisition services. The library employs computer terminals and staff in the production of acquisition output. Assume that the computer terminals are the fixed input (for simplicity, we will ignore any database or other utility charges) and the variable input is personnel. This production scenario conforms with our notion of the short run. We are now in a position to identify three types of cost schedules: total fixed costs, total variable costs, and total costs.

Total fixed costs are those costs incurred by the library, regardless of the size of output—and even if it is closed: depreciation of fixed plant and equipment, insurance, and property taxes. Given the two inputs, one fixed and the other variable, and constant prices, we can define total fixed cost as

$$TFC = (Pct)(ct) \qquad \text{Eq. 5.1}$$

where Pct is the price of a computer terminal and ct is the quantity of computer terminals. Since Pct and ct are both constant, this equation implies that fixed costs will remain constant, regardless of the level of acquisition output.

In contrast to total fixed costs, *total variable costs* depend upon the level of output. In fact, they increase as output is increased. The reason for this is quite simple: although the price of personnel is constant, the library will hire additional staff hours to produce additional units of output:

$$TVC = (Pl)(l) \qquad \text{Eq. 5.2}$$

where Pl is the price of staff and l is the number of staff.

The total cost of producing acquisition output is the sum of the variable and fixed costs of production. Using the equation $TC = (Pl)(l) + (Pct)(ct)$, we note that TC increases as more of the variable input is used. Table 5 shows hypothetical cost schedules for acquisition output where $TC = TVC + TFC$.

Figure 32 shows the corresponding cost curves. Total fixed cost, drawn as a horizontal line, indicates that a cost of $50 will be incurred, regardless of

Table 5
TOTAL COST SCHEDULES

Units of Output	TFC ($)	+	TVC ($)	=	TC ($)
0	50		0		50
10	50		50		100
20	50		85		135
30	50		135		185
40	50		190		240
50	50		250		290
60	50		290		340
70	50		390		440
80	50		510		560

the level of output. Total variable costs rise as output increases. Up to point A, they are shown to increase at a decreasing rate; beyond that point, they increase at an increasing rate. Finally, total costs can be obtained by adding the total variable-cost curve to the fixed cost-curve. Since the vertical distances of the fixed cost curve are equal at all levels of output, the total cost curve and the total variable-cost curve will have the same shape (slope). Stated differently, any increase in the level of output increases total cost and total variable cost by an equal amount.

Next, we examine the basis for the behavior of total cost and total variable cost.

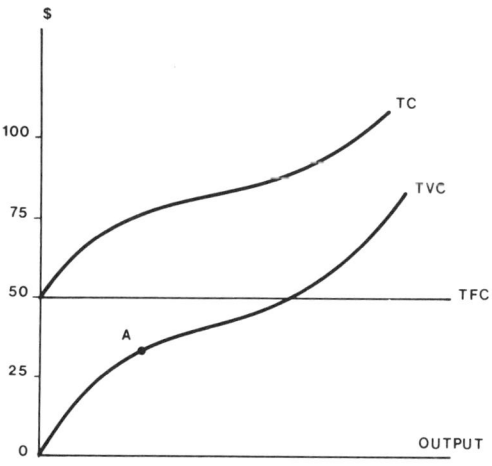

FIG. 32. Short-Run Total Cost Curves

112 Microeconomic Theory

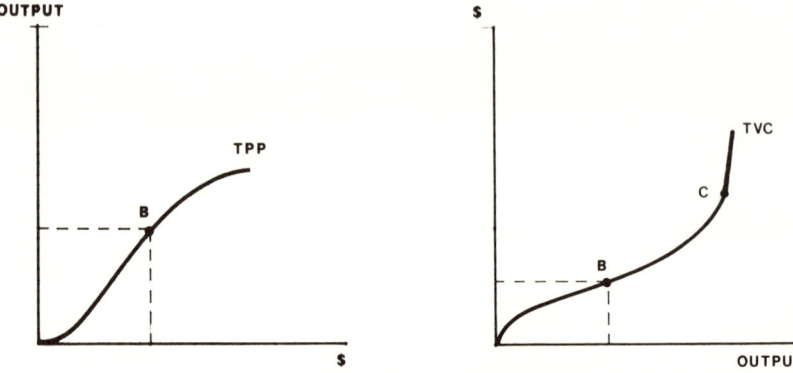

FIG. 33. Total Product and Total Variable-Cost Curves

Behavior of Total Cost in the Short Run

Previously, we indicated that the cost of production is determined by the library's production function and the prices of inputs. In the short-run setting, with input prices constant, the behavior of the production function follows directly from the law of diminishing returns. Keeping this in mind, we see that the behavior of total variable costs is determined by the input price and the production function. Observe that the total product curve in Figure 33 is concave upward from the origin to point B, where the slope of the curve reaches the maximum, indicating that a 1-unit addition to input expands output in greater proportion. It is precisely because the total product curve is determined by the law of diminishing returns that the total variable cost curve is concave downward and then concave upward. In fact, they are mirror images of one another.

In the production of acquisition output, the total product curve shows the amount of staff used to produce each level of acquisition output. In the initial stage of production, the library is employing too few units of personnel in combination with computer terminals; some computer terminals are idle. As we add personnel, the total product increases in greater proportion than increases in input, as specialization and cooperation reduce wasted effort. This is reflected in the upward concave section of the total product curve. If we assume that a staff member's time costs $200 per week, costs rise by $200 while output rises at an increasing rate, by adding one staff member. The result is that total variable costs increase as output expands, but at a decreasing rate; each $200 addition to cost results in output increasing faster than additions to cost.

Thus, in this stage of production the total variable cost curve is concave downward. But beyond point B, each additional unit of labor creates output at a decreasing rate. As a result, the cost of output, total variable cost, rises, indicating that the total variable cost curve is concave upward. If we expanded output beyond point C, the total variable cost curve would be vertical. At this level of output, additions to input add to cost, although they do not add to output.

Average Cost

To better understand the library cost functions, we examine the behavior of per unit acquisition costs: marginal and average costs. There are three separate average cost functions: average fixed costs, average variable costs, and average total costs. These cost functions correspond to the three total cost functions, but the expression of costs in terms of their respective average cost is more convenient for economic analysis of library production.

Average fixed cost per unit of acquisition output is derived by dividing total fixed cost by output (and declines with increases in output):

$$AFC = TFC \,/\, \text{Acquisition output} \qquad \text{Eq. 5.3}$$

As output expands, fixed costs are spread over expanding levels of output. For instance, with a fixed building, per unit costs associated with insurance, lighting, and heat decline as they are spread over a larger level of output.

To obtain average variable cost, we divide total variable cost by acquisition output:

$$AVC = TVC \,/\, Q_a = (P)(L/Q_a) = (P)(1/APPl) \qquad \text{Eq. 5.4}$$

Since $Q_a \,/\, L$ equals the average product of labor, its reciprocal, $L \,/\, Q_a$, is equal to $1 \,/\, APPl$. With the price of labor constant, average variable cost varies inversely with the average physical product of labor. In our discussion of the law of diminishing returns, we demonstrated that as output expands, average product increases at first, reaches a maximum, and then falls. Consequently, the AVC curve reflects the underlying physical characteristics of the production function as expressed in the APP curve. Not surprisingly, this suggests that, at some point, additions to the acquisitions staff cost more in terms of forgone opportunities. At some point, in other words, additions to acquisitions staff would add to the output of an alternative information service at a lower average variable cost.

Average total cost (AC) is equal to the sum of AFC and AVC, which ultimately helps to explain its shape. Using the acquisition production function, we observe that as larger outputs are considered, the efficiency of the fixed input, computer terminals, continues to increase while that of the variable input, staff, increases at a decreasing rate, reaches a maximum, and then decreases. From this, it follows that ATC, reflecting the sum of efficiency of the fixed and variable inputs, slopes downward at first and then, as the efficiency

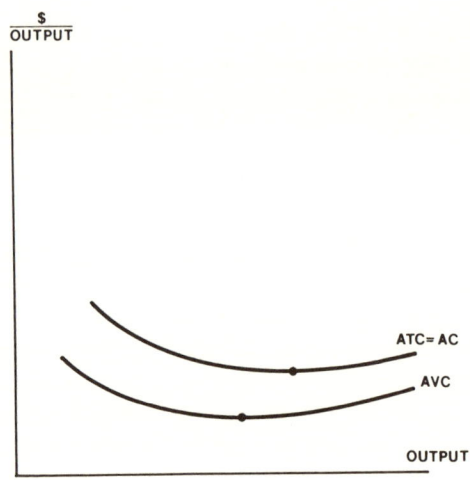

FIG. 34. Average Cost Curves

of the variable input declines, it exerts an upward force on costs. However, since the decrease in average physical product of the variable input is counteracted by the continuing increase in the efficiency of computer terminals, AC reaches a minimum after AVC, as shown in Figure 34.

As we add more and more staff, their per unit contribution to output increases at a decreasing rate. But because AFC is declining, the combined per unit cost of staff and computer terminals reaches a minimum after that of the AVC. Finally, at some point, additions to staff do not add to output, and may actually lead to decreases in output. Thus, even if they were volunteers, the library would not be inclined to use them.

Marginal Cost

Marginal cost is defined as the change in total cost resulting from the addition of a 1-unit increment in output. Total cost is equal to the sum of total variable and total fixed costs. Since fixed cost does not change with changes in output, a change in total cost is entirely the result of a change in variable cost. Symbolically, we can write marginal cost as

$$MC = TC / Qa = TVC / Qa = w(\Delta L) / (\Delta Qa) = w / MPl \qquad \text{Eq. 5.5}$$

Assume that the wage rate of acquisition staff is $10 per unit and that, at some level of output, MPl = 5 units of output. By adding 1 unit of staff, we are able to add 5 units of output (MPl); therefore, an additional unit of output

Supply of Library Services 115

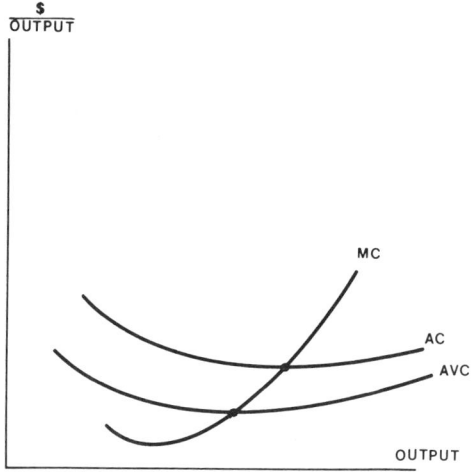

FIG. 35. Average and Marginal Cost

requires 1/5 unit of staff at a cost of $2. Thus, marginal cost is equal to $10/5, or w / MPl.

The shape of the MPP curve forms the basis for the MC curve. With the price of staff fixed, at low levels of output the MPl is rising, so MC must be falling. Eventually, when marginal product reaches a maximum, marginal cost will be at a minimum. And as employment is carried beyond this point, marginal product begins to decline; so, correspondingly, marginal cost must be rising.

The marginal cost of library production is entirely independent of fixed cost, but it is related to average variable cost and total average costs. When marginal cost is below the average cost (either variable or total), average cost is declining. For example, if the average cost of a unit of acquisition output is $4, and producing an additional unit costs $2, the average cost of all units will be lowered. Using the same reasoning, one finds that when the marginal cost curve is above the average cost curve, average cost will be rising as output expands. The marginal cost curve intersects the average curve at its minimum point. When the average curve is neither rising nor falling, a small change in output does not change the average, so the marginal curve must equal the average curve. (See Figure 35.)

The key points to remember when analyzing costs are the production relationships implied by the law of diminishing returns and the assumption of constant input prices. An understanding of the logical significance of these two economic principles assists the information manager in the investigation and representation of production costs.

Short-Run Optimum Output and Cost of Library Production

The library's short-run optimum output occurs when average cost is at a minimum. Assume that the library is combining documents with a fixed facility to produce storage output. At the output for which average cost is at a minimum, the per unit cost of both the fixed and variable inputs is smallest. From this, it follows that the scale of plant is being utilized most efficiently.

At lower levels of output, too few documents are being combined with the fixed facility; the average cost of storing a unit is higher at low levels of output. As we add units of input, we make possible a more efficient utilization of the library, with the result that lower average unit costs accrue as output expands. We can continue adding documents to the site until average cost reaches a minimum. After this point, adding documents to a fixed plant gives rise to rising average costs. Retrieval of documents becomes increasingly difficult.

Of course, the library is not just a storage site; but the conclusion holds for all types of output in the short run and is a direct result of the law of diminishing returns. Thus, use of a fixed site and variable documents for the purpose of producing circulation or reference output would yield similar results. At low levels of output, expanding the level of input yields successively greater levels of output. Intuitively, this makes sense. At low levels of input, there are too few documents to select from. As the number of documents is expanded, the ability to produce a unit of output expands rapidly, to a maximum. After this point, additions to documents create overcrowding, or, in the case of one subject, documents of relatively lower interest. Average variable cost begins to rise; consequently, the average cost of producing another unit of output increases. Therefore, in the short run, without consideration of output price, the optimum output occurs when the average cost is at a minimum.

Long-Run Library Production

The long run describes the period in which the library has sufficient time to vary the quantity of all inputs to produce output at the least cost. What combination of input should the library utilize to produce a given level of output at the least cost? The notion of least cost can be clarified by combining the library's production function and its financial constraint. Isoquants represent the various input combinations that will yield a given rate of output: the library's production function. Isocost lines, analogous to the consumer's budget line, show the alternative input combinations that can be purchased for a given cost. Using these concepts, we can determine the least-cost combination of inputs.

Supply of Library Services 117

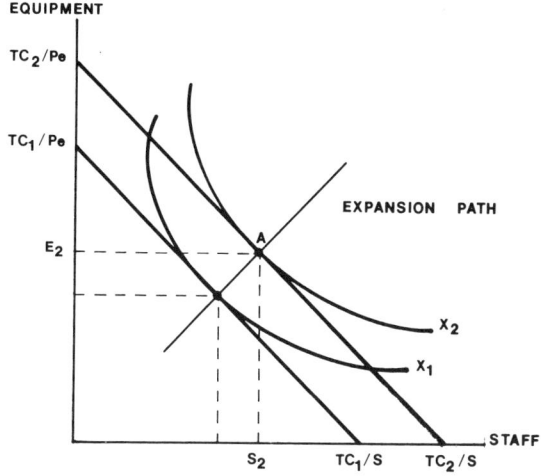

FIG. 36. Optimal Input Combinations

Let's take the simple case of a library choosing between two inputs, equipment and staff, to produce media services output. An isocost line represents the different input combinations of equipment and staff that can be obtained for a given total outlay, TC. With the price the library pays for equipment, Pe, and staff, Ps, held constant, the input combinations that can be obtained from a certain TC can be expressed as

$$(S)(Ps) + (E)(Pe) = TC \qquad \text{Eq. 5.6}$$

where S and E represent staff and equipment respectively. Solving this equation for E, we have

$$E = (TC) / (Pe) - ((Ps) / (Pe))(S) \qquad \text{Eq. 5.7}$$

which denotes a straight line whose slope is minus the ratio of input prices, $-(Ps) / (Pe)$. This indicates that if a unit of staff costs three times as much as a unit of equipment, then employing one more unit of staff—total outlays held constant—implies the library must use three fewer units of equipment. (See Figure 36.)

Bringing together the isocost line and the isoquant permits us to find the least-cost input combination for a given level of output. For any particular total expenditure, the library will produce the maximum obtainable output at the least cost when the library operates on the highest isoquant permitted by its isocost line. This occurs when the isocost line is tangent to the isoquant.

Suppose the library proposes to allocate TC2 to the production of media services. The library is able to operate at any point on the isocost line, but points other than point A represent combinations of inputs which yield lower levels of output for the same expenditure. Alternatively, all points other than A on isoquant X2 yield the same level of output, but at higher costs. By changing the mix of inputs in the direction of point A, the library will be increasing output for a given cost or producing the same output at a lower cost. Thus, points of tangency depict the maximum output for a given cost, as well as the minimum cost of producing a particular output.

At the point of tangency, the isocost lines and the isoquants have the same slope. The slope of the isoquant is equal to the MRS_{se}, and the slope of the isocost line is the ratio of factor prices. This implies that when the library is producing an output in the least costly manner, it will adjust its use of inputs so that the rate at which inputs can be exchanged in production will equal the rate at which inputs can be exchanged in factor markets. In general, the library will minimize cost for a given output (or maximize output for a given cost) by distributing its revenue among inputs in such a way that the marginal product of a dollar's worth of any one input is equal to the marginal product of a dollar's worth of any other input used.

Returning to the media services production case, let us suppose the price per unit of staff is $10 and the price per unit of equipment is $5. What combination of inputs is best? According to our equation, since the price of staff is twice that of equipment, the marginal product of staff should be twice that of the marginal product of equipment. To illustrate, assume that the library is currently operating at a point where the marginal product of staff is 20 units of output, indicating that an extra dollar of staff yields 2 units of output: $MP_s / P_s = 20 / \$10 = 2 / \$1$. At this same point, the marginal product of equipment is 5 units of output, implying that an additional dollar's of worth of equipment will yield 1 unit of output: $MP_e / P_e = 5 / \$5 = 1 / \$1$. The library can obtain more output by adding a dollar's worth of staff than a dollar's worth of equipment. By allocating less revenue to equipment, it will reduce output by 1 unit, but expending this money on staff will increase output by 2 units, for a net gain of 1 unit (costs held constant). Using less equipment tends to increase its MP, and employing more staff tends to decrease its MP. Only when the marginal product of labor is twice that of the marginal product of equipment will the two ratios be equal.

The significance of this point should not be overlooked. Whenever the MP/p ratio of one input to another is not equal, the library can increase output without increasing outlays by shifting revenue from one input to another. Given a fixed site, the library may adjust the number and type of open hours, staff, documents, subjects, and equipment it uses to produce output. Similarly, a multisite library system would allocate monies to open hours, staff, buildings, etc. in such a way that the marginal product of a dollar's worth of any of these inputs was equal. Each facility will have different points of tangency, depending upon the level of output it is producing. At one site, additional outlays may

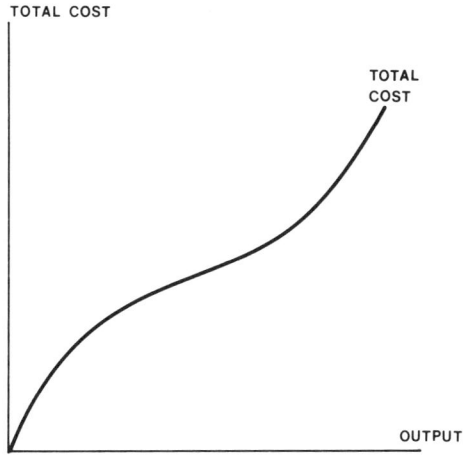

FIG. 37. Long-Run Total Costs

be expended on open hours and less on documents, while at another site additional monies would be allocated for documents and less for open hours (total outlays held constant). The optimum mix depends on what happens as we vary the level of inputs at each library; in all probability, this will differ from site to site. Therefore, an understanding of the relationships between inputs and outputs and between output and cost is crucial to efficient library production.

Long-Run Costs of Library Production

The points of tangency in Figure 36 trace a curve which shows the least costly input combination for each rate of output. With prices of inputs held constant, this curve, known as the expansion path, conveys the same information as the long-run total cost function. Figure 37 shows the library's long-run total cost curve; now that all inputs are variable, there is only one total and average cost function.

It is convenient to think of the long run as a series of alternative short-run production possibilities. While operating in the short run, the library is deciding its long-run strategy—that is, how much and what type of product to produce, which type of equipment to install, which scale of plant to build, and whether or not to train current workers or hire new employees. These planning or investment decisions determine the short-run position the library will occupy in the future. Before making the decision, the library is in a long-run situation; it can choose among a wide variety of inputs. Yet, once the new library is constructed and the equipment installed, the library must operate with these fixed inputs for a period of time which, by definition, is a short-run production possibility.

To gain insight into the long-run adjustment process, let us suppose that the library is faced with three potential scales of plant, each a short-run production possibility. (See Figure 38.) In particular, let us investigate the case where a library administrator is planning to construct a library network. Associated with each scale of plant is a short-run average and marginal cost curve. In the long run, the library can build any one of these possible scales of plant. Which scale of plant is optimum? Since the library will want to produce this output at a minimum average cost, the size of the optimum plant depends upon the output rate it chooses to produce.

Suppose that the library administrator anticipates an output rate of Q1; then the library should construct the smallest scale of plant. In the short run, the firm can produce this output at a lower cost than if it had chosen to employ a larger scale of plant. To produce Q3 units of output, it would not matter whether the library used scale of plant 1 or scale of plant 2, because the average cost is the same in either case. However, for outputs in excess of Q3, the AC of plant size 2 is below the AC of plant size 1. The library would continue to use this scale of plant until output Q5; after this level of output, the library would expand to the scale of operations 3.

The relationship between the library's long-run average cost function and its long-run marginal cost curve further clarifies the production factors which are operating to determine the long- run production optimum. Recall that the marginal curve will intersect the average curve at its minimum. This implies that the SMC will equal LMC, SAC, and LAC at the point where LAC is tangent to the SAC. In Figure 38, at all other outputs other than Q4, the long-run average cost curve is tangent to the short-run curve at a point other than a minimum. This implies that, at any point other that Q4, an information manager can lower long-run costs by rearranging the mix of inputs.

Suppose that the library is operating in short-run situation SAC1; output is Q1 and SAC = LAC and SMC = LMC. The reason why this condition holds can be understood by considering other outputs. At Qo, the SAC1 is above the LAC, which implies that as we move from Qo to Q1, long-run total cost is increasing more than short-run total cost. Basically, at Q1, short-run average cost equals long-run average cost, which means that STC = LTC. Returning to marginal cost, note that in moving from Qo to Q1, long-run total cost increases more than short-run total cost, for a 1-unit increase in output. Thus, the long-run marginal cost curve, to the left of Q1, lies above the short-run marginal cost curve.

As we move to the right of Q1 to Q2, we will be at the minimum point on the SAC1 curve, where SAC = SMC. At this point, LMC is not equal to short-run marginal costs. This indicates to the library manager that, by varying all

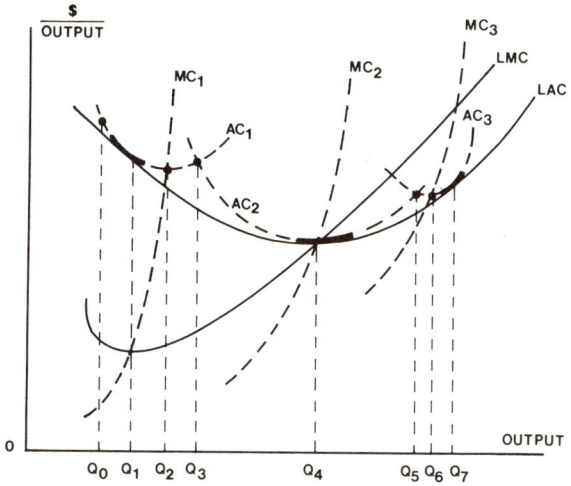

FIG. 38. Short- and Long-Run Cost Curves

inputs, output can be expanded at a lower incremental cost. Also, as we move in this direction, SAC1 rises more than LAC and STC rises more than LTC.

Only when the library reaches an output of Q4 will the optimum condition hold. At all other levels of output the library, in the short run, can reduce its average cost by altering the level of variable inputs and, in the long run, by altering its scale of plant. Once the library is producing Q4 units of output with scale of plant 2, there is no way to reduce average cost, when prices of inputs and technology are held constant.

The long-run average cost curve shows the minimum cost per unit of producing alternative outputs when any scale of plant can be built. In Figure 38, the long-run average cost function is depicted by the solid segments of the short-run average cost curves. The other segments are not included because they are not the lowest average costs. The library could always move onto the long-run curve by varying the level of fixed input.

Shape of the Long-Run Average Cost Function

The long-run total cost curve in Figure 38 is drawn to imply a ∪-shaped average cost function. Much the same as the short-run average cost curve, it suggests that average costs decrease as output expands, reaches a minimum, and increases with further expansion of library output. With the short-run average cost curve, the law of diminishing returns is operating. However, in the long run, when the library can vary all factors of production, the law of diminishing returns is not responsible for the shape of the long-run average cost curve. Instead, returns to scale are operating behind the scenes. Our discussion of returns to scale led us to conclude that increasing returns to scale is operable up to a point, and that beyond this point diseconomies of scale begin to operate, imparting a ∪ shape to the long-run average cost curve. This particular rendition of the long-run average cost curve should not be interpreted to mean that all long-run cost curves have this shape.

Generally, neither increasing returns nor decreasing returns to scale set in at the very outset of library production. Typically, increasing returns are experienced as output is expanded, but the advantages of specialization of staff and equipment give way to the disadvantages of size: control of production procedures becomes increasingly complex, staff morale declines, equipment may not be available. And even though the law of diminishing returns is not operational in the long run, the shape of the long-run cost curve can be traced to the physical relationship between inputs and output—namely, the production function.

In the short run, we suggested, average cost declines due to the indivisibility of equipment which is capable of generating increasing physical average product. Eventually, however, the library's inability to expand its scale of plant causes a decline in the efficiency of the variable input, resulting in rising average costs. Similarly, in the long run, indivisibilities, interpreted as limits on the ability of the firm to expand or contract certain inputs, create the conditions which lead to increasing and decreasing returns to scale. The library cannot continue to hire personnel of equal quality; there is a limit to which the library can reduce or increase the size of its equipment and building. Thus, in Figure 38, if the library is at output Q_4, an attempt to reduce or increase output causes average cost to rise since the library cannot contract or expand all inputs proportionately.

Figure 39 represents the three potential types of changes in costs that can occur when the library changes its scale of operations. Panel A indicates constant returns to scale. In this case, the short-run curves are not rising or falling as the library expands output by expanding its scale of plant. This situation suggests that any forces operating to cause a reduction in costs are exactly offset by forces operating to increase average costs. There are no gains to be made from further specialization in organizational form, whether in labor or equipment.

Panel B represents the case where a library incurs internal diseconomies of scale. In this case, the library can reduce average costs by contracting its size. Internal diseconomies occur as output expands, and bottlenecks are created in the production process; per unit transport costs increase, coordination of production becomes increasingly complex, employee services increase, as does paperwork and adminisitrative expenses. Therefore, the gains from additional library/plant capacity do not compensate for the additional costs indicated by

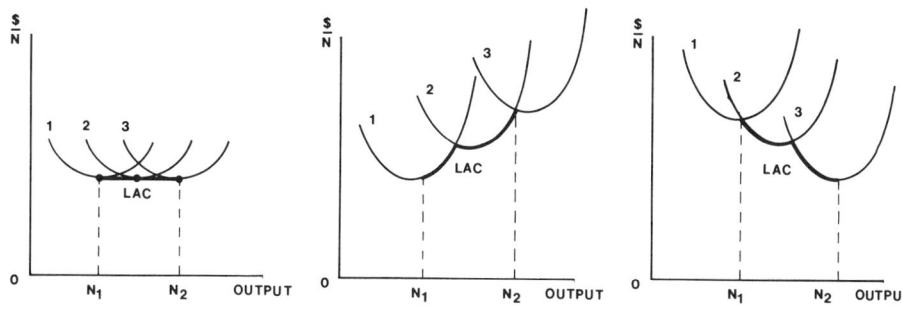

FIG. 39. Economies of Scale

a rising long-run average cost curve. Panel C represents the situation where expansion in library production leads to internal economies of scale.

As we indicated in our initial discussion of returns to scale, output-cost relationship is based on the ability of the firm to take advantage of the benefits which arise from specialization, physical relationship of input (building size, computer capability) to output, and the ability to take advantage of more efficient production processes. In the initial stages of production, with few workers and a fixed site, each employee will be expected to perform numerous tasks. Personnel will not be equally qualified for all of these tasks. As the staff is expanded, the library can hire people with specific task-related proficiencies. Consequently, the productivity of each employee will increase and thereby reduce average cost with expansion in output.

Shifts in the Position of Cost Curves

Both the short- and long-run cost curves have been drawn under the assumption that input prices and technology remained constant. (Recall that we used a similar technique to derive the consumer's demand curve.) The assumption that factor prices, the level of some resource, and the production function are constant is made for the sake of convenience. By doing so, we are able to isolate the behavior of cost with respect to change in output. Consequently, cost curves will shift when we allow for changes in the variables we have held constant.

A change in the price of the fixed resource alters the total fixed and total cost curves; total variable cost is unaffected. The total cost curve shifts up or down by an amount equal to the change in total fixed costs; its slope remains unchanged at all levels of output. For example, assume that the price of a fixed input changes from $15 to $20 and that the fixed amount of input is set at 50 units, changing total fixed cost at all levels of output from $750 to $1000. Obviously, the AFC curve also shifts in response to a change in the price of a fixed resource, but the distance by which the AFC shifts is not the same at all outputs. Simply dividing $1000 at each possible level of output will confirm this fact. Although the AVC and the MC curves are unaffected, the AC curve shifts in the direction of the change in price.

In contrast, a change in the price of the variable input has an affect on the AVC and MC curves; however, it has no affect on the fixed cost curves. A change in the price of the variable input causes the TVC curve to shift upward at each level of output, and TC shifts upward by an amount equal to change in the TVC. Since total variable cost has changed, so have average variable cost and average cost. With average variable cost different at each output, average cost will shift by an amount equal to the shift of the AVC curve at each output. The MC curve shifts in the direction of the price change and intersects the AVC and the AC at their new minimums. In the long run, all inputs are variable; therefore, a rise in the price of either input will shift the LAC and the LMC curves.

Changes in the production function shift the position of the library's cost curves by shifting the underlying product curves. An improvement in the state of technology shifts the total product curve upward, with the consequent upward movement in the average and marginal product curves. Since the respective cost curves, TVC, TC, AVC, AC, and MC, are inversely related to the product curve, they shift downward.

Application: Input Price Change and Library Production

Suppose that the library is currently producing cataloging output by employing labor and network services, both of which are variable inputs. Let's take a look at the effect of a reduction in the cost (unit costs) of network services. First, one should keep in mind that per unit costs vary along a cost curve because of the change in the productivity of inputs with variation in output, not because of altered input costs. Hence, a change in input price leads to a shifting of the entire cost curve. As shown in Figure 40, prior to the price change the library is producing an output of X1 by combining labor and network services at point A on isocost line FG. From the library's expansion path, we can derive the MC and AC curves, shown in panel B.

Your cataloging network announces a reduction in the cost of using the systems catalog services. A lower price for network services implies that the slopes of isocost lines become flatter. If the library were to incur the same total production costs, the new isocost line would be FG". However, let us consider how the change in price affects the way in which the library produces the same level of output. In this case, it would operate at point A', where the original isoquant is tangent to isocost line FG'. The new isocost line, FG', is parallel to isocost line FG", reflecting the lower cost of network services. Isocost line FG" depicts the choice of higher levels of output at the lower network

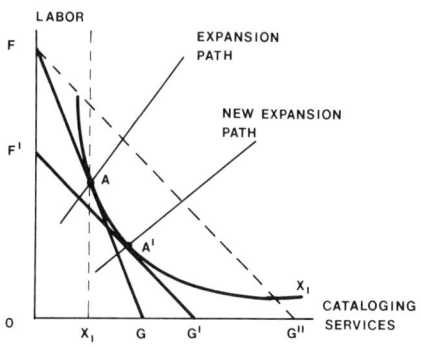 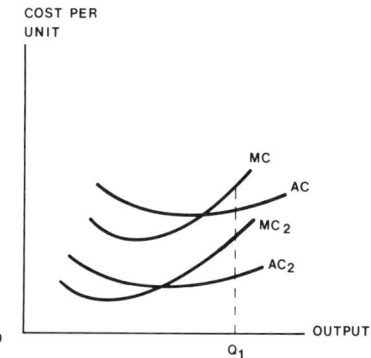

FIG. 40. Input Price Change

price; FG' permits the library to produce the original level of output at a lower total cost. At the new network price, the library substitutes network services for labor.

Similar to consumers, the library has reacted to a change in price by substituting the now lower-priced network services for the now more expensive staff. The lower price defines a new expansion path and, consequently, a new and lower total cost function. By reducing the total cost of producing a given output, the lower network price reduces the average cost of producing that output. And since the total cost of producing any output level has been reduced, the average cost of producing all output levels has been reduced. Similarly, the AC and MC curves are shifted downward, to AC2 and MC2.

Observe that per unit costs can vary as a result of changing output, if input prices are held fixed, or they can vary as a result of a change in the prices or the state of technology. The former is a result of a movement along a cost curve and the latter is the result of a shift in the cost curves. The distinction between these two types of changes is important to remember when analyzing costs and the supply of library services.

Equilibrium of the Library

With respect to the optimal level of output, the library's problem of choice cannot be determined from cost curves alone. Cost curves only provide the library with the minimum costs at which it may produce various outputs. Before we can complete the model of output choice and determine which of the various outputs the library will choose to produce, we must state the library's objective. Then we must specify the demand conditions confronting the library.

Given prices and income, the assumption that the consumer maximizes utility permitted us to solve the consumer's problem of choice. Traditional economic theory postulates that the competitive firm will attempt to maximize profits, and profits are defined as total revenue minus total costs. The assumption that the firm is attempting to maximize profits permits us to determine the output which will maximize profits. But libraries do not receive revenue from the sale of goods and services. Nonetheless, the assumption of profit, or net benefit maximization, in conjunction with cost and demand curves, will allow us to determine the optimal output.

As it applies to a single firm, the behavior of cost is independent of the degree of competition in the product market. Cost curves were constructed on the basis of input prices and the library's production function. The shape of cost curves is determined by forces which apply to all types of libraries. However, the library's demand curve, and consequently its total, average, and marginal benefit curves, are affected by the degree of competition. In this text, we will assume that the library is operating in a purely competitive environment. Advanced students may wish to consult other texts for theories concerning other types of market conditions.

The primary benefit of utilizing the profit maximization model is that it allows us to investigate the way in which a library would operate if it were attempting to maximize net benefits. The purely competitive model assumes that the product the firm sells is substantially the same as that sold by other firms; that there are many sellers, so that any one seller cannot affect the price; and that there are no restrictions on the ability of firms to enter or leave the market. While the first two assumptions hold up for some library services, the last does not. However, as we shall see, the value of the model lies in its power to predict and to provide guidelines for operating a library. With that in mind, we will discuss the demand curve facing the library.

Demand and Benefit Curves

The demand curve of a single firm is directly related to the assumption that the library contributes a relatively small amount of the total supply of information services. Since the library is only one of a very large number of service producers, it cannot affect the price by expanding or contracting output. Thus, in perfect competition, the demand curve for the individual library is drawn perfectly horizontal, or is infinitely price elastic. This implies that the library can provide all the output it wants at the market price.

One implication of the horizontal demand curve is that marginal benefit (revenue) is equal to the price of output. Marginal revenue is defined as the change in total revenue brought about by a 1-unit change in output. Under the assumption of pure competition, price is constant; therefore, marginal

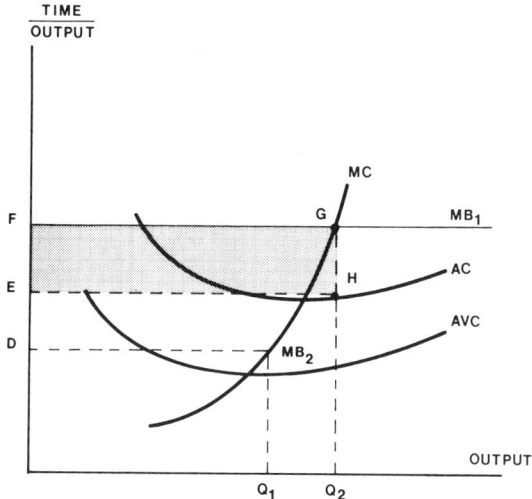

FIG. 41. Short-Run Benefit Maximization

revenue or benefit of an added unit of output is equal to output price. Hence, the demand curve is a horizontal line which lies at a distance above the x-axis equal to the price (value) of the product. In other words, the demand curve for the library is equal to its marginal benefit curve. Although libraries do not sell their goods and services, the demand curve indicates the additional output that consumers are willing to purchase from the library at market prices. Hence, it also reflects the value consumers place on the library's output. These principles serve as the foundation for analyzing the short- and long-run equilibrium positions of the library.

Short-Run Benefit Maximization

We will examine the economics of library production from the vantage point of per unit cost curves. Figure 41 illustrates the library's benefits and costs in per unit terms of time. The library's demand curve is drawn as a horizontal line at the level of 10 units of time. To maximize benefits, the library will produce that output at which marginal cost equals MB1, at Q2 units of output. Net benefit is equal to the shaded rectangle, EFGH. To see why net benefits are at the maximum where marginal cost equals marginal benefit, consider any output less than Q2, or where MB1 > MC, such as Q1. By adding output, since the MB curve is above the MC curve, more would be added to benefit than would be added to cost. As output expands, the addition to benefit from each successive unit becomes increasingly smaller, until Q2, where MC = MB.

It is important to recognize the significance of this point. Suppose that the library is producing a business-documents lending service, and to produce this service it has incurred costs, as represented by the per unit cost curves. The demand curve, represented by the MB curve, indicates the value, in terms of forgone wages, consumers place on the service. If the library provides more documents than are demanded at that price, it will produce lending services whose benefits, to both the consumer and the library, are smaller than costs. This implies that the library could generate added benefits by contracting business-document lending services and, perhaps, generate larger net benefits in another part of the library. As we add more resources to the business-documents lending section, each additional unit costs more in terms of alternative services; and as these items become relatively more limited, their relative value increases. Only when the ratios of MP/p are equalized will the library be in a production situation where MB = MC.

There is no assurance that the library will provide a positive net benefit. In fact, given its invariable scale of plant, the library may suffer a loss. For example, assume that the library has purchased a given number of documents on the assumption that the MB curve would be MB1, but in reality MB2 is the relevant curve. Now the MB curve lies below the minimum point on the AC curve. When this occurs, the best the library can do is to minimize loss. As it concerns the production of document services, the library can liquidate, discard some of its stock (or, in the extreme case, shut down), or keep its current level of documents.

At any price or demand above the minimum of average variable cost, the library will continue to provide business-document lending services. As long as the MB curve is above the AVC curve, the library can cover its variable costs. And it will minimize loss by equating MC with MB. If we assume that MB is—say—15, production of 100 units provides the library with a total benefit of 1500 units. Assume that average variable cost is 10, so that total average variable cost is 1000. Now suppose the library incurs a fixed cost (storage, etc.) of $600. By producing 100 units, the library is able to cover its average variable cost and some of its fixed cost. There is no other output for which the library can reduce its fixed cost. Furthermore, no other output will reduce its loss. For outputs less than 100, MB > MC; consequently, expansion of output reduces losses. Likewise, if output is greater than 100 units, or MC > MB, the library can reduce losses by contracting output.

Finally, if the MB curve falls below the average variable cost, the library may lose less by discontinuing the service. If the library were to continue the service, its loss would be equal to average variable costs plus any fixed costs. Losses are minimized by discontinuing the service. The important point to note is that, in the short run, the library will not liquidate all of its assets the moment the MB curve falls below average costs. Eventually, it will scale back

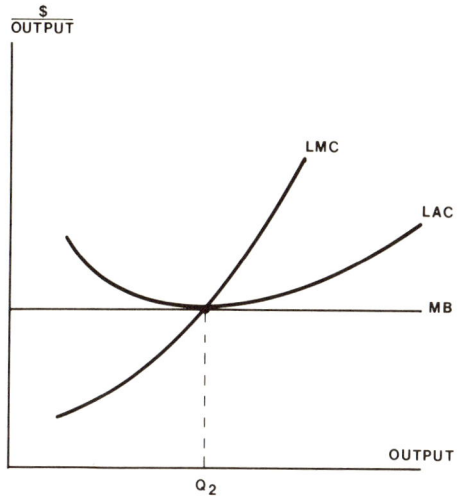

FIG. 42. Long-Run Equilibrium

production, and if the MB curve should fall below the fixed cost curve, it may discontinue the service.

Long-Run Benefit Maximization

Any short-run scale of plant the library has chosen reflects a previous long-run decision. Basically, the same principles apply to long-run production decisions as were used in the short run. To maximize net benefit, the library produces the output at which marginal cost equals marginal revenue. But now the relevant cost curves are the long-run curves and, consequently, long-run marginal cost is set equal to price.

Figure 42 portrays the long-run equilibrium position of the library under conditions of pure competition, as occurring at Q2 units of output. At its long-run equilibrium, the library is operating at the minimum point on its average cost curve, and net benefit is equal to zero. First, we must explain why net benefit is zero at the long-run equilibrium position of the library. Once again, let's assume the library is producing business-documents services, but this time we will add legal-reference services to the product list of the library.

Figure 43A depicts a situation in which the library, having chosen a particular combination of staff, collection, and equipment, is generating a positive net benefit in the production of legal-reference services. In Figure 43B, with the same scale of plant, the library is incurring a negative net benefit in the production of business-document lending services. If we assume that the li-

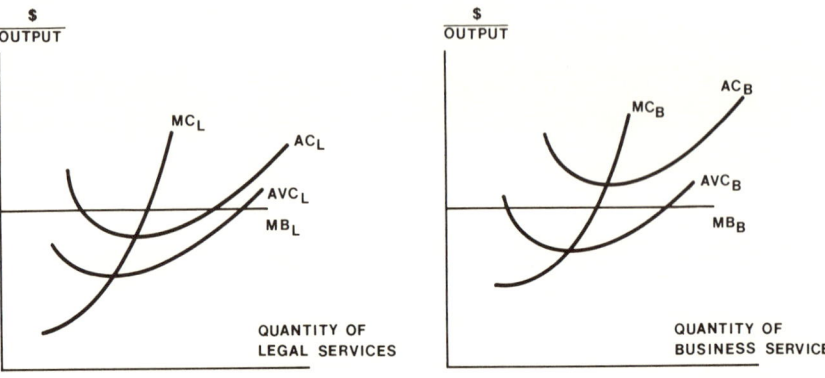

FIG. 43. Long-Run Adjustment Process

brary expects current price (demand) conditions to persist, it would begin making plans to alter the two scales of plant by changing the quantity of specialized factors of production. Why? Because, by committing additional resources to the legal-reference services it will reduce the size of the negative net benefit of business-document lending services; and as resources are subtracted (reduction in specialized inputs), the MP of added resources rises and per unit costs are reduced. With costs reduced and price constant, per unit losses are reduced. But in the process, it is lowering the size of the positive net benefit of legal services, and will continue to do so, until the net benefit of both services is equalized at zero. At this point, no further benefit can be produced by altering the scale of plant of either service.

It is essential to the understanding of long-run equilibrium to emphasize the meaning of zero net benefit. Recall that the concept of cost includes the notion of opportunity costs. When price equals long-run marginal costs, the marginal return to all services is equalized in all alternative production possibilities. Stated differently, no additional gains will be reaped by switching factors of production from one use to alternative uses. Obviously, operating under changing conditions, the long-run equilibrium position, as we have described it, is one that the library will be continually pursuing. The important point to remember is that a long-run equilibrium position implies that the library cannot achieve additional benefits by reallocating resources.

Supply Curve

The preceding section suggests that the MC curve above the shutdown point is the library's supply curve. Operating under pure competition, the library will maximize net benefit by producing an output at which marginal cost is equal to price. By varying price, we derive a series of points depicting the quantity per unit of time the library will supply at an alternative price. Each point on the MC curve shows what the library would produce at a given price. At a price below the minimum average cost, the library would stop providing the service. Thus, the MC curve above the minimum average cost is the library's supply curve.

From our discussion, we know that the library will produce more as the price or marginal benefit of each unit increases, and less at lower prices. The reasons for this are quite simple. As price goes up, the marginal benefit of another unit of output increases; so the library will expand output. However, at the same time, the MC of an additional unit rises. The shape of the library's supply curve and, consequently, the extent to which marginal cost rises are a result of returns to scale. The response of output to changes in price, much like the response of quantity demanded to changes in price, can be measured and expressed in terms of elasticity. Like the industry demand curve, industry supply is derived by the horizontal sum of the supply curves of individual libraries in the industry. Finally, events which cause changes in costs lead to shifts in the firm's supply curve. Reductions in input price and increases in input productivity lead to upward (movement to the left) shifts of the supply curve. Similarly, increases in price or decreases in productivity will cause the supply curve to shift to the right, or downward. The importance of these changes will be investigated in Chapter 6.

Summary

In this chapter we investigated the way in which costs vary with library output. Prior to constructing cost functions, we indicated that the opportunity cost of inputs to the library production process is their value in alternative uses. With alternative uses relatively limited in the short run, opportunity costs will generally be smaller in the short run than in the long run.

Cost analysis and cost modeling require an understanding of the library's production processes. Think of the library as a machine with many interlocking gears, each one a different size and each one setting in motion a series of activities. Our task is to be able to identify these gears, the motions they complete, the energy (costs) associated with these motions, and alternatives. Prior to investigating costs, a library manager must be able to identify production processes, the fixed and variable inputs, and opportunity costs.

Keep in mind that cost curves represent a set of hypothetical propositions. They are used to identify output-cost alternatives, not the library's actual output. Thus, each point on a cost curve is viewed as an option open to the library at points in time. Stated differently, the short and long runs are not particular periods of time. Rather, they provide a convenient way of examining alternatives.

Short-run curves suggest the way in which costs will vary with output with a fixed input. Under these conditions, the law of diminishing returns dictates the shape of cost curves. Long-run cost curves identify how cost will change with output when all inputs are variable. Here, factors which affect returns to scale determine the shape of cost curves. Finally, cost curves are drawn for fixed input prices and a given state of technology. Consequently, changes in input prices and library technology will result in shifting the position of the library's cost curves. The important point to remember is that cost curves should not be viewed as indicators of how costs behaved in the past or will behave in the future.

To gain insight into the long-run adjustment process, we assumed that while the library is in the investment horizon it can choose from a series of service/production options. Basically, once a long-run decision has been made, the library is locked into that position until such time as additional changes can be made. We introduced the concept of isocost lines to determine the least-cost input combination; and price, in conjunction with cost curves, was utilized to determine the optimum output.

Exercises

1. Assume you are the manager of a data search service. To produce the service, you use a fixed resource and a variable resource. What occurs to average fixed costs and average variable costs as output expands?
2. For a given computer memory capacity, what will occur to variable costs as output is expanded? Explain in terms of average product.
3. In terms of forgone opportunities, will the cost of an added open hour be the same for the 20th open hour per week as for the 50th? Explain your answer.
4. With a fixed site and collection, explain why, as output expands, variable costs will begin to rise. Explain in terms of maintenance of documents and equipment, staff, handling of reserves, phone calls theft, and other library production costs.
5. You have completed an analysis of reference questions and have observed that direction questions comprise a large percentage of user requests. Suggest a fixed cost method for reducing the number of directional requests. Using cost curves, illustrate the difference between the two service options: variable cost and fixed cost technique. Explain why you would expect implicit costs to rise in the variable cost case.
6. Explain why, in equilibrium, price will equal MC. In the short run, if price is less than AC but greater than AVC, will the library continue to produce? What will the library do if price should fall below AVC?
7. If marginal benefit stays constant, what will happen to the benefit maximizing output if the price of an input rises?

8. Describe the nature of production cost in the following situation. A library network purchases added computer memory or new reference materials, which results in improved administration of the headquarters and enhances the circulation services of its members.

Suggested Reading

Baumol, William J. "The Costs of Library and Information Services." In *Libraries at Large,* ed. Douglas M. Knight and E. Shepley Nourse. New York: Bowker, 1969. Pp. 216–227.

Bickner, Robert E. "Concepts of Economic Costs." *In Cost Considerations in Systems Analysis,* ed. Gene H. Fisher. New York: American Elsevier, 1971. Pp. 24–63.

Cooper, Michael D. "A Cost Model for Evaluating Information Retrieval Systems." *Journal of the American Society for Information Science* 23:5 (September–October 1972). Pp. 307–312.

Mansfield, Edwin. *Microeconomics: Theory and Applications.* 4th ed. New York: Norton, 1982. Chap. 7.

6
EQUILIBRIUM ANALYSIS

One of the main objectives of economic theory is to analyze the process by which prices are created. Prices are determined by supply and demand. *Supply* summarizes the process by which producers combine inputs to maximize profits, and *demand* portrays the consumer's utility maximizing choices. Neither side of the market, by itself, can determine market price. Operating together, a condition of balance, known as *equilibrium,* is achieved. In this chapter we bring together the theory of consumer choice and production. The objective is to find out how each side of the market, reacting to economic variables, operates to establish price and quantity. Having shown how the state of equilibrium is achieved, we can begin to investigate the result of changing market conditions on the quantity of information that will be supplied and consumed.

Initially, we focused our attention on consumer behavior. Next we examined the nature of input productivity and costs. Our aim is to orchestrate the two components of the market so that we can analyze the operation of library services in terms of price and quantity. The choices made by information managers are difficult; they involve distinct tradeoffs among types and quantities of inputs and outputs. The theory of production brought us part of the way toward understanding the impact of library policy within the context of production costs. The theory of consumer choice permitted us to investigate the way in which library prices affect consumption of information services. In each case, we have treated price as given. Now, we put the two sides together, as price and quantity are determined in the market.

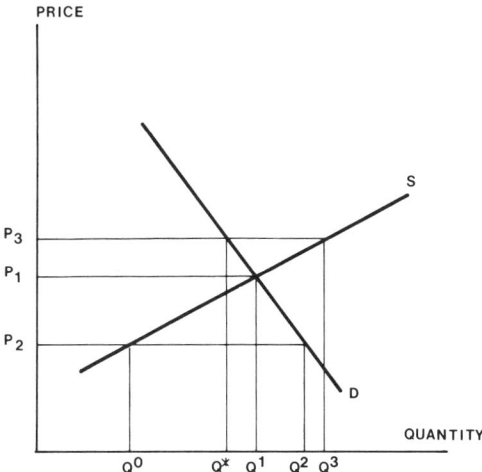

FIG. 44. Equilibrium

Determination of Price and Quantity

Equilibrium is defined as the intersection of the supply and the demand. The justification for this proposition is best understood by looking at a state of disequilibrium. Figure 44 portrays the market for reference service in equilibrium; price is P1 and quantity is Q1. Suppose that the market price was momentarily lower than P1, say P2. At this price, P2, consumers are willing to purchase Q2 units of reference service, but the supply curve indicates that the library will only produce Qo. The quantity demanded, Q2, is in excess of the quantity offered on the market, Qo. The plans of consumers and producers are inconsistent. Library service consumers will not be able to purchase the amount of reference they desire, and some of them will start to bid up the price (form lines). Library staff notice that consumers are willing to pay a higher price and will begin to reevaluate the current resource allocation. The change in market conditions suggests that the staff will move resources to reference services. As they shift resources to reference service, MC (in terms of opportunity costs) begins to rise. The process continues until demand equals supply at P1,Q1.

What if the market price were at some higher level than P1, such as P3? At this point, the quantity that producers of reference service are willing to supply, Q3, is in excess of that which consumers are willing to purchase, Q*. Here, there is downward pressure on price. Unsold (unused) reference service will lead the library to lower its reference inventory, shown as a movement down the supply curve. At any price other than P1, one or the other process will be set in motion until equilibrium is achieved. In essence, markets work to achieve a condition of balance. Since any other state cannot persist, we will always be in a state of equilibrium; that is, price adjusts to make quantity demanded and supplied equal.

A wide range of economic problems can be analyzed on the assertion that markets must "clear." With more than one price, there are further gains from exchange, and the market has not yet "cleared." Hence, one of the primary uses of equilibrium is the analysis of changes in supply and demand and the concomitant prediction of what will occur to price and quantity.

Changes in Supply

Inventory Control

Suppose that a multisite library alters the method by which it circulates its inventory. To find out what occurs to equilibrium price and quantity, let us describe the initial market conditions. Before the change, the library controls the circulation of inventory with a relatively labor-intensive production technique. To control circulation and lend its materials, the library relies on the use of library cards, date stamps, and item-transaction cards. The transaction card, or a duplicate, is kept as a record of item transactions. From these records, each site is able to determine which materials are overdue and assess late charges. Consumers are allowed to borrow materials at any site and return them to any site without penalty.

To notify consumers of overdue materials, the library combines staff, transaction records, notices, and stamps. Personnel review transaction records for a specific due date to determine which items have not been returned. Library staff then prepare overdue notices for mailing. Given the current production function for circulation, each site is unaware of the return of its materials to other locations. Consequently, "overdues" will be sent for materials that have already been returned.

Since circulation records are filed by date and not by title, author, or subject, these files cannot be used to reserve materials. Instead, as returned materials are readied for shelving they are checked against a list which is kept up to date manually. Furthermore, each site keeps track of its circulation independently of the others. If a library gets a reserve, it will search materials as they are returned. The library will not check other locations to see if the item is on their shelves. Also, let's assume that if a particular site does not own a requested item, it forwards the request to a centralized processing center. If the library system owns the item, this center will check its location file to determine which locations own the item. Having verified ownership, staff members attempt to locate the reserved item by telephoning member libraries. If a library has the material, it will be sent to the library nearest the requesting consumer, and the patron will be notified by phone or postcard. If no location has the item on its shelves, the centralized processing center will ask one of the locations to place a reserve on the item. This library will search for the material for a specified period of time. If the material is found, it is sent to the requesting branch; if it isn't found, the process is started over again.

Now let us assume that the library decides to employ a new circulation technique. The new method keeps track of all circulation records simultaneously, regardless of which library owns or circulates an item. It permits member libraries to more efficiently determine the status of the library system's inventory. Furthermore, it produces all overdues and notifies staff that an item which has been checked in is on reserve. With this information, we will be able to examine what occurs to the price and quantity of circulation services. To simplify matters, we will not analyze the production technique to fill requests for items not owned by the library system, the delivery technique to distribute items from location to location, or the manner in which patrons are notified about reserved items. Instead, we will focus on the productivity of labor.

Assume that the new circulation system raises the total product of labor. This is tantamount to a downward shift of the average and marginal cost curves. Before we investigate what occurs to the price of circulation services, let us discuss the changes in the library's production function. As circulation increased, before the investment in the new system, the amount of staff time devoted to this function had to increase too. First, the number of records that had to be searched for overdues increased. Second, it seems reasonable to assume that the quantity of overdues which had to be prepared, as well as the number of items placed on reserve, increased. Thus, in the short run, the amount of time available for other library services decreased. Alternatively, there could have been some combination of delays in circulation duties and delays in other services. As output increased, the opportunity cost of labor increased. With the introduction of the new system, the quantity of time utilized to produce a unit of circulation services has been reduced. Time devoted to reserves and inventory control, including detection of overdue items and the production of notices, has been reduced. The average and marginal amount of effort required to produce a unit of circulation services has been reduced, implying a reduction in the average and marginal cost of processing circulation information. Stated differently, each unit of output can be produced with less labor than was previously required.

Figure 45 depicts both the original demand-and-supply curve and the new supply curve. On the assumption that demand remains unchanged, the price of circulation services has been reduced and the quantity demanded has increased. Consumers spend less time in lines; there are fewer delays in receiving requested items; and transactions related to erroneous overdues have decreased. The amount of reduction depends upon the shapes of the demand-

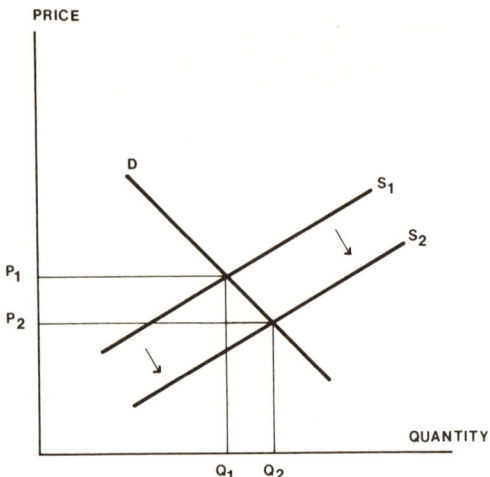

FIG. 45. Technological Innovation

and-supply curves. The more elastic the demand curve, the greater the response to a change in price. Likewise, the shape of the supply curve affects the market price and quantity. A supply curve with a low elasticity implies a relatively small response to changes in market conditions. With the passage of time, regardless of the initial shape of the supply curve, the ability to respond to changing market conditions is greater, and so is the response of quantity demanded and quantity supplied.

Delivery Policy and Market Price

Let's examine changes in demand and library inventory distribution policy in a multisite library. The library has several inventory control options: inventory can be stored centrally or decentrally; items may or may not be requested; items may be shipped directly to the patron or to the requesting site; items can be returned to any site or must be returned to the owning site. The library can combine these inventory control options in several ways. For example, it can store items centrally, allow requests, ship them directly to the patron, and allow the patrons to return the items to any site. Each combination of storage, delivery, and return options has a different impact on the library and the consumer. In this section, we will analyze the impact of an increase in demand, given library delivery policies.

We will assume that the library houses the items centrally, allows requests, ships reserved items to patrons, and allows them to return items to any site.

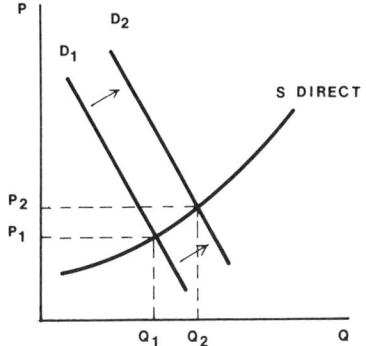 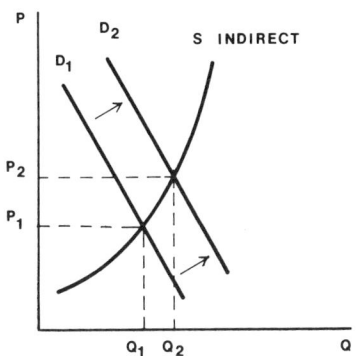

Fig. 46. Direct vs. Indirect Delivery Method

When demand increases, what happens to production costs and time price? If we assume that the library's inventory and loan policy is fixed, output cannot be expanded significantly and time price increases. As demand increases, more time will be expended on shipping, decreasing the amount of time available for other library services. Therefore, the opportunity cost of expanding output increases. The library will move up its marginal cost curve, and time price will rise. The extent to which both price and output increase depends upon the elasticity of supply.

Now let us alter the policy described in the preceding paragraph. Assume that we change the way in which items are shipped to the patron, all else remaining the same. Instead of shipping the item to the patron, we ship it to the requesting site. In this case, the library must unpack the item, notify the patron, and hold the item for a specified period of time. Obviously, as demand increases, the opportunity cost per unit cost will be greater in this case than in the previous one. More time will be spent handling items. In addition, time prices, in terms of wait and travel, are relatively higher than in the item-to-patron delivery example. This conclusion is not surprising; items will first be shipped to the library, unpacked, and then be retained on a reserve shelf for a fixed time period. Graphically, the difference between the two systems can be represented by two supply curves, one lower and perhaps more elastic than the other, as shown in Figure 46.

On the other hand, the library may opt to distribute inventory in a decentralized mode. Assume that patrons can request items from any site, that they are shipped directly to the patrons, and that they can be returned to any site. The primary difference between this production technique and the centralized/ship-to-patron technique is the potential of a more complex return-to-owning-site shipping system. Therefore, both time and production costs may be relatively higher than the centralized/ship-to-patron delivery method.

The library could opt for a no-request policy, decentralize inventory, and have items returned to owning sites. In this case, its cost curves would be lower than for the other production situations. Splitting up the collection among many sites, not allowing requests, and having the consumer return items to the owning sites lowers production costs. The reason is that staff will no longer have to contact patrons and items will no longer spend time on reserve shelves or have to be shipped from one location to another. In addition, a reserve list will not have to be maintained. Thus, items can be checked out, returned, and be readied for use at a lower cost. On the assumption that demand had increased, price will be lower, and output higher, than with the aforementioned circulation techniques.

Changes in Demand

Shift in Tastes

Suppose that a change occurs in tastes, with the result that library consumers are more favorably disposed toward computer-related materials and less favorably disposed toward historical materials. The demand for computer materials has increased; however, because inventory cannot be expanded, short-run output cannot be increased substantially and, consequently, price increases. On the other hand, demand for historical materials has dropped, reducing the price and quantity. Yet, the history service capability (inventory) of the library will not be reduced immediately because the library can still cover variable costs (per unit opportunity cost of storage).

The change in market conditions triggers a process of adjustment. Resources will be shifted from history services to computer-related services. In the short run, if variable inputs can be redeployed from history to computer services, they will be withdrawn from history and shifted to computer-related services. The process of adjustment is not complete until the library has had a chance to change the operating capacity of each service. In terms of cost, the library is producing computer services at an output greater than the minimum average cost; history services are operating at an output less than the minimum of average cost. (See Figure 47.)

In the long run, a change in taste will lead to additional adjustments. Diminished demand for history services will result in a reduction in the number of new purchases, and items currently in the library's stock will either be weeded or allowed to age and fall into disrepair. The transfer of funds from one service to another results in shifts of the supply curves. The supply curve of history will shift to the left, causing a rise in price, whereas the supply of computer services will shift to the right, resulting in a decrease in price. The transfer of resources from history to computer services will cease when the

Equilibrium Analysis 141

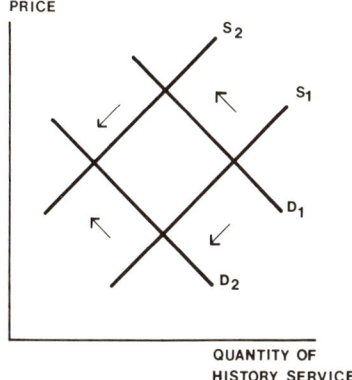
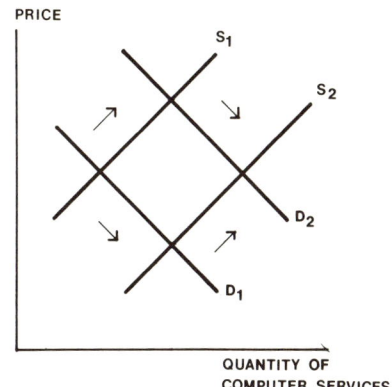

FIG. 47. Allocation Process

history price has increased and costs have been reduced to the point where losses are avoided.

Based on the analysis in this section, we can observe what would happen if the library manager did not behave as we have suggested. Assume that the library manager does not shift resources from history to computer-related services. At the new level of computer demand, the price of service has increased, and so has quantity. But, given the choice not to increase the service capability, represented as a constant supply, item availability decreases. Lines will persist in the long run, items will fall into disrepair, and some items will be sent to the bindery, resulting in a further decrease in item availability. If substitutes for library service exist, some consumers will choose to go elsewhere. The loss of consumers will continue until the price of library computer-related service decreases to the level of other producers.

While the use of computer-related services begins to decrease, no increase takes place in the use of history services. In fact, with history-service capability kept constant and a reduced demand, a net loss will persist in the long run. But this type of behavior is inconsistent with our assumption that library managers operate so as to maximize net benefit. By switching from history to computer-related services, library use will increase while income is held constant. Therefore, it seems reasonable to assume that the library manager would redeploy expenditures.

Household Information Production and Library Economies

Imagine that as a result of changes in the way consumers produce goods and services, demand for information has increased. The impact of this change

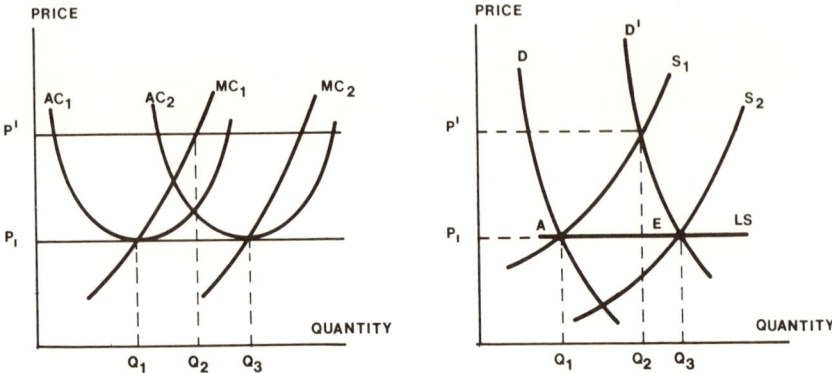

FIG. 48. Long-Run Supply and Constant Costs

on the equilibrium price and quantity depends upon the shape of both the demand and the supply curve. To simplify matters and to gain insight into the process of adjustment, we will concentrate on the shape of the supply curve, which, you recall, depends upon returns to scale.

To begin, let's analyze the constant-cost production possibility. A library that is characterized by the absence of internal economies, or diseconomies, is said to be subject to constant returns to scale. Figure 48 shows the long-run equilibrium under constant-cost conditions. To derive the long-run supply curve for library services, we take some equilibrium position as a starting point and trace the effects of the shift in tastes until the library returns to a long-run equilibrium. Although the right-hand side of the diagram is traditionally reserved for industry analysis, it will be useful for understanding the constant-cost library. As shown in Figure 48, the initial output is Q1, and price is P1.

Once the demand curve moves up, the immediate response will be constrained by short-run production conditions. The library increases output with existing plant and equipment. Consequently, we move upward to the right on the MC curve; market price rises to P′, at which Q2 units are produced. At this price, the library is producing a net benefit. But the existence of net benefits suggests that the library will increase its scale of plant, shown as a movement along its long-run average cost curve to AC2, MC2. Given constant per unit costs, as output expands the average wait time for an item is reduced, price falls, and the process of adjustment ceases when net benefit is zero. Hence, the short-run supply curve shifts to the right, until the new short-run supply curve intersects D′ at point E, where price has been restored to its original level.

Point E is a second point on the long-run supply curve. Granted that the market demand is D′, library output expands until it reaches Q3 and price P.

The long-run supply curve connects points A and E, indicating that the constant-cost library supply curve is characterized by a horizontal line. With an infinitely elastic supply curve, the long-run price remains constant.

To summarize: in the constant-cost situation, expansion does not affect prodution costs. Since the cost curves do not shift, price must fall to its original level and net benefit returns to zero. At higher prices, net benefits would persist and the library would continue to expand.

In contrast to the constant-cost production scenario, the library may be characterized by internal economies or diseconomies of production. Unlike the constant-cost situation, with output expansion, production that is subject to internal diseconomies leads to higher costs. Therefore, the long-run supply curve is positively sloped. The decreasing cost case is characterized by a negatively sloped supply curve; price will be lower in the long run. For instance, economies of scale in book stock may result as the libary expands. Library materials may be shared among a larger population, thereby reducing per unit costs. Note that a decreasing cost situation should not be confused with a change in the state of technology. A change in the state of technology results in a shift of the cost curves, whereas a change in the level of output is a movement along a supply curve.

Although the reasons are different, the same three types of long-run supply curves apply to industry production. The shape of industry supply curves is determined by the extent to which external economies or diseconomies are present. Unlike returns to scale, economies or diseconomies emerge from forces which operate outside a library's control. For example, as new libraries are formed (and other information firms too), they increase their demand for inputs. But some inputs may only be available in larger quantities at higher prices. Consequently, the cost curves of all information firms rise as output expands, indicating a positively sloped long-run industry supply curve. And existing firms end up producing the same amount as in the initial period. Alternatively, the expansion of an industry may lead to reductions in the cost of an input, such as communication costs. Firms' cost curves shift downward; thus, a movement to the right along the long-run supply curve results in lower market prices. To summarize, if external effects are present, expansion or contraction of industry output can cause the cost curves of individual libraries to shift.

What distinguishes internal from external economies is that internal economies arise from the control of the library over its own resources whereas external economies operate outside the library's control. Internal effects are illustrated as movements along the library's cost curves; external effects result in shifts of the library's cost curves. Hence, it is important to distinguish between external and internal economies when one is predicting the shape of the outcome of changes in market conditions.

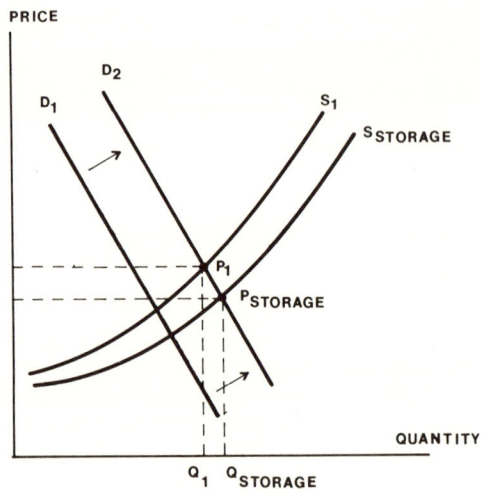

FIG. 49. Seasonal Variations in Demand

Seasonal Variations in Demand

The demand for certain types of library services shifts in response to changes in the seasons. Just as the response of nonlibrary service consumption to changes in seasons is crucial to understanding the markets for these goods, the behavioral response of library consumers to changes in seasons is important to the analysis of library markets.

Suppose that the demand for garden-and-house improvement-related services increases in the early spring and continues to increase until early summer, after which it begins to diminish. In sharp contrast to this situation, the demand for school-related services begins to decrease as summer approaches. What we see is that the consumption of particular library services varies widely over the year. Let us concentrate our analysis of seasonal demand on the increase in demand. As illustrated in Figure 49, demand curve D2, increased demand, with supply constant, S1, leads to higher prices. The extent to which price rises depends on the inventory policy of the library. Through use (general wear and tear, theft), the stock of a particular library service will be reduced during the peak demand period, but it can be built up again during the off-peak (and previous) periods. If the supply is not increased during the off-season, then the price increase will be relatively greater than for the case in which stock is replenished. In addition, the speed with which the library is able to rebuild stocks affects the price (in terms of wait time) of library service. For example, if the time between order and receipt is long, items may arrive after demand has shifted in one or the other direction. In essence, until stock is increased, price is higher.

Information Search Technique

To locate documents, library staff and patrons employ a variety of search techniques, including the library catalog, other indexes, signs, and browsing. Prices and income guide consumers to the optimal search method. We will show how the introduction of a change in the ability to search for information affects the price and quantity of information services. To begin, we assume that the time cost of information search is a function of staff and client production functions. Viewing information search in this manner permits us to use isoquants to portray information search activity. Production of search activity is achieved with varying combinations of user and staff time. Each isoquant represents the maximum output that can be generated from different input combinations. A reduction in the amount of staff time implies an increase in the amount of user time required to produce the same level of output.

If the quality of staff or other library search aids increases, the total time required to locate an item is reduced. A similar result occurs if the ability of the consumer to locate information increases. Any improvement in the technology of information search changes the output obtainable by varying one input with the other fixed. This means that the total product curves shift upward. With isoquants, an improvement in production technique results in a shifting in of isoquants toward the origin, as shown in Figure 50. This, in turn, leads to a new production expansion path with lower long-run production costs. The long- and short-run cost curves shift downward; supply increases, lowering the price of information search and increasing quantity—given no change in demand.

The relative use of staff or patron time will depend upon which input has increased its marginal and average product. If the ability of staff to locate information has increased, given no change in user capability, there would be an increase in requests for staff assistance. Note that the increased ability of staff has permitted an increase in output at lower prices, and that the slope of the isoquant would also have changed. This situation contrasts sharply with that of an increase in demand holding supply constant; in this case, price increases.

Another analytical approach to a change in production technique involves thinking of the library consumer as having a self-supply curve for information services.[1] Assume that, given the availability of a library catalog, the consumer's ability to produce search activity is improved. In Figure 51, without the catalog, the consumer's supply curve is S1, and with the catalog it is S2. Given a demand curve, the price of search activity is lower with a catalog. Next,

146 Microeconomic Theory

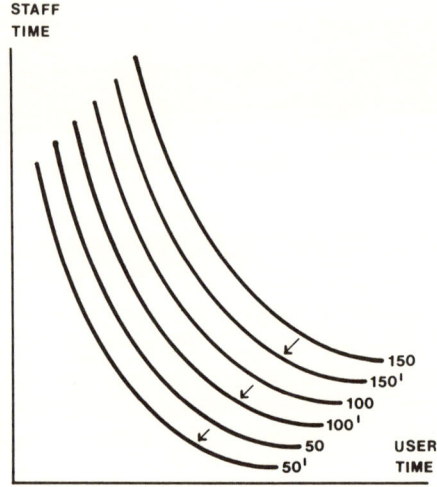

Fig. 50. Information Search

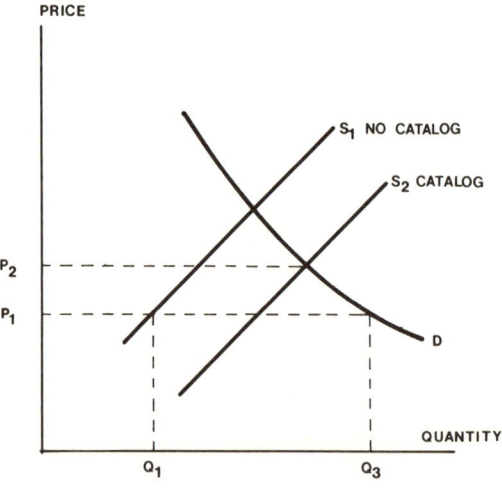

Fig. 51. Consumer Demand for Information Search

assume that, given current library policy, the price of using staff assistance is P1. Given the availability of a catalog, at this price the user will supply Q1 units of self-service and will purchase Q3–Q1 units of staff assistance. Observe that, with a catalog, staff prices higher than P2 result in reliance on self-supply (or alternative sources). Returning to our original point, we see that the introduction of a new technique results in a downward shift of the supply with a lower price and higher quantity. Interested readers may wish to examine the change in search effectiveness by using indifference curves. Here, the change can be represented as a change in the price of one of two services: self/alternative vs. library supply.

Path to Equilibrium

Much of this chapter has focused on equilibrium levels of price and quantity. In reality, disequilibrium, rather than equilibrium, is the usual state of affairs. A library is continually buffeted by changes. Long-run adjustments take time; as the library begins to readjust resources, underlying market conditions may have changed, so that the library is moving toward a state of equilibrium that is continually shifting. However, the fact that supply-and-demand curves are continually moving in response to changes in economic variables does not undermine the usefulness of theories based on equilibrium. On the contrary, although a library may never fully attain a position of equilibrium, the tendency to move toward equilibrium permits us to use equilibrium analysis to predict the direction of change.

To start our analysis of the path to equilibrium, let's assume that the quantity supplied (in terms of service capability) of children's fiction is a function of the price in the previous period. Current acquisitions are based on previous market conditions. On the other hand, we will assume that library consumers make choices based on current prices. Assume that the demand and supply for children's services are as shown in Figure 52; price in the previous period was Po. Operating under the assumptions we have listed, the amount the library will be able to supply in period 1 will be Q1. Yet, with Q1 being supplied, the price will be P1. With a price of P1 established in the first period, the supply curve indicates that Q2 will be supplied in the second period. Given the supply-and-demand curve in Figure 52, this process will go on until price and quantity converge at the intersection of the two curves. Notice that the relative slopes of the demand-and-supply curves determine the nature of the adjustment cycle. Finally, the primary purpose of this rather simple model is to highlight the mechanics of change when time lags are present in library production.

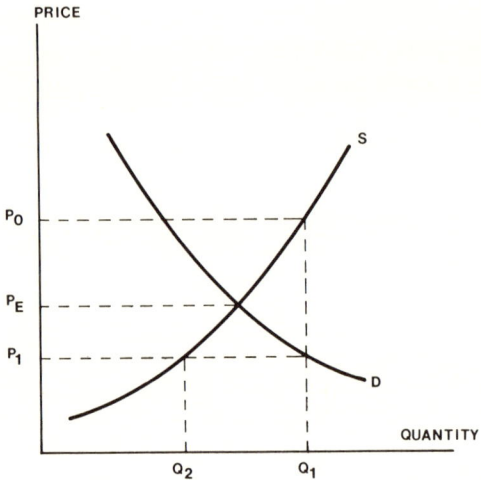

Fig. 52. Path to Equilibrium

Summary

The market for library services is comprised of consumers and producers. The demand curve reflects the condition of wants in terms of the quantity of a good that would be purchased at various prices. Tastes, prices, and income play a major role in determining demand. Initially, we assumed that tastes and income were constant, which allowed us to analyze the impact of changes in price and derive the demand curve. Once we derived the demand curve, we were able to illustrate changes in taste, prices of other goods, and income.

The library as producer was examined in the context of inputs and output. We saw that the supply curve for a good generally slopes upward, its shape determined by input prices, the state of technology, and the length of time to which the supply curve pertains. Finally, we linked the two sides of the market together to illustrate how the equilibrium price and quantity are obtained. Equilibrium was defined as a position that markets tend to move toward. If price exceeds the equilibrium price, there will be an excess of supply, and market forces will operate to lower price. Conversely, if price is less than the equilibrium price, there will be excess demand, and market forces will operate to push price up. Shifts in either the supply or the demand curve tend to change the equilibrium price and quantity. In the short run, the response in price is greatest. As the library moves toward the long-run position, the response in output tends to be the larger of the two. Actual outcomes depend upon the elasticity of both the demand and the supply curves.

Exercises

1. Suppose that a library's acquisition techniques result in a six-month delay in the availability of new publications. What will happen to the price and quantity of library services if the delay is reduced? Which curve shifts, and in what direction?
2. Assume that a library purchases a phone-answering device which permits clients to find out the library's hours of operation. This service functions when the library is closed. Compare transaction costs with and without this device.
3. The price of paperbacks increases relative to hardbacks. Predict the library's reaction.
4. Use the path-to-equilibrium approach to analyzing the demand and supply of librarians.

References

1. Robert M. Mason and Peter G. Sassone. "A Lower Bound Cost Benefit Model for Information Services," *Information Processing and Management* 14:2 (1978): 71–83.

Suggested Reading

Buckland, Michael K. *Book Availability and the Library User.* New York: Pergamon, 1975.
———. "Toward an Economic Theory of the Library." In *Economics of Information Dissemination: A Symposium,* ed. Robert S. Taylor. Syracuse: School of Library Science, Syracuse University, 1973. Pp. 68–80.
Dorfman, Robert. *Prices and Markets.* 2nd ed. Englewood Cliffs, N.J.: Prentice-Hall, 1972.
King Research, Inc. *Library Human Resources: A Study of Supply and Demand.* Chicago: American Library Association, 1983.

II Applications and Extension of Microeconomic Theory

7

QUANTITATIVE METHODS

The first portion of this text supplied information managers with basic tools for analyzing economic phenomenon. Although a general framework is necessary, operating in a risk-filled environment suggests the need to increase the precision with which we can predict, which involves employing models that incorporate estimates of future events. The first two chapters in Part 2 are devoted to an investigation of statistics for making decisions in an uncertain world. Following this, we introduce general expenditure evaluation guidelines for library projects, such as library buildings and security systems. In Chapter 11, we will examine public library finance and its implications for the supply and pricing of library services.

Introduction to Quantitative Methods

Suppose someone handed you records containing the circulation history of 20,000 items. Next, they ask you to make some conclusions about the past and future circulation of library materials. Essentially, your problem is to take a large volume of raw data and organize them into a format which permits you to study the main characteristics of circulation records. Statistical methods help to organize data and uncover principles and trends at work behind information. In subsequent chapters, we will use statistical methods to probe several key resource- allocation concerns in information management: number and type of inventory to order and the affect of staff levels on the time that consumers spend waiting in lines.

Our first step in statistical analysis is to define our problem—to draw some conclusions about the past circulation of library materials. You have also been asked to make some inferences about future use, based on these records. Immediately, one key question comes to mind: Exactly what types of conclusions does the manager want me to make? (More on this later.) Luckily, the data have already been collected otherwise, this would have been your first task. Next, you must go about the job of interpreting the data.

The most common technique for organizing statistical data is to group information into a relatively small number of classes. *Frequency distribution* tables or diagrams are used to organize data into a more compact form, without obscuring the essential information in the data. Essentially, we group the circulation histories according to some observable characteristic, such as how often a particular title was circulated (this can also be listed within a range of use). We might also be interested in how often people enter the library at a particular time of day. A frequency diagram shows the percentage of people who visit the library at particular times of day (or range). The reduction of data into classes or intervals may result in the loss of some detailed information; however, well-designed frequency distributions permit us to compute key characteristics with fewer computations.

Assume that the information manager has asked you to describe some basic mathematical properties of these circulation records. Given a data series, we might consider deriving some measure of central tendency, such as the average use in a particular subject or the most commonly occurring value in a series of circulation records, known as the *mode*. The latter is often synonymous with *maximum popularity*. To compute the average or arithmetic mean, you simply add all the times items that have circulated and then divide by the number of items in the class. The *mean* is the most widely used measure of central tendency in statistics, but because it is affected by every value of observation it may be distorted by a few extreme values.

The *median*, the value larger than or equal to half of the terms and equal to or smaller than the other half—is not distorted by the value of observations. Where there is a vast difference between the number of times an item has been borrowed, the median gives a better picture of the level of activity than the mean. For instance, suppose we wish to find the median number of times an item circulates. Given nine items and the number of times each has circulated, we calculate the median by taking the number of items in an array, ordered from lowest to highest circulation, add 1, and divide by 2—indicating that in this case the fifth item is the median. Unlike the mean, the median will remain the fifth item, regardless of whether one or two items have extremely low or high circulation. Consequently, the median is usually a more revealing measure of activity.

The *average* and the median, two selected measures of central tendency, are generally not sufficient to describe the data that are analyzed. In addition, statisticians have developed measures of *variance* or *dispersion*. These measures indicate the extent to which items in a series are scattered about the average. Usually, measures of dispersion are used to form a judgment about the reliability of the average or, if the extent of variation is known, to control it. The concept of dispersion is also important in forecasting. For example, we might have two groups of circulation records:

(X) 34, 58, 7, 26, 20, 10, 56, 45

(Y) 32, 30, 32, 36, 29, 35, 32, 30

each with the same arithmetic mean. Intuitively, we know that group X has a higher dispersion measure than group Y. Now if you were told that there was another unlisted number in each series, you would be more certain about your prediction being accurate in series X than in series Y.

The most commonly used measure of dispersion is known as the *standard deviation*. It takes on particular significance when a frequency distribution is bell shaped or normal. Briefly, it describes what percentage of items in a normal-shaped distribution falls within a given distance from the mean. When we analyze circulation histories, the standard deviation allows us to picture the distribution of circulation more accurately. For example, the average number of days a book is out on loan only tells us that half of the items will be out less time and that the other half will be out more time than the average. But, as we shall see, the standard deviation permits us to calculate the maximum number of items that would be on loan a given percentage of the time.

Decision Making with Risk

To make decisions in a world of uncertainty requires that we take into account the level of risk associated with decisions. Probability, in conjunction with certain modeling techniques, allows us to estimate the numerical likelihood of possible outcomes. In these sections, we will introduce some of the probability theory to be used in Chapters 7, 8, and 9.

Throughout the course of a manager's work, decision situations arise which involve assessing an uncertain future. We have all noticed that there are certain times when the post office, the grocery store, the roads, and our libraries are congested, and other times when they are not. We may wonder why people choose to come to the library at these times, but the simple fact that this pattern is observable is useful to us as decision makers. Given events of this type, an information manager can employ models which rely on probability theory to predict future occurrences.

Probability

Probabilities generally fall into two categories: objective and subjective. Objective probability is based on historical evidence. For example, to find out the objective probability of people coming to the library at a certain hour who want to use seats, we would rely on previous counts or samples of this event. *Sampling* implies drawing upon a part of a larger population in order to make inferences about the larger group. For example, we might want to examine the frequency of use of the library's microfiche catalog readers, the number of times a particular document is used, the number of times a piece of equipment needs repairs, or the use of the library's automated catalog. To obtain this type of information, we could make observations of use at specified intervals of time and, from this information, make inferences concerning total use. To make inferences, we rely on probability theory.

However, there will be times when a pattern is broken; and this may indicate a random event or reflect the beginnings of a new trend. Probability theory permits us to test whether or not such random events reflect a significant change from an established pattern. Frequently, we cannot rely on historical evidence for assigning probabilities. In instances such as these, managers may rely on their own estimation of an outcome, based on their previous experience or intuition.

Measuring Probability

Assume a library operation in which a number of outcomes can take place. We define probability as a number that describes the likelihood of a particular outcome. One might ask: What is the probability of people coming to the library at a certain time? Or the probability that we will have a given number of requests for a particular type of material or author/title? Or we might be interested in knowing what patrons will do when they visit the library: Will they use the catalog? Will they borrow one or more books? Or will they perform some combination of these activities? The probability of any one of these activities can be expressed as the *chance* that it will happen.

To determine the likelihood that a patron would use the catalog, we could examine past records or observe people coming into the library during a specified period. In probability theory we refer to this as an *experiment;* the set of all possible outcomes of an experiment is called its *sample space*. When the number of people who enter the library is studied, the possible *outcomes* would be all the people who entered the library. Let's assume that we have information which shows that of every 100 people who enter the library, 60 use the catalog. Based on our sample, we might state that the probability of a person using the catalog is 60/100. If we repeated this experiment many times, we would state that the probability of a particular event is the proportion of times, or relative frequency, that this event occurs in the long run. Mathematically, given a situation which occurs a large number of times, N, the probability of an event, E, which occurs n times is

$$P(E) = n / N \qquad \text{Eq. 7.1}$$

Quantitative Methods 157

For example, if we observe N people coming into the library, the probability of their coming at a certain time, E, is the number of people who come at that time, n, divided by N.

Based on our definition of probability, P(E) must have a value between zero and 1. An impossible event will have a value of zero; an event that is certain to occur must have a value of 1. In other words, if an outcome is impossible, the number of times the outcome, or n, will occur is zero: $0 / N = 0$. If an event is certain, its probability must be equal to 1. If all of the people come in at three o'clock, then $n = N$: $100 / 100 = 1$. Since the number of times n occurs cannot be negative, its probability cannot be less than zero. Can fewer than zero people come into the library? And since n cannot exceed the number of times the outcome takes place, N, its probability cannot exceed 1.

Rules of Probability

Most decision makers are concerned with two conditions: the case where one or another event will occur, and the case where two or more events will occur. Note that when we discuss probability we can speak of mutually exclusive or nonmutually exclusive events. For instance, we may either pass or fail a test; when we toss a coin, on any toss either heads or tails will turn up, but not both. When library patrons attend the library, they are not restricted to only one activity. However, it is possible to state library events in terms of mutually exlusive activities. The consumer can either use the catalog or not use the catalog; borrow one book, or two books, but not one *and* two books; etc.

Given a set of mutually exclusive and physically exhaustive events (all events listed), the sum of the expected number of outcomes of n trials must equal N. Thus, if our sample space is 20 people visiting the library, the sum of the expected number of times 1 person, 2 persons, and so on up to 20 must equal 20, since there are no other possible outcomes. Further, when all the mutually exclusive outcomes of an experiment exhaust the physically possible outcomes, the sum of all probabilities in their frequency distribution must equal 1. It seems reasonable to assume that if something is going to occur, the certainty of its occurrence, or the sum of all possible alternatives, should equal 1. For example, given a fair coin, the probability of heads is 1/2 and that of tails is also 1/2; the sum of all possible outcomes is 1.

A single probability, like the probability of a person borrowing a given number of books, is called an an *unconditional* probability. Often, however, we are interested in the probability that a library patron will consult the librarian or borrow a book. If these events are mutually exclusive, we can express the probability of either of two possible outcomes as the sum of their individual probabilities:

$$P(A \text{ or } B) = P(A) + P(B) \qquad \text{Eq. 7.2}$$

158   Applications and Extension of Theory

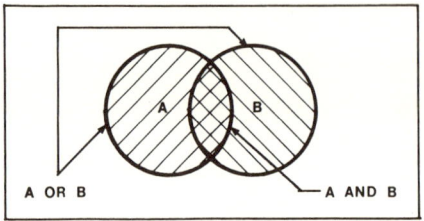

FIG. 53. Addition of Nonmutually Exclusive Events

Thus, if the probability that a person will consult the librarian is 1 in 10 and the probability that he or she will *not* is also 1 in 10, the probability that one or the other will occur is 1/10 + 1/10 = 1/5, or .20.

The *addition* rule for events that are not mutually exclusive—events that can occur simultaneously—seeks to avoid double counting. For instance, since a novel can be both a mystery and a romance at the same time, the probability of selecting either a romance or a mystery must account for the fact that we could choose them together, or

P(A or B) when A and B are not mutually exclusive

= P(A) + P(B)—P(A and B)   Eq. 7.3

where P(A and B) represents the simple intersection of two sample spaces. Figure 53 illustrates the concepts in Equation 7.3. The event A or B is indicated by the heavy line, and events A and B are shown by the hatched wedge in the middle. So as not to double count, we must subtract the area of the hatched wedge.

In many situations, we will want to go further than simply find out whether or not the library visitor has consulted the catalog or the reference librarian. We may wish to know whether or not they consulted the librarian and checked out materials, or whether they consulted the librarian and didn't check out materials. When two events such as these occur, the outcome of the first event may or may not have an effect on the second event. Events which have no effect on the probability of the occurrence of another event are statistically independent. If consulting the librarian and checking out materials are viewed as independent of one another, the probability of these events occurring together or in succession, *joint probability,* is simply

P(LC) = P(L)P(C)   Eq. 7.4

In terms of coin tossing (using a fair coin), we might ask the probability of getting tails on two successive tosses. It is simply P(T1)—the probability of tails on the first toss multiplied by the probability of tails on the second toss, P(T2), or (.5)(.5) = .25. Likewise, if a person's use of the librarian and borrowing privileges are not related to one another, we determine the joint probability of borrowing and reference use as the product of the single or marginal probabilities. Or, if the client's borrowing of library materials has no relation to his or her use of the catalog, then the probability of a visitor using the catalog X times and taking out Y items is the simple product of the two probabilities of event X and event Y.

In addition to the single and joint probability, there is a conditional probability. This refers to the probability that a second event (B) will occur, given that another event (A) is known to have occurred. For example, the probability of finding an item on the shelf may be enhanced, given that you consulted the catalog. Generally, the probability of event B, given that event A has occurred, is written

$$(B/A) \text{ or } P(B/\text{then } A) \qquad \text{Eq. 7.5}$$

When they are independent, $P(B/\text{then } A) = P(B)$. While this may seem confusing at first, recall that an independent event can have no effect on another event. Consequently, if the existence of A has no effect on the probability of B, then the single probability of B has not been altered. As it concerns the library client, we are referring to the situation in which, having consulted the catalog, the probability of the library visitor's finding an item is simply equal to the probability of finding an item.

On the other hand, we may wish to know what the conditional probability is in cases of statistical dependence:

$$P(A/B) = P(AB) / P(B) \qquad \text{Eq. 7.6}$$

where $P(A/B)$ is the probability of event A, given the condition that B has occurred. Unlike independent events, like flipping coins or tossing dice, statistical dependence refers to the case where the probability of some event is dependent upon or affected by the occurrence of some other event, such as the probability of drawing a playing card without having replaced cards already selected.

To obtain a better understanding of the use of this equation, consider Figure 54. The shaded area denotes that event B, consult librarian, has occurred; the darker region indicates that the event AB, consult librarian and check out one book, has occurred. We know that once a person has consulted the librarian, the only way we can observe the person borrow a book, A, is for event AB to occur. Hence, the ratio of $P(AB)/P(B)$ indicates the probability we will observe event A, given that B has already occurred.

A simpler example should help clarify this complex but important notion of probability. Imagine you are given a box with 10 library items that have been coded: four Rs that have X marks, one R with a Y mark, three Ms with an X mark, and two Ms with a Y mark. Suppose you pick an R from the box. What is the probability that it has an X on it? We can ignore the Ms, since

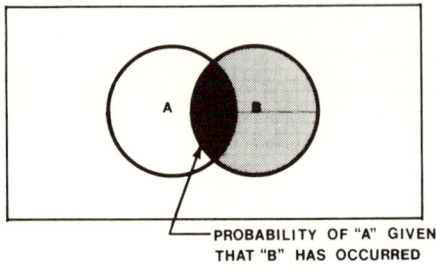

FIG. 54. Conditional Probability

we know we have picked an R. Hence, our first step is to compute the simple probability of X and Y, having chosen an R, or

$$P(X/R) = 4/5 = .8 \qquad \text{Eq. 7.7}$$

$$P(Y/R) = 1/5 = .2 \qquad \text{Eq. 7.8}$$

Note that to determine the probability of an X, given an R, P(X/R), we divided the probability of Xs and Rs, or 4 out of 10, by the probability of Rs, or 5 out of 10:

$$P(X/R) = P(XR)/P(R) \qquad \text{Eq. 7.9}$$

Having determined the conditional probability formula under statistical dependence, we can derive the formula for joint probabilities under statistical dependence by solving Equation 7.9 for P(XR):

$$P(XR) = P(X/R)P(R) \qquad \text{Eq. 7.10}$$

which means that the probability of events X and R happening together or in succession equals the product of probability of event X, given that R has occurred, and the probability that event R will occur. Returning to our previous example of marked library materials, we have the probability of picking an X and an R together or in succession:

$$P(XR) = P(X/R)P(R) \qquad \text{Eq. 7.11}$$

$$P(XR) = (.8)(.5) = .40 \qquad \text{Eq. 7.12}$$

Our answer makes sense in light of the fact that 4 out of the 10 balls have Rs and Xs.

Finally, to determine marginal or single probabilities under statistical dependence, we sum the probabilities of all the joint events in which the simple event occurs. The probability of picking an X is equal to the sum of the joint probability of picking an X and an R, plus the joint probability of picking an X and an M, or

$$P(X) = P(XR) + P(XM) \qquad \text{Eq. 7.13}$$

$$P(X) = (.40) + (.30) = .7 \qquad \text{Eq. 7.14}$$

which, once again, can be verified by inspection: 7 out of the 10 items have Xs.

Summary

In this chapter we have introduced basic probability concepts which will assist us in decision making in a risk-filled environment. We defined probability as the numerical likelihood that an event will occur: the proportion of times an event will occur divided by the number of trials. Further, we discussed several key properties of probabilities, including rules for computing joint and conditional probabilities under conditions of independence and dependence. From an information management point of view, conditional probabilities can be quite useful. We can apply them to database searching, to reference and catalog evaluations, and to determine the likelihood of a person's completing one activity after having completed another. In the next two chapters we will explore several applications of probability theory to practical information management.

Exercises

1. Assume that 50 people enter the library during the day and that 30 of them ask for assistance. What is the probability that people who enter the library will ask for assistance?
2. Given the following circulation records, compute the mean and the median number of circulations:
   10   15   16   35   5   10   11
3. In symbolic notation, write the formula for the conditional probability under dependence for the likelihood that a patron, having consulted a librarian, will check out library materials.
4. The information manager notes that from zero to 5 reference questions are asked during each hour. Based on past experience, the following probabilities are assigned to each occurrence:
   $P(0) = .05$
   $P(1) = .11$
   $P(2) = .20$
   $P(3) = .31$
   $P(4) = .27$
   $P(5) = .06$
   1.00

a. Are these valid probability assignments?
b. Let X be the event that three or fewer questions are asked in one hour. Find P(X).

Suggested Reading

Ellis, Richard B. *Statistical Inference: Basic Concepts.* Englewood Cliffs, N.J.: Prentice-Hall, 1975. Chap. 3.

Rowley, Jenny E., and Peter J. Rowley. *Operations Research: A Tool for Library Management.* Chicago: American Library Association, 1981. Chap. 3.

Sanders, Donald H., Franklin A. Murph, and Robert J. Eng. *Statistics: A Fresh Approach.* 2nd ed. New York: McGraw-Hill, 1980.

8
PRODUCTION DECISIONS

Managers of information services cannot know in advance what the costs and use of their services will be. Because of this uncertainty, we make estimates of these variables and use our forecasts to make resource-allocation choices. Most of the models disussed in this chapter rely on probabilities to make these estimates. We will show how *breakeven analysis* can analyze library storage decisions, how *inventory control* models permit us to predict the future use of library materials, and how queuing models can be used to analyze the operations of library activities.

For information managers, one objective is to respond quickly to changing market conditions. This requires directing procurement, scheduling, work flows, and inventories in new ways. To this end, we will expose information managers to useful quantitative models. We will be utilizing concepts which require some understanding of statistical methods: standard deviation, correlation, and regression. This is presented in in such a way that even readers with a limited statistical background can acquire an appreciation for the uses of statistical techniques.

Breakeven Analysis: Graphic Approach

Breakeven analysis is an application of cost functions (covered in Chapter 5). Breakeven charts are used to predict the effect of output rate on costs, revenues, and profits. They can also be employed to produce projections of the effect of price changes on use, equipment selection on costs, and change in use and/or costs on purchase decisions. In information management, breakeven analysis can be applied to the determination of whether or not a library

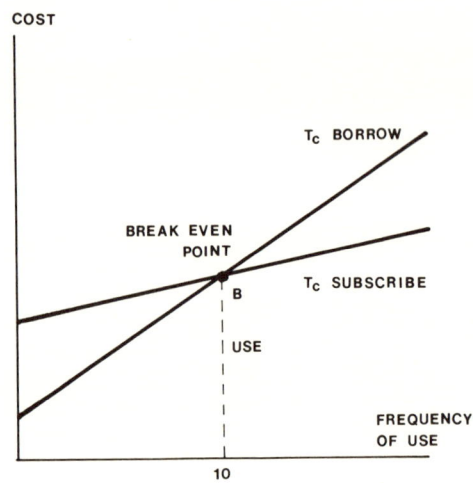

FIG. 55. Breakeven Chart

should purchase a particular material, which type of storage technique to use and when, and when to use manual or automated reference techniques.

Typically, breakeven analysis is used for short-run production decisions. Hence, the most common approach to breakeven analysis involves assuming that the library's production costs are constant in the relevant range of output. Our objective in applying breakeven methods to library resource allocation is to determine the level of use, known as the *breakeven point,* above which a library should select a particular material or process and below which an alternative should be chosen. The variables that are used to predict the breakeven point include fixed costs, variable costs, and number of uses.

Let us apply breakeven analysis to the purchase-or-borrow decision facing a serials manager. Subscribing to a serial involves a number of fixed and recurring costs, including ordering, inventory control, use costs (retrieval, binding, shelving), storage, weeding, and the annual subscription cost. For the purchase problem, the library's fixed costs include existing storage costs and those fixed costs associated with the selection and ordering process, such as machinery and furnishings. Variable purchase costs include labor, purchase-order forms, labels, and so on. Fixed borrowing costs involve storage costs for bibliographic tools, machinery, and furnishings. Variable costs include bibliographic verification, forms, stamps, and external borrowing charges. Figure 55 illustrates the standard breakeven chart as applied to a library's purchase-or-borrow choice. Given the assumption of constant per unit costs, the library's total cost is plotted as a straight line. For simplicity, we assume that the cost to the patron of waiting for materials does not effect the breakeven point.

Production Decisions   165

For libraries that *do* sell their services, the revenue line would show price times quantity sold. Since most libraries do not sell their products and services, we do not show a revenue line. Instead, we express revenue in terms of the number of uses. The breakeven point, B in Figure 55, indicates the point at which marginal cost of borrowing is just equal to the marginal cost of purchasing. Thus, by plotting the costs of borrowing, subscribing, and number of uses on the same diagram, we are able to see that when use is under 10 per year, the library minimizes costs by using external sources. After 10 uses per year, the library minimizes costs by subscribing to a journal. Observe that the breakeven point is dependent upon the library's costs and use. Consequently, a change in these variables will affect opportunity costs and, therfore, the decision of the library. Also, note that application of the breakeven point to all serials will tend to minimize wait time in the aggregate. In other words, the serials will be subscribed to and stored in relation to their popularity.

Library Storage

The breakeven model can be used to analyze the question of how and where to store library documents. In this section we will present a simple mathematical method for computing the breakeven point for library storage problems.[1] As with the own-or-borrow decision, the storage decision concerns itself with fixed costs, variable costs, and use. Fixed costs are those that are independent of use, such as building and existing shelving. However, variable costs depend upon the amount of usage an item receives. For example, the library has the option of storing its serials in a manner that requires staff to retrieve items for the consumer. Every time a patron requests materials, a staff member must be notified; next, the item must be retrieved and given to the consumer. Finally, items which have been retrieved must eventually be placed back in the storage area. These costs involve labor and, perhaps (depending upon the location of the requested item) travel expenses, phone charges, computer time, and mailing charges. Thus, the more use materials receive, the higher will be total retrieval costs.

Suppose that you have two storage options, S1 and S2. Storage site 1 represents the case in which the opportunity cost of space is relatively high—for example, a room which has a variety of information service uses: one that is open to the public. On the other hand, storage site 2, either an off-site location or a room closed to the public, involves lower space costs but higher retrieval costs. For a given serial, how would you go about deciding which storage option minimizes total costs? To answer this question, the manager must have data on use and costs. Costs include a fixed storage cost, space, and a variable retrieval cost, labor.

Assume that the cost of storage in site 1, $Cs1$, is $5 per item and the cost in site 2, $Cs2$, is $2 per item. Also, let's assume that retrieval costs, $Cr1$ and

Cr2, are 50¢ and $1 respectively. How can we find the crossover point? By definition, at the crossover point the costs of the two systems will be equal. Let us define the total cost of storage in either site as

$$(\text{Cost of storage}) + (\text{Cost of retrieval})(\text{Number of uses}) \quad \text{Eq. 8.1}$$

Intuitively, one can see that items which are used quite often should be housed in the site which has lower retrieval costs. The reason for this is quite simple: as use goes up, fixed costs remain constant, while variable costs increase. Storing high use items in a low-retrieval-cost option decreases the total cost of production. To determine the point at which the cost of option 1 is equal to option 2, we introduce an equation which sets the cost of each option equal to one another and solve for the number of uses. We are looking for the number of uses at which the cost of each storage site is equal. To compute the breakeven point, X_t, we first set the cost of site 1 to site 2:

$$Cs1 + (Cr1)(Xt) = Cs2 + (Cr2)(Xt) \quad \text{Eq. 8.2}$$

Next we solve for Xt, as follows:

$$Cs1 - Cs2 + (Cr1)(Xt) = (Cr2)(Xt) \quad \text{Eq. 8.3}$$

$$Cs1 - Cs2 = (Cr2)(Xt) - (Cr1)(Xt) \quad \text{Eq. 8.4}$$

$$Cs1 - Cs2 = (Xt)(Cr2 - Cr1) \quad \text{Eq. 8.5}$$

$$(Cs1 - Cs2) / (Cr2 - Cr1) = Xt \quad \text{Eq. 8.6}$$

Observe that the crossover point occurs when the added cost of storing in site 1 equals the added cost of storing an item in site 2. Equation 8.6 suggests there is a direct relationship between the ratio of storage cost differences to the difference in retrieval costs. As the difference in storage costs increases relative to the difference in retrieval cost, the breakeven point increases.[2] This solution agrees with our intuitive sense that high-use materials should be housed in locations where retrieval costs are low relative to storage costs. Now, substituting the cost figures, we can solve for the crossover point:

$$Xt = \frac{\$5 - \$2}{\$1 - \$.50} = \frac{\$3}{\$.50} = 6 \quad \text{Eq. 8.7}$$

Equation 8.7 indicates that, below 6 uses, an item should be stored in site 2 and, above 6 uses, in site 1. A similar model can be developed to assist the library manager to decide when to store serials in hardcopy or microform. In both cases we can also incorporate storage constraints which limit the options of the library.

Breakeven analysis can also be used to assist in determining when to use a print or on-line form of an index. The breakeven model also is useful for examining equipment-selection problems. Equipment affects the library's production function and, therefore, its costs. Hence, we can use breakeven analysis to determine the effect different types of machines would have on the breakeven point. Final selection would depend upon the library's rate of production.

However, the model, as we have presented it, has several limitations which need to be recognized. First, it is wise to limit the area of study. If too many services are included on a single breakeven chart, too many variables will be summarized and essential information about particular services will be concealed. The assumption of linear costs is realistic only over a narrow range of production. Essentially, breakeven analysis is a useful tool for short-term planning. In the long run, the cost-volume-use relationships are subject to change, suggesting that the breakeven point will change too. Finally, each component of the model, library cost, use, and cost to patron—is influenced by each other, as well as by outside factors. Hence, one must test the nature of these relationships and be cognizant of the effect of change on the breakeven point.

Inventory Models

One of the primary activities of a library is to lend items to the public for a specified of time. The library manager may therefore wish to procure an adequate and comprehensive supply; however, scarce revenue places a limit on the ability to purchase inventory. To help us determine how many copies of an item, or how much revenue, to devote to different subjects or types of materials, we will examine several inventory models.

Multiple Copies

A problem familiar to information managers is how many copies of an item to purchase. It has been shown that an increase in the number of copies of an item, given a level of popularity, increases the availability of an item.[3] Yet, the library manager is confronted with scarce resources. Thus, there is a tradeoff between number of titles and number of copies. We must decide how much money should be allocated to duplicating copies of items in high demand and how much should be spent on additional titles.

To estimate the optimal number of copies of a given title to order, we will utilize a simple inventory control model.[4] The library will be represented as a supply room where persons come to borrow items, to be returned at a later date. Some items are requested more frequently than others. Given a limited budget, we assume that a library objective is to reduce delays. To implement the model, we must collect data within an observation period on the number of loans and the length of time a copy is kept on loan. We compute the average length of time all copies were kept, and determine the standard deviation.

The *standard deviation* is a statistical measure of the tendency for data either to group or disperse around their average. For instance, we might observe the

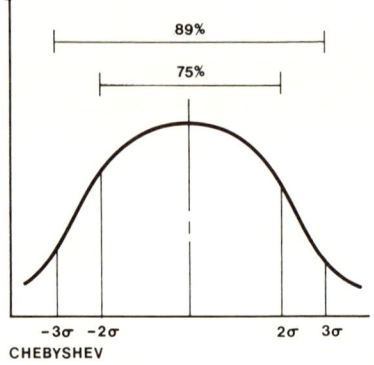 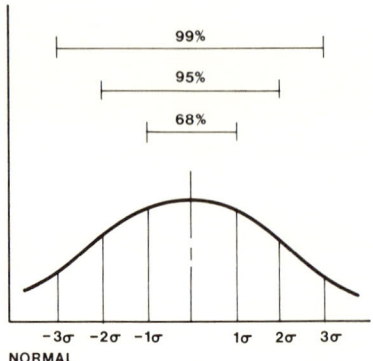

FIG. 56. Standard Deviation

number of people at the reference desk in an hour. Over a period of time, say a month, we gather observations and plot them on a frequency diagram. Having gathered the data, we can compute the mean and the standard deviation. (Recall that the mean indicates the average number of people at the reference desk in one hour: the central axis of the distribution. Think of the mean as a stable point of reference in the distribution of persons gathering at the reference desk.) To gain further insight into the distribution, we compute the variance or the average deviation from the mean. The variance is computed by dividing the sum of the squared deviations by the number of people. However, we would be talking about "squared people." To get the measure of dispersion back into the same units as the observed value, we take the square root of the variance, known as the standard deviation. Completing this computation makes intuitive sense, since we are reversing the original squaring process.

The standard deviation permits us to determine where the values of a frequency distribution are located in relation to the mean (the spread or shape of the curve). Again, it is a statistical measure of the tendency for observations to disperse around their own average. For instance, suppose the mean number of people at the reference desk is 10 per hour. What proportion of our observations lies between 10 and 13 people per hour? We can determine this proportion by a theorem developed by Chebychev, a noted Russian mathematician. He proved that, whatever the shape of a frequency distribution, at least 75 percent of the observed value will fall within plus-and-minus 2 standard deviations from the mean, and at least 89 percent of the values will lie within plus-and-minus 3 standard deviations of the mean. If you had been told that the standard deviation was 1.5, you would be able to state that 75 percent of the observed values would fall between 10 and 13 persons per hour. In other words, the probability of 13 people being at the reference desk in an hour is 75 percent, as shown in Figure 56A.

Production Decisions 169

There is also mathematical proof (but we shall spare you the manipulations) that approximately 67 percent of all values in a bell-shaped distribution (normal curve) lie within plus-and-minus 1 standard deviation from the average, and that about 95 percent of all values lie within plus-and-minus 2 standard deviations. If you have no reason to suspect that the distribution is normal, use Chebyshev's theorem.

The basic formula for computing the number of copies to purchase is

$$N(95\%) = \text{Nav} + 2s \qquad \text{Eq. 8.8}$$

where N(95%) is the number of items needed to fulfill at least 95 percent of the requests made by library users, Nav is the average number of books out on loan per period of time, and

$$\text{Nav} = (N/T)(\bar{A}) \qquad \text{Eq. 8.9}$$

where N equals the number of times a particular title has been borrowed within a specified period of time, T is the period of time, and A is the average length of time all copies were kept out. We cannot simply use Nav as a guide to the number of copies needed for N(95%), and the reason for this is quite simple: an average provides information about usage in only 50 percent of the cases, but we want to achieve a higher level of success. Since we are dealing with probabilities, we cannot achieve 100 percent certainty; therefore, we will attempt to arrive at a level of 95 percent. Assuming a normal distribution, N(95%) requires that we add 2 standard deviations to Nav. In essence, our objective is to determine the number of copies of a single item necessary to meet at least 95 percent of the demand for that item within a specified period of time.

The formula for computing the standard deviation from a sample of observations is

$$S = \sqrt{\frac{\Sigma(A_i - \bar{A})^2}{N - 1}} \qquad \text{Eq. 8.10}$$

where A_i is the length of time, in days, that a single item was off the shelves each time it was borrowed; $\bar{A}$ is the average length of time all such items were borrowed; and N is the number of observations. Assume that we have gathered data which show that, within 50 days, a particular item, of which the library has several copies, was borrowed 10 times and that the average loan period, $\bar{A}$, was 7.8 days. Using the data provided in Table 6, we shall illustrate how to compute the number of copies we need to satisfy 95 percent of the demand.

Given the number of observed days as 50, we calculate Nav as follows:

$$S = \sqrt{\frac{\Sigma(A_i - \bar{A})^2}{N - 1}} = \sqrt{\frac{67.6}{9}} = 2.7 \qquad \text{Eq. 8.11}$$

$$\text{Nav} = (N/T)(\bar{A}) = (10/50)(7.8) = 1.56 \qquad \text{Eq. 8.12}$$

$$N95\% = \text{Nav} + 2s = 1.56 + 5.4 = 6.96 \qquad \text{Eq. 8.13}$$

Table 6

STOCK LEVEL CALCULATION TABLE

No. Loans	Ai	Ā	(Ai–Ā)	(Ai–Ā)²
1	5	7.8	–2.8	7.84
2	6	7.8	–1.8	3.24
3	10	7.8	2.2	4.84
4	12	7.8	4.2	17.64
5	4	7.8	–3.8	14.44
6	7	7.8	–0.8	.64
7	10	7.8	2.2	4.84
8	11	7.8	3.2	10.24
9	7	7.8	–0.8	.64
10	6	7.8	–1.8	3.24
	78			$\Sigma(Ai-\bar{A})^2 = 67.6$

Based on this result, we predict that 95 percent of the time we would have no more than 7 copies on loan at a given time. Having fewer than this number indicates that added copies are needed to meet future demand. Unfortunately, the out-of-print status of many items may limit our ability to buy additional copies. However, if the material is general in nature, we may be able to identify substitutes. Observe that we assumed a normal distribution. Under most circumstances, when the number of observations is over 30, this is a reasonable assumption. Actually, the number of observations can be much lower; but when you are unsure of the shape of the distribution, refer to Chebyschev's theorem.

Beware of the limitations on using this model. One must make allowances for use of an item by the repair department; short-term demand, such as assignments that will not be repeated in the future; obsolescence rate; and lost and damaged books. Any one of these factors will affect the need for added copies. For example, if one counts lost and damaged items as a part of the total inventory, one might underestimate the need for more inventory. Note that even when demand is short-lived, as it might be for a best-seller, one might be able to use past data to predict the number of items that should be held for future publications of this author.

Revenue Allocation

COLLECTION ADEQUACY   In the example above, we examined the question of how many copies of an item to purchase. Next we analyze the more general question of whether additional monies should be spent on a given class of materials. As it concerns collection adequacy, the information manager is confronted with two types of production decisions: quality and quantity of a particular section of the library. Our concern will be to provide a method that will assist in setting the quantitative mix of materials among subject areas. There are several methods of assessing collection adequacy; and the first model is based on simple statistical techniques for testing hypotheses based on sample proportions.[5]

A vendor claims that it can deliver 75 percent of your order within 6 weeks. These figures give the appearance of good service, but you can't be sure that the numbers are reliable. How was the 75 percent figure arrived at? Did the vendor base this percentage on orders shipped to one library or to many libraries? Are all the vendor's customers in the same state as the vendor or are they spread out over a large region of the country? What types of libraries were served: small libraries, with relatively few orders for popular fiction, or academic libraries? You are told by one of your employees that a certain section of the library requires additional resources. You don't know whether or not this is correct. Both the vendor and your employee have made a statement whose reasonableness you wish to test.

Suppose you have performed a test that shows that the vendor ships a certain percentage of orders within 6 weeks. We will summarize a method of determining whether or not the results of your test (sample) are significantly smaller or larger than the vendor's, to warrant acceptance or rejection of the vendor's statement. In this instance, it makes sense only to check whether or not the vendor's claim is too high. Our answer will be probabilistic. Depending on the size of the difference between our values and the vendor's, we either reject or accept the hypothesis.

When testing a hypothesis, we need to decide on the level of significance or the confidence interval that guides us in our decision. A general rule of thumb is to set the level of significance at .05, which implies that we would accept our hypothesis if our test shows a 95 percent chance of being correct. Associated with the testing of hypotheses are two possibilities. We may reject a hypothesis when it should have been accepted; this is known as a type I error. On the other hand, we may accept a hypothesis which should be rejected; this is known as a type II error. Levels of significance can be set to limit the size of these two types of errors. In practice, one sets the level of error in accordance with the level of the stakes involved in a decision.

The confidence interval can be used to test hypotheses about the population. Perhaps the most useful procedure in testing a hypothesis involves testing the *null* hypothesis, which states that there is no difference between the sample figure and the hypothesized population figure. Usually, we want to reject the null hypothesis or, equivalently, show that the sample figure is different from the hypothesized population figure at some specified level of significance. As it concerns this example, the null hypothesis will be that the proportion of items currently being used in a given section of the library matches the proportion of the entire population it comprises.

The first steps in determining the adequacy of the collection are defining the class of materials, counting the number of items in the class, and determining the percentage of the collection that this section represents. We are going to test, say, the adequacy of adult level math materials. The statistical significance of any difference between inventory and use depends upon the size of the total population. Consequently, we should determine whether or not the class of materials will be expressed as a percentage of the entire collection or just a portion of it. In this example, we will assume that adult math materials compete with all other books, except juvenile fiction, and comprise 2.25 percent of the defined collection.

In any test such as this there will be some level of error, and the statistical method permits us to determine the acceptable level of error. To determine the adequacy of a subset of the collection, we must formulate a decision rule. In particular, we wish to formulate a rule which permits us to decide if the sample proportion varies too far from the information manager's estimate of use. In this instance, type I error is defined as incorrectly stating that usage is significantly different when it isn't. Type II error is defined as a test which is not sensitive enough to detect a change when one has actually occurred. The sample size can be determined by a formula that takes into account the percent chance of each type of error. Our decision is to accept a 2 percent chance of a type I error, but a 10 percent chance of a type II error as high as 3 percent use, implying a 23 percent change from the null hypothesis.[6]

Having set the levels of acceptable error, we compute the sample size from

$$n = \left[\frac{(Z\ \text{Type I})\sqrt{Po(1-Po)} + (Z\ \text{Type II})\sqrt{P1(1-P1)}}{P1 - Po}\right]^2 \quad \text{Eq. 8.14}$$

where n is the sample size; Z Type I and II are standard units associated with specified levels of error, and may be found in standard statistical tables; Po is the proportion of the collection associated with the null hypothesis; and P1 is the proportion associated with the type II error. Given this equation, we find that we require a sample size of

$$n = \left[\frac{(2.06)\sqrt{(.0225)(.9775)} + \sqrt{(1.28)(.03)(.97)}}{(.03) - (.0225)}\right]^2 \quad \text{Eq. 8.15}$$

$$n = \left[\frac{(.304) + (.218)}{.0075}\right]^2 = 4844 \quad \text{Eq. 8.16}$$

Now we are ready to determine whether or not a significant shift has occurred in use. To accomplish this, we use a common statistical technique, known as the one-tailed test of a hypothesis:

$$\bar{P} = P + Z\ \text{Type I}\sqrt{\frac{(P)(1-P)}{n}} \quad \text{Eq. 8.17}$$

Where P̄ is the decision value, Z Type I is the standard Z unit associated with a specified type I error, P is the proportion of items in the section being studied, and n is the sample size. The plus sign is used when one wishes to test whether or not use is high in proportion to inventory. We use a minus sign when we wish to determine whether inventory is excessive.

Suppose we find that use of the advanced math section is 3.25 percent of the defined collection population. We test to see if use has increased significantly in proportion to inventory, as follows:

$$\bar{P} = P + Z \text{ Type I } \sqrt{\frac{(P)(1 - P)}{n}} \qquad \text{Eq. 8.18}$$

$$\bar{P} = (.0225) + (2.06)\sqrt{\frac{(.0225)(.9775)}{4844}} \qquad \text{Eq. 8.19}$$

$$\bar{P} = .0225 + (2.06)(.0021) \qquad \text{Eq. 8.20}$$

$$\bar{P} = .0268 \qquad \text{Eq. 8.21}$$

The decision value, 2.68 percent, is less than the sample proportion of use, implying that a significant increase in use has occurred. This indicates that, in this section of the library, additional volumes would add to circulation. Comparison with other sections of the library, and taking into account differentials in cost per volume, would provide a more accurate indicator, in terms of use, of the value of an additional volume.

Let us summarize the steps we used to evaluate collection adequacy. First, we stated the hypothesis to be tested and the alternative hypothesis. That is, we set out the possible decisions: to accept or reject that a significant increase in use had occurred. Next we chose a region of acceptance and level of error associated with type I and type II errors. We base these decisions on how important it is to reject the null hypothesis and be wrong, compared to being more careful and not having a powerful test. Finally, we based our test on a sample of use. The test we have demonstrated will be more reliable if use is measured during different periods of the year. Sampling should be made in such a way as to limit reuse of the same item during the sample period.[7] We based our decision to accept or reject the null hypothesis on the significance of the difference between the sample value and the decision value.

PREDICTING FUTURE USE *Regression analysis* can be used to help information managers determine the nature of the relationship between variables. We will show how regression analysis can be employed to predict the future use of library materials. In regression analysis, the primary goal is to define a mathematical relationship between two variables. Based on this equation, we will make our predictions. Our attention will be restricted to two variables. The variable to be predicted, called the *dependent* variable, is usually plotted

174   Applications and Extension of Theory

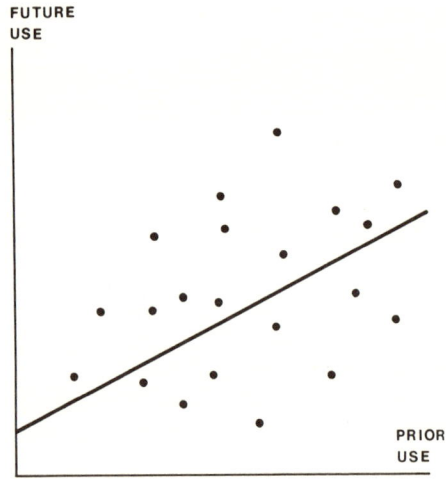

Fig. 57. Regression Diagram

on the vertical axis and is customarily referred to as Y. The variable whose value will be used to make predictions, the variable that Y is dependent upon, is known as the *independent* variable. It is plotted on the horizontal axis and is denoted by the letter X.

The relationship between two variables can take several shapes; however, our discussion will be limited to relationships which can be explained by linear equations. The first step in regression analysis is to determine if there is a logical relationship between the two variables. Fortunately, based on previous research,[8] we can assume there is a basis for using linear regression, in conjunction with other models, to predict library use based on prior years' use. Having established a logical relationship between two variables, our next step is to plot data in a scatter diagram, as shown in Figure 57.

The line in Figure 57 is referred to as a regression or estimating line. The general equation for a straight line, where the dependent variable Y is determined by the independent variable X, is

$$Yc = a + bX \qquad \text{Eq. 8.22}$$

where Yc is a computed value of Y, given prior years' use, X, and the regression equation. It (Yc) is the equivalent of a value of Y read from the regression line. The value *a* is the y intercept; *b* is the slope of the line, and represents how much each change in X changes Y. Both *a* and *b* are constants, and do not vary for a given straight line.

Now that we know what a regression line looks like, how do we go about finding an equation that best fits the scatter diagram in Figure 57? Statisticians have developed a procedure that minimizes the error between the estimated points on a regression line and the observed values. First let us point out that the best-fit regression line has two mathematical properties: the positive deviations of the scatter points above a best-fit regression line and the negative deviation will cancel out the negative deivations below the line, and the sum of such deviations will be equal to zero. However, two different lines which appear to fit the same scatter diagram may have zero as the sum of positive and negative deviations. Hence, we cannot simply use these properties to guide us to the best-fit line. Essentially, the problem with this method is the canceling effect of the positive and negative values. Yet, using the absolute value ignores the magnitude of error. We would rather have a few small errors than one or two large ones. The technique of squaring the individual errors before we add them permits us to magnify large errors and also cancels out the positive and negative value. In effect, we will be looking for the estimating line that minimizes the sum of the squares of errors, which is more commonly referred to as the least-squares method.

Using the criterion of least squares, we are able to determine whether one estimating line is a better fit than another. But there are many such lines for a given set of data points. Luckily, statisticians have developed two equations which permit us to estimate the best-fitting line. The first formula allows us to calculate the slope:

$$b = \frac{\Sigma XY - n\bar{X}\bar{Y}}{\Sigma X^2 - n\bar{X}^2} \qquad \text{Eq. 8.23}$$

where b is the slope of the best-fitting line, X represents the values of the independent variable, Y equals the values of the dependent values, $\bar{X}$ is the mean of the values of the independent variable, $\bar{Y}$ is the mean of the values of the dependent variable, and n is the number of data points.

The second equation permits us to compute the Y intercept of the line whose slope is equal to b:

$$a = \bar{Y} - b\bar{X} \qquad \text{Eq. 8.24}$$

where *a* equals the Y intercept; *b* is the slope; and $\bar{Y}$ and $\bar{X}$ are the mean values of the dependent and independent variables, respectively.

Suppose that an information manager is interested in the relationship between prior use of library materials and expected future use. To determine this relationship, the manager has gathered information concerning four items currently in the library's collection, as shown in Table 7. Out first step in calculating the regression line is to calculate the values needed for each equation. The sum of all Xs is 16; the sum of Ys is 8; the mean of X values is 4

Table 7
CIRCULATION HISTORY

Item	Year 1–Use(X)	Year 2–Use(Y)
1	6	3
2	4	2
3	4	2
4	2	1

and the mean of Y values is 2; the sum of each XY combination (6)(3) + (4)(2), and so on, is 36; and the sum of all values of X squared is 72. Now we are ready to use the equations to find the constants of our regression lines:

$$b = \frac{36 - 32}{72 - 64} = 4/8 = 2 \qquad \text{Eq. 8.25}$$

$$a = 2 - (2)(4) = 2 - 8 = -6 \qquad \text{Eq. 8.26}$$

To determine the estimating equation that illustrates the relationship between the prior year's use and the next year's use, we substitute the values of a and b into the generalized formula for a straight line:

$$Yc = -6 + 2X \qquad \text{Eq. 8.27}$$

Given circulation in a prior year, this equation permits the information manager to estimate next year's circulation. For instance, an item which had been used five times last year would be estimated to have a next-year circulation of

$$Yc = -6 + 2(5) = -6 + 10 = 4 \qquad \text{Eq. 8.28}$$

Now that we have dazzled you with the power of our computations, be aware of the fact that one should not use an estimating equation for making predictions beyond the range of observable values. The relationship between X and Y may be quite different beyond the available data. Consequently, values below or above observable values should only be used with caution, if at all. Regression analysis should not be used to infer a cause-and-effect relationship. Although one may exist, other factors may also be at work; therefore, we simply state that a degree of association exists. One must be careful, when using historical data, to estimate future trends. Conditions in the library may change, thereby negating past relationships. Finally, one should not forget to attempt to establish a logical relationship between the two variables, or we may make a spurious or meaningless prediction.

The simple relationship we have examined, between a prior year's use and the next year's use, seems to demonstrate that, in general, use falls over time. But we have not taken into account an item's use over a long period of time. Morse has developed a time correlation model of materials' use, based on a set of equations known as the Markov process.[9] In the Markov model, the behavior of a system at a given period of time is determined only by its state at the last period, and only indirectly by states of earlier periods. In effect, the model suggests that if an item was used m times last year, the probability that its use will be n times in the next year is $Tmn = P(n/m)$. The latter term, known as a conditional probability, is dependent on m and n, but only on the prior-use history of the item via the value m. Thus, changes in the item's popularity will be accounted for more heavily than in a simple time-correlation model.

In this model, a particular class of items, which are used m times in a given year, should have an average use the next year of $N(m)$, where $N(m)$ depends entirely on m. Individual item use will be clustered around the average value $N(m)$: $N(m)$ = mean number of uses during year $t + 1$, given that the sample had m uses in year t. Thus, if in a class of library materials we counted 50 items which had 3 uses in the first year, 20 of which had zero use in the next year; 10 of which had 1 use in the next year; 7 had 2 uses in the next year; 6 of which had 3 uses in the next year; 3 of which had 4 uses the next year; 2 of which had 5 uses the next year; and 2 of which had 6 uses the next year, we would compute $N(m)$ as

$$N(m) = ((0)(20) + (1)(10) + (2)(7) + (3(6)$$
$$+ (3)(4) + (2)(5) + (2)(6)) / 50 \quad \text{Eq. 8.29}$$
$$N(m) = 1.52 \quad \text{Eq. 8.30}$$

indicating thus the predicted use of an item which was used 3 times in year t will be 1.52 times in year $t + 1$.

Having computed many such $N(m)$'s for a given class of books and a series of m values, we could plot them on a graph. With $N(m)$ on the Y-axis and m on the X-axis, we would use the method of least squares to derive a formula for predicting next year's use. Morse's linear formula for predicting book use is $N(m) = \alpha + \beta m$. This means that all items of a given class that circulate m in a given year should have an average circulation—$N(m)$—the next year, where $N(m)$ is dependent solely on m and parameters α and β. Parameter β measures the rate at which the popularity of a class of materials diminishes over time, and α measures the mean use which an item in a given class will eventually reach over time.

To derive his model of book use, Morse assumed that the process of book circulation is random. Briefly, this does not imply that library consumers pick items at random. Instead, it suggests that, unless forewarned, information managers do not know when a particular consumer will arrive at the library or what items he or she will select. In this sense, the use of library materials is a random process to the information manager. In addition, we are unable to predict the behavior of a single item, yet we can predict the average use of a class of materials.

A few words of caution are in order. When one is conducting a study of the use of library materials, one should take into account the affect that loan period has on use. A separation of materials by loan period might alleviate this problem. Also keep in mind that this model is not intended to account for other factors which may affect book use, such as user frustration due to cataloging, demographic characteristics of users, and the possible emergence of new trends or products. However, we are able to use the model to determine two key characteristics of items in a given subject class. In particular, the parameters α and β permit us to detect the behavior patterns of items in a given subject class. Chen suggested that a large α indicates that items have a long shelf life.[9] On the other hand, the smaller the value of β, the faster that circulation of items in a given class reaches a steady state; that is, the faster they lose popularity. Consideration of the values of these two parameters can assist in shaping purchase and weeding policies. Items that belong to a class of materials with a short life span could be weeded more often and, depending upon initial usage, perhaps be replaced more often.

The model developed by Morse and Chen supply the information library manager with useful quantitative information concerning the library's inventory. We have summarized just a few components of their book-use model. Several other key circulation variables can be determined by using their model, including the average length of time an item is off the shelf and the need for duplicating copies.

CORRELATION BETWEEN CIRCULATION AND INVENTORY *Correlation analysis* is a statistical method to determine the strength of the association between two variables. Often, correlation analysis is used in conjunction with regression analysis to measure the degree to which we have reduced the error in predicting based on our regression formula. Both regression and correlation provide us with measures of relationships. Regression describes the nature of a relationship and the rule for predicting the value of one variable vis-à-vis a known and related variable(s), whereas correlation quantifies the accuracy of our estimating equation.

Rather than measure the degree of correlation between circulation history and future use, we will explore the correlation between current inventory, use, and acquisitions. As we shall see, this type of correlation requires a technique that differs from that which describes how well the regression recipe actually explains the relationship between two variables. But for readers who are interested in determining the correlation coefficient of a regression equation, we will briefly discuss its meaning and supply its equation.

First, let us examine the coefficient of determination which is developed from the variation of the Y values around the regression line and their own mean. One way of interpreting it is to look at the amount of variation in Y

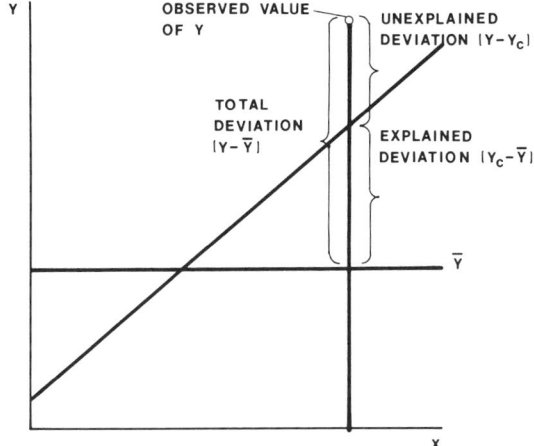

Fig. 58. Correlation

that is explained by the regression line. Figure 58 shows a regression line, an observed value of Y, and $\bar{Y}$, the mean of the Y values. If we use the mean alone to estimate the value of one Y value, then we would expect a great deal of variation between our estimate and the value of Y as expressed by $(Y - \bar{Y})$, the total variation. However, when we use the regression line as the basis of estimating Y, we get a better estimate. Notice that the regression line is closer to most of the points in the scatter diagram. But even though the regression equation accounts for part of the deviation between Y and its mean, $(Yc - \bar{Y})$, the remaining portion of the total distance, $(Y - Yc)$, remains unexplained. Thus, the total deviation between Y and its mean is the sum of the explained and unexplained variation. When we consider the total variation for the entire scatter diagram, it is equal to the sum of squared total variations from their mean: Total variaton = explained variaton + unexplained variation, or

$$\Sigma(Y - \bar{Y})^2 = \Sigma(Yc - \bar{Y})^2 + \Sigma(Y - Yc)^2 \qquad \text{Eq. 8.31}$$

The coefficient of determination, r^2, simply expresses the portion of the total variation of Y, which is explained by the dependent variable:

$$r^2 = \frac{\text{sum of the squares of explained variation}}{\text{sum of the squares of the total variation}} \qquad \text{Eq. 8.32}$$

With a bit of algebra, we obtain

$$r^2 = \frac{\Sigma(Y - \bar{Y})^2 - \Sigma(Y - Yc)^2}{\Sigma(Y - \bar{Y})^2} \qquad \text{Eq. 8.32}$$

$$r^2 = 1 - \Sigma(Y - Yc)^2 / (Y - \bar{Y})^2 \qquad \text{Eq. 8.33}$$

Using values we would have already computed in our regression analysis, statisticians have developed a short-cut method of determining r^2:

$$r^2 = \frac{a \Sigma Y + b \Sigma XY - n\bar{Y}^2}{\Sigma Y^2 - n\bar{Y}^2} \qquad \text{Eq. 8.34}$$

We cannot expect to explain more than 100 percent of the variation in Y; consequently, the value of r cannot exceed 1. When there is perfect correlation, its value will be 1. If every value of Y lies on the estimating line, the sum of the variation around the mean would be zero. Any value divided into zero is simply zero; consequently, $1 - 0 = 1$. Conversely, when there is no correlation, the coefficient of determination will be zero.

The coefficient of correlation is simply the square root of the coefficient of determination. However, although the coefficient of determination can be expressed in terms of percentages, the coefficient of correlation only provides a scale, between plus-and-minus 1, indicating the direction of the relationship. The closer r is to its limit of plus-or-minus 1, the stronger the correlation. The sign of r is determined by the slope of the regression line, b. When the slope is negative, the correlation or relationship is inverse. In demand theory, this is the case for the price-quantity relationship. Likewise, the value of r will lie between 0 and 1 when there is a direct relationship between two variables, as there is between price and quantity in supply theory.

Information managers will frequently encounter situations where the correlation technique used to describe the strength of the regression equation is an appropriate method of analyzing relationships between two variables. Yet, these tests are based on normally distributed populations or large samples, but we cannot always be sure that our population is normally distributed. For these cases, we need statistical alternatives which do not make restrictive assumptions about the shape of a distribution. These measures are commonly referred to as distribution-free or nonparametric statistics; inferences may be made regardless of the shape of the distribution.

Typically, nonparametric methods are used when a sample is too small to make assumptions about the distribution of a population. In certain instances, we will not have numerical values which allow us to measure the size of the difference between two or more values: rank or ordinal data. Actually, the use of rank or ordinal data can be viewed as an advantage. Sometimes the number of computations in a correlation analysis is so large that a nonparametric test simplifies the test. One disadvantage of distribution-free tests is that they tend to ignore some amount of information. For instance, when data are ranked, the number 154.2 can be replaced by a simple one-digit number. Yet, we have lost some information. We lose even more information if the size of the number doesn't change its rank. Nonparametric tests can be used when we have nominal data such as male and/or female, and there is no implication of higher or lower.

Table 8
CIRCULATION, SHELFLIST, ACQUISITIONS

Subject	Circulation	Rank	Shelflist	Rank	Acquisitions	Rank
Crafts	2,760	2	4,951	1	675	1
Business	4,520	1	3,012	3	542	2
Psyc.	1,890	4	987	6	321	4
Religion	750	7	1,230	4	57	8
Computer	1,500	5	945	8	311	5
Health	2,476	3	3,421	2	475	3
Amer.Hist.	1,012	6	962	7	225	6
Biog.	235	9	423	10	35	9
EuropeTrav.	430	8	1,000	5	89	7
Physics	175	10	625	9	29	10

There are many nonparametric tests, but we will focus on the rank-order correlation technique devised by Spearman whose formula is one of the simplest and easiest to use. McGrath utilizes this formula as a way of allocating library revenues between subject areas.[11] The underlying assumption of his approach to collection development is that demand guides what is produced: what is used in the first period determines what will be purchased in the second period.

We will use Spearman's formula for to analyze the relationship between the rank order of inventory-circulation and also between acquisition-circulation. To implement the model, one must first choose the number of subjects to test for. Given a large circulation, the larger the number of categories the more accurate the test. On the other hand, if too many categories are chosen, the count in each category will be too small for statistical confidence. McGrath suggests testing 30 to 60 categories.[12]

Spcarman's formula for rank correlation between any two variables, X and Y, is expressed by the Spearman rank correlation statistic, r:

$$r = 1 - \frac{6\Sigma d^2}{n(n^2 - 1)}$$ Eq. 8.35

where n is the total number of subject divisions and d is the difference between the ranks for the two variables to be correlated: d = Rank(X) − Rank(Y). For our purposes, Rank(X) is equal to the circulation rank and Rank(Y) is equal to the rank of each shelflist category or acquisitions rank.

Suppose you have been given the information found in Table 8. Using Spearman's forumla, what would you be able to state about the relationship between circulation and shelflist, as well as between circulation and acquisitions?

182   Applications and Extension of Theory

The computation for the correlation between circulation and the library's shelflist is

$$r = 1 - \frac{(6)(40)}{1000 - 10} \qquad \text{Eq. 8.36}$$

$$r = .75 \qquad \text{Eq. 8.37}$$

The rank correlation coefficient between circulation and shelflist suggests a fairly high rate of agreement between past acquisitions and current use. The correlation coefficient between current use and current purchases, .97, suggests that current acquisition policies are in agreement with current use.

Now a note of caution. As is true of all statistical methods, correlation analysis is subject to error and misinterpretation. The r scale is not linear; that is, it cannot be interpreted as a percentage. For example, an r of .8 does not indicate that the regression equation "explains" 80 percent of the total variation in Y. Instead, as we get closer to either plus-or-minus 1, the relationship becomes closer, or "better fitted."

One must be careful to rank all series in a consistent manner; otherwise, the formula cannot be used. Another problem associated with correlation is the possibility that a change in conditions will violate one or more of the assumptions. In this case, we would not want to use past trends to estimate future trends. Thus, changes in the makeup of the collection, changes in course requirements, and the like require a new test. Frequent monitoring of the collection may militate against errors associated with these types of altered market conditions. Finally, correlation analysis should not be used to prove a cause-and-effect relationship, nor to find relationships between variables which do not have a common bond, such as a ranking of ice cream flavors and a ranking of most-often-asked reference questions.

ECONOMIC ORDER QUANTITY   Not only do we face the problem of monitoring library materials inventory and purchase policies, we are also concerned with the inventory process of such items as forms, pencils, stamps, copier paper and, envelopes. The economic order quantity is primarily useful for analyzing inventory control of these types of items.[13] There are two basic inventory decisions: How much should be ordered and When should this quantity be reordered? Several costs are involved in the inventory process—namely, ordering, carrying costs, and lost sales or lost production. The objective of the model is to minimize costs. This is achieved when there is a balance between costs associated with ordering and carrying inventory and the cost of not having inventory, in terms of lost sales or lost production. In essence, there is a tradeoff between keeping small inventories and ordering frequently, and keeping large inventories and ordering infrequently. The former results in high ordering costs and the latter in high holding costs. The economic order-quantity formula supplies a method for finding an optimal compromise between these two positions. It computes the minimum inventory needed to fulfill a given demand.

Ordering costs include the costs associated with getting items into the library's inventory. These costs are incurred every time an order is placed, from the issuing of the purchase order to the receipt, routing to appropriate storage facilities, and paying vendors. Upon receipt, the deliveries must be checked against the original purchase order for verification of price, quantity, and other specifications. Labor, paper, and computers constitute the primary ordering costs. Holding or carrying costs include the cost of capital, possible obsolescence of inventory, and warehousing.

Inventory is kept to meet potential demands, and to be of value, an inventory model must specify the nature of demand. For a given library item, it may be known or unknown or predictable or unpredictable. The manager's job is to match, as best as possible, inventory with potential use while minimizing costs. The simplest economic order quantity (EOQ) model assumes that demand for an item is known and has a constant, or nearly constant, rate. For example, a library system may utilize request forms at a rate of 1000 per day, or 7000 units per week, and so on. Furthermore, we will assume that the entire order arrives in inventory at one point in time and that inventory will not be allowed to go below requirements. Given these assumptions, an inventory manager will not have to be concerned with lost sales.

Now let us apply the EOQ model to how many book jackets to order and when to order them. After careful analysis, we find that the library system utilizes an average of 1000 per week or 52,000 per year. These jackets are ordered from the vendor in cases of 100 each, for a total of 520 cases per year. In addition, for each order the library incurs a processing cost of \$25, and there is a holding cost of 70¢ per case.

Determining how many cases to order involves creating a balance between ordering costs and inventory costs. To solve for this tradeoff, we characterize total (variable) costs as the sum of the inventory and holding costs. If we assume that Q equals the size of the order quantity, then our how-much-to-order decision involves solving the equation for a value of Q which minimizes total variable costs. In general, as the order quantity increases, ordering costs decline and holding costs increase. Total costs are at a minimum when the two costs are equal.

The inventory process can be described as receipt of inventory level Q, from which clients are served until the stock is depleted, at which time another order of Q units will arrive. Given the assumption of a uniform rate of demand, we can illustrate the inventory process as shown in Figure 59.

The average inventory, 1/2Q, is the amount the library will have on hand one-half of the time during any ordering cycle. In effect, total carrying costs are a function of the average inventory held and the per unit holding cost. Let

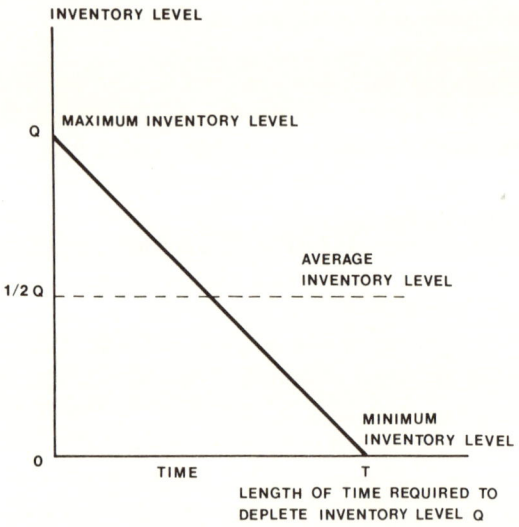

Fig. 59. Inventory Control Model

I = carrying charges as a percent of the value per unit and c = value of a unit. Then total annual inventory holding costs, TC, can be expressed as

$$TC = (1/2)(Q)(Ic) \qquad \text{Eq. 8.38}$$

With the cost of a case of book jackets set at $20 per case, the carrying cost is .035, or 70¢. Observe that the total carrying cost rises as the order quantity, Q, increases.

To compute the annual ordering cost, we let D equal the annual demand for book jackets, indicating that we will place D/Q orders per year. Total annual ordering costs, TO, are simply the cost of placing an order, Co, multiplied by the number of order placed per year, D/Q:

$$TO = (D/Q)(Co) \qquad \text{Eq. 8.39}$$

Given an annual demand and fixed ordering costs, the larger the size of the order the smaller the annual ordering costs. Now from microeconomic theory we know that the rule for minimizing production costs is to have MC1 = MC2. This occurs when the two lines intersect and when the total reordering cost is at a minimum:

$$(1/2)(Ch)(Q) = (D/Q)(Co) \qquad \text{Eq. 8.40}$$

Using simple algebra, we solve for Q and find that

$$Q = \sqrt{\frac{(2)(D)(Co)}{Ch}} \qquad \text{Eq. 8.41}$$

Substituting the appropriate values from our example, we find that the order quantity that minimizes total annual inventory costs is

$$Q = \sqrt{\frac{(2)(520)(\$25)}{(\$.70)}} = \sqrt{\frac{26{,}000}{.70}} \qquad \text{Eq. 8.42}$$

$$Q = 192 \text{ cases} \qquad \text{Eq. 8.43}$$

Solving equation 8.40 for an order quantity of 192 cases results in a total inventory cost of approximately $68 per year. A quick check of the economic order-quantity equation reveals that a library will want to order large quantities, Q, and therefore store high average inventories when holding costs are low, ordering costs are high, and yearly consumption is high.

Now that the inventory manager knows *how much* to order, he or she needs to know *when* to order. The reorder point is determined by demand, and by the time required for an order to be processed and received (lead time). In terms of inventory level, we can express the reorder level, Ri, as a function of demand per day, D, and the lead time for a new order in days, L, or

$$Ri = DL \qquad \text{Eq. 8.44}$$

The library's book jacket inventory is used at an average of $(52{,}000) / (5 \text{ days/wk})(52) = 200$ jackets per day. If the lead time is 30 days, we would reorder when the inventory reaches a level of $(30)(200) = 6000$.

Using the information we have at hand, it is a simple task to compute the order cycle. The frequency with which we will reorder inventory is a function of the rate of demand, D, the order quantity, Q, and the number of days we operate per year. More generally,

Reorder cycle = (number of days per operating year) / (D/Q) Eq. 8.45

Given a rate of demand of 520 and an EOQ of 192, we find that $520 / 192 = 3$ orders per year. If we place 3 orders per year and we operate 260 days of the year, we can express the cycle time as

$$T = \frac{(260)(Q)}{520} = \frac{(260)(192)}{520} = 96 \text{ days} \qquad \text{Eq. 8.46}$$

The EOQ model, based on a constant rate of demand, assists the manager in meeting demand with minimum inventory cost. The application of this type of model is particularly useful when the library has a limited amount of storage space and when capital earns income for either the library or its budgeting agency. An inventory manager may wish to take into account the possibility of fluctuating demand, as well as the possibility of delays in receipt of the order. The order quantity and reorder point could be increased to serve as a precaution against higher-than-expected demand or delays in receipt of incoming orders.

The EOQ model can be applied to situations where quantity discounts are offered by vendors. There are, moreover, two approaches to handling the decision to order large quantities: cost comparison or price change. In the former, we simply compare the total cost per year with and without the discount. In the latter, we solve for the point at which the reduction in ordering cost is equal to the added carrying costs. Other applications of the EOQ include computing the optimum production lot size, such as the number of library material request forms to print, and inventory situations in which the rate of demand can be stated in terms of probabilities, such as the rate of demand for forms which the public uses in a library. It could also be employed to analyze the number of trips consumers might make to the library and the relative "size" of their use per trip.

Waiting-Line Models

Everyone who has used a library has experienced waiting-line situations, such as waiting at the circulation desk to check out materials or at the reference desk for the librarian to finish with the preceding client. If clients accumulate in lines, the transaction cost of library use increases and quantity demanded decreases. To lower the wait time, additional staff or check-out terminals can be added. However, the addition of staff or extra circulation terminals adds a cost to the system. A manager's aim is to balance the benefits of better service with the added costs.

Waiting-line or *queuing theory* is a statistical technique which allows us to describe or predict a system's operating characteristics, such as the average number of people waiting in line, the average time an individual spends waiting for service, and the percentage of times that an arriving person will wait, as well as the percentage of time that service facilities will be idle. Inventory models rely on certain assumptions concerning the rate at which customers arrive, the rate at which they are served, and the manner in which they are served. Given this type of information and the costs for added equipment, staff, or lost use, the library manager will be in a better position to evaluate decisions concerning the number of terminals to purchase, the number of microfiche catalogs to buy, and the number of staff to hire.

Let's assume that we are investigating reference service at a library with one reference librarian. This is an example of a single-channel or single-server waiting line; that is, clients form a single line which is serviced by a single processing station.

To implement the model, we will make several assumptions:[14]

1. The probability of a person arriving in the next time period does not depend on the time the last arrival occurred: arrivals are random. In other words, people do not arrive in a consistent pattern. For example,

during one five-minute period 10 people may arrive; during the next, 3 people. Even though arrival rates are random, if we observe the process over a sufficient period of time, we will be able to calculate the total number of persons arriving per period of time.
2. Service time is random; the probability is that the time it takes to answer one patron's question is not related to the previous patron's question. The first customer may be serviced in 2 minutes, but the next may require 10 minutes. The time it takes to answer questions is related to the nature of the question, but not to any previous requests for service.
3. The method of determining who is served next (referred to as queue discipline) operates on a first-in-first-out basis.
4. All patrons who want service will wait for service. No one leaves the line or balks at entering the system when a given number of people are in line. (In the next section, a queuing model will be developed to include the notion that customers will balk if a certain number of people are already in the system.)
5. The average arrival rate, number of persons arriving for service per time period and average service rate, and the number of persons served do not change over the time period under study.
6. Arrival rates do not exceed service rates. Think of P, or the ratio of arrival rate to service rate, as an indicator of traffic intensity. Basically, traffic intensity measures the likelihood of a queue forming. If the arrival rate exceeds the service rate, the ratio will be more than 1. Given no balking, this implies that the queue will grow increasingly larger since, on average, more units will arrive than can be served per time period.

To use the model, we need to know the average number of arrivals per time period, A, and the average service rate, S. Having determined these values, we can solve for a number of queue-related variables. First, we want to compute the traffic intensity or the probability that a line will form, which is

$$\text{Probability of a queue forming: } P = A / S \qquad \text{Eq. 8.47}$$

This is simply an application of the classical method of determining probability. The chance of a line forming is simply the ratio of the average number of people arriving to the average number of people who can be served.

For example, if an information manager observes that, on average, 5 people per hour use reference service and the answer rate is 10 questions per hour, then the probability of a line forming is 5/10, or 1/2. Another way of looking at this variable is to observe that P indicates that, on average, the librarian's time will be utilized half the time answering reference questions. The other half of the time, $1 - P$, will be spent "idle," or not answering reference questions. Depending on the nature of the reference librarian's duties, a given

188   Applications and Extension of Theory

amount of "idle" time may be required to handle administrative tasks or backlogs (we assume no backlogs). Given a constant service rate, as the average number of people requesting service increases, "idle" time decreases and the probability of a line forming increases.

Rather than bore you with the mathematical derivation of the queuing models listed below (Equations 8.48–8.52), we will investigate their use in terms of library managment.

Average number of persons in queue: $N = P^2 / 1 - P$ Eq. 8.48

Average number of persons waiting in line plus being served:

$$Ns = P/1 - P \text{ or } A/S - A$$ Eq. 8.49

Average time a person spends waiting in line:

$$Tl = P / (1 - P)S$$ Eq. 8.50

Average wait in line plus being served: $W = 1 / S - A$ Eq. 8.51

Average "idle" time of library staff: $Its = 1 - A/S$ Eq. 8.52

Let's suppose that, in the library under investigation, a reference librarian can serve an average of 30 persons per hour and that clients arrive at an average rate of 15 per hour. Using these figures, we can use queuing equations to analyze reference service:

Probability of queue: $P = 15 / 30 = .50$ Eq. 8.53

Average number of persons in queue:

$$N = (.50)^2 / (1 - .50)$$ Eq. 8.54

$$N = .25 / .50 = .50$$ Eq. 8.55

Average number of persons waiting in line plus being served:

$$Ns = .50 / (1 - .50)$$ Eq. 8.56

$$Ns = .50 / .50 = 1$$ Eq. 8.57

Average time a person spends in line:

$$Tl = .50 / (1 - .50)30 \text{ hr.}$$ Eq. 8.58

$$Tl = .50 / (.50)30 \text{ hr.}$$ Eq. 8.59

$$Tl = 1/30 \text{ hr.} = 60/30 = 2 \text{ minutes}$$ Eq. 8.60

Average time a person waits in line plus being served:

$$W = 1 / (30 - 15) \text{ hr.}$$ Eq. 8.61

$$W = 1/15 \text{ hr.} = 4 \text{ minutes} \qquad \text{Eq. 8.62}$$

Average "idle" time of library staff:

$$\text{Its} = 1 - (15/30) = .50 \qquad \text{Eq. 8.63}$$

These formulas illustrate an interesting relationship between staff "idle" time and patron wait time. For example, assume a situation in which the reference staff can serve an average of 30 persons per hour with an average arrival rate of 10 persons an hour. In this case, the time a person spends in line decreases to 1 minute, while the average "idle" time changes from 50 percent to 67 percent. This simple model allowed us to calculate several important characteristics of the reference service of a library. These same formulas can be used to examine a change in the ability of the library staff to answer questions. Intuitively, we recognize that a less experienced staff member increases all the variables except "idle" time.

Complex queuing models, known as multichannel models, permit the manager to analyze situations in which additional staff are assigned to the reference desk or another computer terminal. Using a two-channel model, one could compare the difference between the added cost and added usage in additions to reference staff against the cost and benefit of additions of staff to other departments. One can also develop a model which permits "balking" by consumers or by the librarian; the latter is known as *allowing a backlog*. In this instance, the queue would no longer be first in-first out. Queuing models have been applied to resolve the optimal number of copies a reserve library should have given a loan period[15] and the optimal number of open hours.[16]

Simulation Method Queuing

The quantitative methods presented in the previous sections emphasize an analytical approach in which mathematical solutions are possible. However, there are sytems which are too complex to be modeled in this way. Computer simulation or experimentation of library operations is one of the more effective methods for modeling problems which are too complex to be solved by using a mathematical method. The computer is programmed to describe the logical implications of an operating system; several experiments or "runs" through a system are completed and we then study the behavior of a library operation. Simulation has been applied to numerous practical information-service management activities, including reserve book activities,[17] seating capacity,[18] loan and duplication policy,[19] and mail delivery.[20] In this section, we will apply simulation to a waiting-line situation. Our objective will be to describe a system, and not to solve for an optimal solution.

Most simulation models rely on probabilities to describe the problem at hand. In general, probability situations are quite complex, but computer sim-

Table 9

REFERENCE DESK ACTIVITY

Number of Customers Arriving	Probability
0	.15
1	.45
2	.19
3	.14
4	.07

ulation makes it possible to solve the many computations needed to describe the situation being analyzed. We will rely on a Monte Carlo method of simulation, one that relies on a random device, such as a roulette wheel, for choosing the next event in a library operation. A computer, by acting like a person throwing a cube with 10 sides, numbered 0 through 9, generates a table of random numbers. Suppose we set these numbers up in a table of 100 two-digit random numbers from 00 to 99; each of the two-digit numbers has a 1/100 = .01 chance of being selected. Now assume that, during a given period of time, the probability of 5 people entering the library and looking for a place to sit is .20. Since each two-digit combination has a .01 chance of occurrence, we can let 20 of these numbers correspond to the probability of 5 customers arriving. Hence, any time a number between 00 and 19 is observed, we will state that 5 people have entered the library looking for seating.

Let's also suppose that the library has an information desk to which customers go for a variety of services. Currently, one person is assigned to the information desk: a single-channel queuing system. When a person comes to the desk, the staff member takes his or her request and attempts to fulfill it. If another customer arrives at the information desk, this second person waits in line and is served on a first-in-first-out basis. But if more than 4 people are in line, a customer will leave, or balk.

Based on observations of information desk activity during a one-hour period of time, the information manager has developed a table of arrival probabilities. In addition, the assistant noticed that three types of questions were asked: (1) questions that take 2 minutes to answer, (2) questions that take 7 minutes to answer, and (3) questions that take 9 minutes to answer. The probability associated with each type of question is .49, .39, and .12, respectively. In modeling the system, we will examine what happens during time intervals of 5 minutes. With the Table 9 data, the data on types of questions and an understanding of the random-number technique, we can portray the operation of the reference desk as in Table 10.

Now that we are in a position to simulate events at the information desk, let us begin our experiment just as the library opens and observe what occurs in 5-minute periods (Figures 60–64). Our first step is to pick a random number

Table 10
PROBABILITIES OF REFERENCE ACTIVITIES

Interval	Arrivals	Question Type	Probability
00–14	0		.15
15–59	1		.45
60–78	2		.19
79–92	3		.14
93–99	4		.07
00–48		1 (2 min)	.49
49–87		2 (7 min)	.39
88–99		3 (9 min)	.12

FIG. 60. Operation in First 5 Minutes

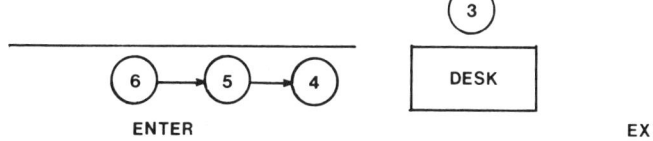

FIG. 61. Operation in Second 5 Minutes

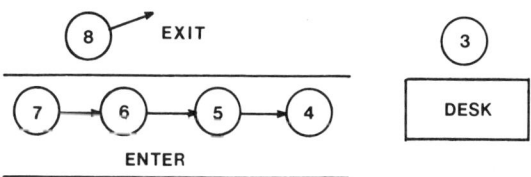

FIG. 62. Operation in Third 5 Minutes

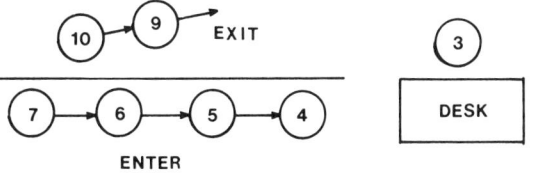

FIG. 63. Operation in Fourth 5 Minutes

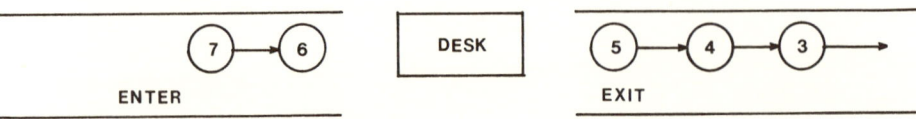

Fig. 64. Final State

to indicate the number of library clients who arrive for service. Next we pick another random number to determine the type of question each client will ask. For the sake of convenience, we have reproduced the first 12 two- digit numbers from a row of random numbers:

63 27 15 99 86 71 74 45 11 02 15 14

The first number is 63; two customers (1, 2) arrive. The second number is 27; the first customer asks a question, which takes 2 minutes. The second customer can be waited on during the first period.

The third number is 15; the second customer asks a question which takes 2 minutes to answer, leaving 1 minute in the first time period.

The fourth number is 99; four customers (3, 4, 5, 6) arrive at the desk. The next number is 86; the third customer's question will take 12 minutes to answer and will not be finished until 1 minute into the fourth period.

When we enter the second time period, the next number is 71, and two more customers (7, 8) enter the system. However, they cannot be served, since the third customer is still waiting for an answer. There are four people in line, so the 8th customer leaves.

We enter the third period; the next number is 74 and two more customers (9, 10) enter the system. But they cannot be served, since the third client is still being waited on. There are still four people in line; hence, customers 9 and 10 leave the system.

We enter the fourth time period and the third customer is finished, leaving 4 minutes. The next number is 45, indicating that the fourth customer will take 2 minutes, leaving 2 minutes in this time slot. The next number is 11, so the fifth customer can be served in another 2 minutes. We have finished the fourth period, and two customers are still waiting in line.

We have simulated the operation of the information desk during a period of 20 minutes (four 5-minute intervals). This is too short a time to draw any general conclusions about the operations of a library's information desk. Furthermore, we observed the library as it was opening. Most information managers are concerned with the operation of a system during its steady-state or normal operating condition—that is, when a number of people are already in the library. A technique for accomplishing this is to run the simulation model for a period of time that is long enough for the system to have gained a steady-state condition. During this phase, we wouldn't collect data on the operations of the system. Once a steady-state has been achieved, we would begin to observe the system and gain a better understanding of the operations of the information desk during the course of normal operating hours.

In developing the simulation model, we followed the logic and the relationships of the actual operations of our hypothetical library information desk. Simulation models that do not adequately reflect the real system cannot be relied upon to provide a reasonable picture of the library. One technique for validating a simulation model is to compare simulated results with current or past observations of the behavior of the actual system. This can be accomplished by running the simulation model using real-world observations. When divergences occur, one should check the simulation model. Another check of the model's internal consistency is to compare the simulated probability distribution with the corresponding distributions of the real operating system.

Summary

Information managers are confronted with a host of complex management problems, from deciding how many people should work in a given production situation to how many chairs to purchase for a library. Resource allocations can be based, in part, on examining how the consumer uses the library: How often does a consumer visit the library and how often does he or she use a particular service? What is the variation of use between types of clients? Can we observe a pattern of use that can be correlated with time of day, week, season? Do people who visit the library at a particular time use it differently than those who attend at other times? Does the length of stay affect use? As they concern the collection, similar questions may be asked: What is used? How often and when? Does age affect use? If so, does it differ for classes of materials?

We require theories and methods which allow us to test how well the library is satisfying the needs of its users. We may also wish to predict what will happen to the performance of the operating system as we duplicate copies, reduce the loan period, add seating, reduce staff, and so on. In this chapter we discussed several approaches to handling these questions: breakeven analysis, hypothesis testing, economic order quantity, regression, correlation, and queuing. We can use these models to experiment with the operations of information services and get a better picture of the results of our decisions. Models help us in forming conditional forecasts. If the operating system or some outside influence should change, our predictions become unreliable. Above all, then, theoretical and statistical analysis can be useful in peeling back our ignorance about the library and, as such, should be viewed as a guide to decision making, not a substitute for judgment.

Exercises

1. Your library has two possible methods of storage. The cost of storage method 1 is $2 per item and for method 2 it is $1 per item. The cost of retrieval is 25¢ and 50¢ respectively. Compute the breakeven point.
2. Suppose your book vendor claims that 4 out of 5 orders will be received within 6 weeks. Using a sample size of 100 and setting the probability of a type 1 error to 1 percent ($Z = 2.33$), test to see if the vendor's claims are too high.
3. For the following set of data, plot the scatter diagram, develop the estimating equation that best fits the data, and predict Y for $X = 6$ and 11.

    X 8 12 10 7 13 5 9   13 14 8
    Y 3   5   6 2   7 1 5.3 7.5 8   3.2
4. A library uses a computer terminal to check out materials. Assume the situation can be approximated by a simple queue and, on average, 15 customers arrive per hour and the average service rate is 2 minutes. Calculate the
    a. Probability of a queue forming
    b. Average time a user spends in line
5. Describe the steps in a simulation of the microfiche catalog for reader use.

References

1. Richard A. Stayner, "Economic Characteristics of the Library Storage Problem," *Library Quarterly* 53:3 (July 1983): 313–327.
2. Ibid., p. 320.
3. Michael K. Buckland, *Book Availability and the Library User* (Elmsford, N.Y.: Pergamon, 1975).
4. Robert S. Grant, "Predicting the Need for Multiple Copies of Books," *Journal of Library Automation* 4:2 (June 1971): 64–71.
5. Gregory R. Mostyn, "Use of Supply-Demand Equality in Evaluating Collection Adequacy," *California Librarian* 35 (April 1974): 16–23.
6. Ibid., p. 21.
7. Ibid., p. 20.
8. Ching-chih Chen, *Applications of Operations Research Models to Libraries* (Cambridge, Mass.: M.I.T. Press, 1976); Philip M. Morse, *Library Effectiveness: A Systems Approach* (Cambridge, Mass.: M.I.T. Press, 1968).
9. Morse, *Library Effectiveness*, Chap. 5.
10. Chen, *Applications*, p. 67.
11. William E. McGrath, "A Pragmatic Allocation Formula for Academic and Public Libraries with a Test for Its Effectiveness," *Library Resources and Technical Services* 19:4 (Fall 1975): 356–369.
12. Ibid., p. 363.
13. Richard I. Levin and C. A. Kirkpatrick, *Quantitative Approaches to Management* (New York: McGraw-Hill, 1965), chap. 5.
14. Michael Halperin, "Waiting Lines," *Reference Quarterly* 16:4 (Summer 1977): 297–299.

15. M. Bommer, "The Development of a Management System for Effective Decision Making and Planning in a University Library" (Ph.D. dissertation, University of Pennsylvania, 1971).

16. Morse, *Library Effectiveness*, Chaps. 3 and 4.

17. J. V. Baumler and J. L. Baumler, "A Simulation of Reserve Book Activities in a College Library Using GPSS/360," *College and Research Libraries* 36 (1975): 222–227.

18. J. J. Cook, "Increased Seating in the Undergraduate Library," in *Case Studies in Systems Analysis in a University Library*, ed. B. R. Burkhalter (London: Scarecrow Press, 1966), pp. 142–170.

19. M. K. Buckland et al., "Systems Analysis of a University Library" (University of Lancaster Occasional Papers, No. 4) (Lancaster, England: University Library, 1970).

20. M. J. Probst Reed, "Computer Simulation: A Tool for Analysis of Library Service," *Journal of Library Automation* 9 (1976): 117–136.

Suggested Reading

Chatterje, S., and B. Price. *Regression Analysis by Example.* New York: Wiley, 1977.

Chen, Ching-chih, ed. *Quantitative Measurement and Dynamic Library Service.* Phoenix: Oryx 1978.

Dykman, Thomas R., and Joseph I. Thomas. *Fundamental Statistics for Business and Economics.* Englewood Cliffs, N.J.: Prentice-Hall, 1977.

Freud, J. E., and F. J. Williams. *Elementary Business Statistics: The Modern Approach.* 3rd ed. Englewood Cliffs, N.J.: Prentice-Hall, 1978.

Goyal, S. K. "A Systematic Method for Reducing Over Ordering Copies of Books." *Library Resources and Technical Services* 16 (Winter 1972): 26–32.

Levin, Richard, and C. A. Kirkpatrick. *Quantitative Approaches to Management.* New York: McGraw–Hill, 1965.

Longley-Cook, L. H. *Statistical Problems and How to Solve Them.* New York: Barnes & Noble, 1970.

Rowntree, Derek. *Statistics Without Tears: A Primer for Non-mathematicians.* New York: Scribner, 1981.

Weinberg, George, and John A. Schumaker. *Statistics: An Intuitive Approach.* 2nd ed. Belmont, Calif.: Wadsworth, 1969.

9

INFORMATION ECONOMICS

Management decisions range from the relatively simple task of ordering supplies to the complex process of scheduling, negotiating contracts, and planning for the future. Each choice involves an assessment of alternative courses of action. In Part 1 of this text, we made the simplifying assumption that consumers know with certainty present and future prices and that firms know their cost and demand functions. Although adequate for many situations, the assumption that certainty prevails in the decision-making process is inadequate in cases where there is a large element of risk. Risk is based on our inability to know the future. When events are uncontrollable, the repercussions of our decisions may diverge from what we planned. Risk refers to situations where the relative probabilities of each possible outcome are known, and the only unknown is the outcome. Since risk affects the potential outcome of our decisions, techniques which enable the manager to estimate possible outcomes supply us with a valuable tool for guiding decisions under risk.

Several methods are available for incorporating risk into the decision-making process, and these techniques involve a series of steps: defining the problem, dividing it into its components, identifying potential courses of action, and identifying and assessing the probability of uncontrollable events. Once these steps have been taken, we assign costs and benefits to potential outcomes. Finally, using one of several quantitative methods, we evaluate our choices. Each approach, or decision rule, is useful under different operating environments, so a variety of decision theory options is presented. The conditions defined in each method permit an individual to make choices which are consistent with his or her attitude toward risk and uncertainty.

Our study of decision making under conditions of risk begins with an examination of projects which involve few decision alternatives and potential future events. Payoff tables assist us in structuring this type of decision situation and illustrate the fundamental concepts of decision theory. To extend the model, we will discuss probability and the use of decision trees in developing an optimal decision strategy.

Payoff Tables: Computer Memory Application

Payoff tables, like flowcharts, condense the decision process into its primary components and clarify the logic of the decision process. They provide us with a convenient form for structuring the decision situation. To illustrate the decision theory approach using payoff tables, let us examine the case in which information managers attempt to decide upon the optimal computer memory size for a cataloging network.

Assume that a group of information managers is setting up an automated information network and that, though the model and brand of computer have been chosen, the memory size has not. Having defined the nature of the problem, our next step is to identify the alternative courses of action, commonly referred to as decision alternatives. For the sake of simplicity, we will limit the number of alternatives to three computer memory sizes: A1, large; A2, medium; and A3, small.

The optimal decision strategy will depend upon the managers' ability to assess market acceptance of the network's services: cataloging, interlibrary loan, acquisitions, serials control, and processing labels. While the events which shape market acceptance are not known, the manager is often able to identify a variety of possible future levels of acceptance. Hence, the next step in the decision theory approach is to identify the future events which might occur. These future, and uncontrollable, events are known as *states of nature*. It will be assumed that we have listed all of the possible states of nature and that they are defined in such a way that one—and only one—of these listed states of nature will occur; that is, they cannot overlap. In this example, we will limit the number of acceptance levels to three: S1, high; S2, medium; and S3, low.

To decide which size computer memory to purchase, the information managers must estimate the level of profit associated with each combination of memory capacity and level of market acceptance. Profit, in decision theory terminology, is known as the payoff resulting from the outcome of a decision, given that a particular state of nature occurs. Payoff Table 11 summarizes the possible courses of action our team of network managers may take. Although we have chosen to state entries in monetary terms, they can also be stated in output, time, etc. We denote the payoff for any given entry in the payoff table

Table 11
NETWORK PAYOFF TABLE

Decision Alternatives		States of Nature		
		High Acceptance S1	Medium Acceptance S2	Low Acceptance S3
Large memory	A1	$300,000	$200,000	−$25,000
Medium memory	A2	225,000	125,000	50,000
Small memory	A3	150,000	90,000	75,000

as $P(A_i, S_j)$ where A_i denotes a decision alternative and S_j denotes a state of nature. Thus, in Table 11, the payoff associated with decision alternative A1 and state of nature S2 can be represented as

$$P(A1, S2) = \$200,000.$$

We have illustrated the first three steps in the decision-making process: identification of the decision alternatives, possible states of nature, and the payoff associated with each decision alternative and state-of-nature combination. To use the information presented in the payoff table effectively, we must choose, and apply, a criterion for evaluating our options and identifying the best strategy.

Decision-Making Rules under Uncertainty

Information managers may be confronted with situations in which the probabilities of each possible outcome cannot be assessed, more commonly referred to as a *condition of uncertainty*. Although economists and statisticians have devised rules for making decisions under uncertainty, each rule has its limitation. They are often criticized for their constricted view of the factors which may affect an outcome. Each rule attempts to formalize a manager's subjective view of a given situation; it is therefore up to the manager to choose the rule which—according to his or her attitude toward risk, financial resources, and any other considerations that may apply—is most appropriate. Hence, no single rule applies to decision making under uncertainty. However, they do allow us to analyze and structure the decision process under different operating conditions.

The three most common decision criteria—the maximin (or minimax), the maximax (or minimin), and the minimax regret—are used in situations when the decision maker is unable or not confident enough to attach probabilities to alternative states of nature. An additional decision criterion, Hurwicz's rule, permits us to modify the extreme positions taken by the maximin and max-

Table 12
MINIMUM PAYOFF

Decision Alternatives	Minimum Payoff	Maximum of Minimum
A1	−$25,000	
A2	50,000	
A3	75,000	$75,000

imax decision criteria. Since each of these rules may lead to a different decision recommendation, we will examine the nature of each criterion.

Maximin Decision Criterion

The maximin decision rule illustrates the pessimistic or conservative view of making choices. A pessimistic network manager would reason that, no matter what course of action is chosen, "nature" would conspire to create a situation of maximum disadvantage. Thus, the conservative approach suggests that the best, or safest, course of action would be to make the best of a bad job—in other words, to maximize the minimum possible payoff (profit, cost, etc.). Using the payoff table information, we first list the minimum payoff associated with each decision alternative. From this new list, an information manager would choose the memory capacity which results in the maximum payoff.

As Table 12 illustrates, a small memory yields the maximum of the minimum payoffs. Hence, the pessimist, concentrating on the worst-case scenario, chooses a course of action which limits payoffs but avoids extreme losses. The network manager, by choosing the small memory capacity, guarantees a minimum profit of $75,000.

Perhaps the next choice a network management team must make is to select a computer maintenance contract. Assuming a similar outlook, the team would attempt to minimize costs. In this instance, we list the maximum cost for each decision alternative and recommend a course of action corresponding to the minimum of the maximum costs—the minimax.

Maximax Decision Criterion

While the maximin decision criterion paints a pessimistic picture, a more optimistic outlook might be appropriate. In this case, the network manager would opt to use the maximax decision rule and select the outcome which maximizes the maximum payoff.

To implement this rule, we first determine the maximum payoff for each decision variable and then select the course of action which provides the max-

Table 13
MAXIMUM PAYOFF

Decision Alternatives	Maximum Payoff	Maximum of Maximum
A1	$300,000	$300,000
A2	225,000	
A3	150,000	

imum payoff. Using a similar approach to the maintenance contract problem, the maximax rule reverts to the minimin criterion, which minimizes the minimum cost value.

Table 13 summarizes the decision maximax process as applied to the computer memory selection problem. Based on the information in this table, we would recommend selecting the large memory. The optimal strategy concurs with the network managers' optimistic view of future events. Use of the maximax criterion provides the possibility of obtaining the best of all payoffs, but it also exposes the network to the potential of a net loss.

Hurwicz's Rule

The maximin and maximax decision criteria illustrate two extreme attitudes toward an uncertain future. Hurwicz's rule, however, permits us to modify our position. Based on Hurwicz's rule, we construct a new table with the use of a constant that permits us to modify the extreme position of the maximin and maximax decision criteria. On a scale of 0 to 1, it represents the subjective attitude of the decision maker. Typically, it is selected on the basis of prior knowledge or intuition. If the managers adopt a 1/2 constant, we would reconstruct our payoff table as shown in Table 14, which indicates that either the large or medium memory capacity could be selected.

As with the other criteria, the appropriateness of the constant depends on the attitude of the manager toward risk, available financial resources, and other aspects of the decision environment. Before we examine methods of decision making using probability, let us examine an additional criterion for decision making, under uncertainty, without using probabilities.

Table 14
THE HURWICZ PAYOFF TABLE

Decision Alternatives	Minimum	Maximum	(1/2)(Min + Max)
A1	−$25,000	$300,000	$137,500
A2	50,000	225,000	137,500
A3	75,000	150,000	112,500

Table 15
MINIMAX REGRET CRITERION

Decision Options	States of Nature			Maximum Regret
	S1	S2	S3	
A1	0	0	$100,000	$100,000
A2	75,000	75,000	25,000	75,000
A3	150,000	110,000	0	150,000

Minimax Regret Rule

Suppose we had chosen to adopt the maximin strategy and that, after the introduction of network services, we find that the actual state of events is S1. From Table 11, we know that profits would amount to $150,000. Hindsight indicates that option A3, yielding a profit of $300,000, would have been the optimal course of action. A cautious network manager has sacrificed profit, or opportunities. Lost opportunities, or regret, for any decision can be expressed as the difference between the maximum, or optimal, payoff for a given set of circumstances and the payoff actually experienced:

$$R(A_i, S_j) = P^*(S_j) - P(A_i, S_j) \qquad \text{Eq. 9.1}$$

where $R(A_i, S_j)$ equals the regret associated with decision option A_i and state of nature S_j, and $P^*(S_j)$ equals the best payoff under state of nature S_j. We can construct a regret matrix from a payoff table by computing the regret value associated with all combinations of a given decision alternative and state of nature. Each payoff entry is replaced with a regret value that is found by subtracting its entry from the largest entry in its column (Table 15; refer also to Table 11):

To make a final recommendation, we first identify the maximum regret for each decision option. Then we select the alternative which corresponds to the minimum of the maximum regret values. In this instance, the decision criterion indicates that the medium memory capacity is our optimal course of action. Each decision rule we examined reflects a different philosophy of the future. A major limitation of the decision rules presented in this section is that they do not include information concerning the probabilty of future states of nature. In order to more conveniently illustrate decision making using probability, we will first explore sample spaces. Tree diagrams help us to visualize experiments, their sample space, and the process of computing the probabilities of complex events. Having accomplished this, we will introduce two decision criteria for making choices under uncertainty by using probabilities.

Library Expansion

Assume that a library has embarked on a program of facility expansion. Our first step, therefore, is to define the experimental outcomes. When the list of

202   Applications and Extension of Theory

all possible outcomes has been listed, we have identified the same space. For the sake of simplicity, we will divide project completion into design and construction phases. The architectural firm assigned to the job will monitor project costs and scheduling, but library management cannot be sure of the time required for each stage of construction. Having a reliable estimate of completion time will affect crucial monetary decisions. For example, if we find that there is a reasonable probability of late completion, the director may request changes: increasing the construction budget to account for overtime or additional labor, or delay in hiring new library staff.

To make a decision, the library director has requested a management team to conduct research into the completion time of similar library projects. Suppose the library director has learned that, at similar construction sites, the design phase has been completed in either 1, 2, or 3 months. Completion time for the construction stage has been either 5, 6, or 7 months. Thus, we are faced with three mutually exclusive completion times for each stage of the project. To determine the total number (sample space) of experimental outcomes (sample points), let us introduce a simple counting rule for an experiment consisting of multiple steps.

Basically, we take the sum of the outcomes for each possible event and compute their product. For example, when we toss a coin we have 2 possible outcomes. If we toss one coin and then another, we have $(2)(2) = 4$ possible outcomes. Applying the counting rule to the library construction project, we find that the number of experimental outcomes is equal to $(3)(3) = 9$. The sample space, $S = ((1,5),(1,6),(1,7),(2,5),(2,6),(2,7),(3,5),(3,6),(3,7))$, is best visualized in a tree diagram (see Figure 65). Next, having listed the potential outcomes, we estimate the probabilities of the various events. Our research revealed 50 projects with similar construction characteristics. The results of the team's study are shown in Table 16.

For the purposes of this example, we will rely on the relative frequency method of attaching probabilities. To compute the probability of an outcome using the relative frequency method we divide the number of outcomes for a given completion time by the total number of projects: $P(d,c)$ = number of projects with completion time t/total number of projects. Using the information provided in Table 16, we compute the probability of a particular outcome as shown in Table 17.

The probability of an event's occurring is equal to the sum of the probabilities of the sample points which comprise the event. Thus, to determine the probability of completing the project in less than 8 months, less than or equal to 8 months, equal to 8 months, or more than 8 months, we find the sample points which correspond to these completion times. Letting E denote completion time in 8 months we express the event as

$$E = ((1,7),(2,6),(3,5)) \qquad \text{Eq. 9.2}$$

Information Economics 203

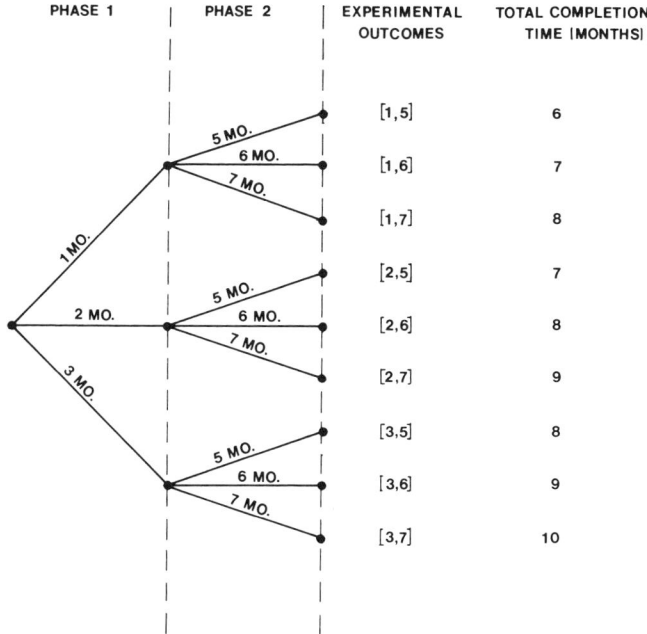

FIG. 65. Library Construction Tree Diagram

Table 16
SURVEY RESULTS

Phase 1	Phase 2	Sample Point	Number of Projects
1	5	(1,5)	3
1	6	(1,6)	5
1	7	(1,7)	6
2	5	(2,5)	5
2	6	(2,6)	8
2	7	(2,7)	6
3	5	(3,5)	4
3	6	(3,6)	7
3	7	(3,7)	6
			50 = Total

Table 17
PROBABILITIES OF COMPLETION TIME

(1,5)	6months	P(1,5) = 3/50 = .06
(1,6)	7months	P(1,6) = 5/50 = .10
(1,7)	8months	P(1,7) = 6/50 = .12
(2,5)	7months	P(2,5) = 5/50 = .10
(2,6)	8months	P(2,6) = 8/50 = .16
(2,7)	9months	P(2,7) = 6/50 = .12
(3,5)	8months	P(3,5) = 4/50 = .08
(3,6)	9months	P(3,6) = 7/50 = .14
(3,7)	10months	P(3,7) = 6/50 = .12
		1.00 = Total

and its probability as

$$= P(1,7) + P(2,6) + P(3,5) \qquad \text{Eq. 9.3}$$

$$= .12 + .16 + .08 = .36 \qquad \text{Eq. 9.4}$$

The probability of the project being completed in 8 months or less is equal to .62; the probability of its being completed in more than 8 months is equal to .38. Although we have computed probabilities by using tree diagrams, we have not devised rules for making decisions. In the next section we will investigate two criteria for using probability to make choices under uncertainty using probability.

Decision Making under Uncertainty Using Probability
Expected Monetary Value and Expected Opportunity Loss

Often, information managers are faced with decisions for which they can develop a good probability estimate of a variety of outcomes. In cases such as these, we can apply either the expected monetary value or expected opportunity-loss decision critieria. The expected monetary value rule refers to the process of identifying and choosing the alternative which yields the highest expected value.

The expected monetary value of an outcome is found by multiplying the probability of each outcome by the value of that occurrence and summing the products:

$$\text{EMV}(D_i) = \sum_{j=1}^{N} P(S_j)V(D_i, S_j) \qquad \text{Eq. 9.5}$$

where EMV(Di) denotes the expected monetary value of decision alternative

Di, P(Sj) equals the probability of occurrence of state of nature Sj, and N equals the number of possible states of nature. In other words, we compute the expected monetary value of a decision alternative by summing the weighted payoffs for each alternative. The weight for a payoff is equal to the probability of the respective state of nature. Given that one and only one state of nature can occur, the probabilities of all states of nature must satisfy the following conditions:

$$P(Sj) \geq 0 \text{ for all states of nature } j \qquad \text{Eq. 9.6}$$

$$\sum_{j=1}^{N} P(Sj) = P(S1) + P(S2) \ldots P(Sn) = 1 \qquad \text{Eq. 9.7}$$

To illustrate the use of the EMV, let us consider a new business software package for our accounting department. There are two possible decisions: to purchase or not to purchase the new system. The two possible outcomes are success or failure. (In this example, we will only evaluate two new software packages.) Also, assume that we have estimated that success will result in increased productivity. Success equals the net gain in productivity and cost equals purchase price, training, and maintenance. The expected monetary value is the sum of the probabilities of either event occurring:

$$Ev(Op) = ((Ps)(Bs)) + ((Pf)(Cf)) \qquad \text{Eq. 9.8}$$

where Ev(Op) is the expected value of the new operating system, Ps is the probability of success, Bs is the benefit of success, Pf is the probability of failure, and Cf is the cost of failure. In the case of not purchasing, we assume that there is no effect on productivity; consequently, the expected monetary value is zero.

Suppose that management has reason to suspect that the probability (for both systems) of success is .45 and the probability of failure is .55. Productivity increases from system A1 result in a gain (over the expected lifetime of the software) of $15,000; its cost in terms of purchase price and maintenance (over the expected lifetime of the software) is $4500. System A2 results in a net benefit of $12,900 at a cost of $3200. Using these figures, we calculate the expected monetary value to be

$$EV(Op) = .45(\$15,000) + .55(-\$4,500) = \$4,275 \qquad \text{Eq. 9.9}$$

$$EV(Op) = .45(\$12,900) + .55(-\$3,200) = \$4,045 \qquad \text{Eq. 9.10}$$

In this example, we would have chosen to purchase operating system A1. Of course, we have other options for allocating revenues, and we might compare, in productivity equivalencies, the expected gains from different information investments.

Another situation where one can apply this rule would be the case in which a library is in the process of evaluating an investment in access to an automated

206   Applications and Extension of Theory

cataloging system. Once again, the two possible decision alternatives are to purchase or not to purchase and the two possible states of nature are system success or failure. The expected value of not buying the system is zero. If the library is one of the first users of the cataloging system, we don't know anything and cannot compute reliable probabilities. In this case, we could simply give a 50/50 chance for success or failure.

An alternative version of the expected monetary value is the expected opportunity loss. This criterion is employed in conjunction with the regret concept developed in the section Minimax Regret Rule. Essentially, the expected-opportunity-loss rule weights each regret value with the probability of a state of nature:

$$EOL(D_i) = \sum_{j=1}^{N} P(S_j) R(D_i, S_j) \qquad \text{Eq. 9.11}$$

Use of either criteria will always yield the same recommendation. Thus, only one rule need be applied to the selection process. Of the two approaches, the expected value rule is the one most frequently applied. However, since many decision makers think in terms of what possible benefit a given action may cause them to forgo, the opportunity-loss approach has an analytical advantage. Further, the expected-opportunity-loss method supplies an information manager with an indication of the value of collecting sample information.

Decision Trees

A decision tree is useful for representing, in a logical progression, the constituent parts of the decision process. It reveals the places where the manager has control and the places where chance plays a primary role. We use squares to denote decision situations and circles for chance situations. The number at the end of each branch refers to the payoff (cost or benefit) associated with a specific sequence of events. In essence, the decision tree summarizes each possible chain of events associated with a decision. For example, given the choice to purchase an automated acquisition system, the library must next decide which system to purchase. Once a particular system has been selected, the state of nature or chance event will occur. We use a decision tree to illustrate each possible sequence of events associated with the purchase of an acquisition system (Figure 66).

Let's assume that an information manager is in the process of choosing an acquisition system and that there are three alternative systems, A, B, and C. Each system is associated with a net benefit, plus some probability of future events occurring. Figure 66 depicts the decision-making process. The information manager is responsible for selecting the particular decision branch to take, and his or her objective is to select the best branch. Yet, the chance

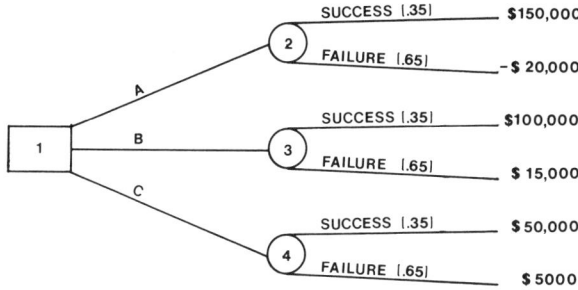

FIG. 66. Acquisition System Decision Tree

branches are not under the control of the manager; therefore, the particular branch to be followed from a chance node depends upon the probabilities associated with the branches.

To compute the expected monetary value of being at a specific chance node, we use a process known as backward induction. This requires that we work from the right-hand side of the decision tree and weight each potential payoff by its probability of occurrence. Assume that there are two states of nature, successful and not successful, and that we have calculated the probability of both payoffs. The expected benefit value of being situated at nodes 2, 3, and 4 is computed as follows:

EMV(node 2) = .35($150,000) + .65(−$20,000) = $39,500   Eq. 9.12

EMV(node 3) = .35($100,000) + .65($15,000) = $44,750   Eq. 9.13

EMV(node 4) = .35($50,000) + .65($5,000) = $20,750   Eq. 9.14

If the acquisition manager is interested in maximizing the expected monetary benefits (time saved) system, we would recommend choice B. Observe that decision trees assist us in arriving at an optimal decision strategy. The value of a decision tree lies in its ability to illustrate the sequential nature of library managment problems. First, we consider the alternative decisions and states of nature. Next, we determine probabilities for each state of nature and compute the expected monetary value for each chance branch. Using the EMV, we select the decision branch leading to the state of nature which supplies the best EMV. An additional benefit of this approach is that it forces us to analyze the effect of the assumptions we make. Finally, we have chosen to represent the process by using a simple series of choices. Real-world problems involve a series of "trees," one for each major choice.

Expected Value of Perfect Information

Before making a decision, we may have the option of gathering information regarding the likelihood of events. Statisticians call an initial hunch an *a priori* probability; after information has been sought, we have what is known as a *posterior* probability. For example, if you are considering the purchase of a new word processor, you might initially assess the chance of its meeting your requirements as .5 and the chance of its not meeting your needs also as .5. After you gather information from a consultant, other librarians, and consumer literature, your beliefs may be revised to .75 for success and .25 for failure.

Information managers have access to sources of information in the form of empirical data and subjective opinion, as well as to experts/consultants. The decision maker can either request a subset of a consultant's knowledge of the problem, then use this information to revise beliefs, or the consultant's beliefs about the problem. For example, if a library is about to purchase an automated circulation system, the library could ask the consultant to provide technical knowledge about the feasibility of automating certain tasks and what type of computer systems would be required. On the other hand, we may simply ask the consultant to give us an opinion about the likelihood of a given system's working. (Of course, we will want to evaluate the consultant too!) With new information, we revise our initial (prior) probability distribution. We can also weight the value of the consultant's information, given our judgments about him or her. Bayes's theorem provides a formal model for revising probabilities. However, rather than illustrate the formal mechanics of Bayes's theorem, we will examine methods of determining the value of information.

Decision tree analysis can be utilized to compute the value of information. We have two alternatives: to make a choice, based on additional information, or to choose the best alternative without information. The difference between the two options provides us with the expected value of information. To highlight the process of determining the value of information, we will examine the expected value of perfect information and the expected value of sample information. In each case, to derive the value of information, we take the expected value of the information alternative and subtract the contribution of the next-best alternative.

Perfect information allows us to eliminate all uncertainty. Although we would not expect to obtain perfect information, an example will aid in understanding the technique of appraising the value of additional data and provide us with an upper-bound value of information. Let us assume that a library is choosing among three different methods of handling a problem, and each plan has the potential to contribute to the success of a new project. The success of each plan depends on the type of equipment used to produce a project. We will assume there are three types of machinery that the library can employ: A1, A2, A3. In addition, we have some beliefs about the probability of particular market conditions. Table 18 summarizes these conditions (S1–S4), our decision alternatives (A1–A3), the probability that an event will occur, and the expected monetary value, without added information. With perfect information, we would choose the highest payoff for each potential situation. From

Table 18
PAYOFF TABLE FOR LIBRARY MACHINERY

| States | Decision Alternatives | | | |
of Nature	A1	A2	A3	Probability
S1	54	32	45	.40
S2	24	32	20	.25
S3	28	20	25	.20
S4	28	30	20	.15
EMV	37.4	29.3	31	

Table 19, we find that the expected monetary value, with perfect information, is 39.7; thus, the value of the information is $39.7 - 37.4 = 2.3$

Another way of viewing this problem is to examine the value of perfect information for each possible state of nature. For example, if the information indicates that condition S1 will prevail, then the change in contribution is $54 - 54 = 0$; with S2, it would be $32 - 24 = 8$; if condition S3 had prevailed, the contribution of perfect information would be $28 - 28 = 0$; and if S4 had prevailed, its contribution would be $30 - 28 = 2$. Since we can't know which condition the new information will indicate, we calculate the expected value of perfect information as $(0)(0.40) + (8)(0.25) + (0)(0.20) + (2)(0.15) = 2.3$.

Perhaps the simplest method of deriving the value of perfect information is the opportunity-loss approach. Mathematically, we can express the EVPI as

$$\text{EVPI} = \sum_{j=1}^{N} P(Sj)R(d^*,Sj) \qquad \text{Eq. 9.15}$$

where d^* denotes the optimal decision prior to obtaining information, $P(Sj)$ equals the probability of state of nature Sj, N is the number of states of nature, and $R(d^*,Sj)$ is the opportunity loss for d^* and state of nature Sj.

Table 20 shows the opportunity losses associated with our machinery decision. The minimum expected opportunity loss, 2.3, is associated with plan

Table 19
CHOICE WITH PERFECT INFORMATION

States of Nature	Choice	Payoff	Probability
S1	A1	54	0.40
S2	A2	32	0.25
S3	A1	28	0.20
S4	A2	30	0.15
EMV		39.7	

Table 20

OPPORTUNITY-LOSS TABLE

States of Nature	Decision Alternatives			Probability
	A1	A2	A3	
S1	0	22	9	.40
S2	8	0	12	.25
S3	0	8	3	.20
S4	2	0	10	.15
EOL	2.3	10.4	8.7	

A1. Observe that this is consistent with the fact that plan A1 has the highest expected payoff.

To summarize, due to uncertainty, and no matter what the manager does, a course of action may be selected which is not optimal. The expected value of perfect information (EVPI) is equal to the expected opportunity loss of the optimal decision. That is, the expected opportunity loss of the best available decision action is the difference between the best possible outcome and that associated with a given decision alternative. If it is assumed it is possible to obtain perfect information, this difference would equal zero. Hence, the EVPI is equal to the expected opportunity loss associated with the best plan.

Expected Value of Sample Information

We have shown how the addition of probabilities affects the optimal decision under uncertainty. In order to update knowledge or assure ourselves about potential states of nature, we may seek additional information, through experimentation, literature search, or consultants. In this section, we will summarize a method for deriving the value of information through a consultant's advice.

Suppose an information manager is in the process of selecting an automated cataloging vendor. To increase the likelihood of choosing the correct vendor, the manager is considering hiring a consultant, and our task is to estimate the value of such services. Let us assume that, prior to hiring a consultant, the manager feels that the likelihood of choosing the best vendor is 35 percent. Also, once a vendor has been chosen, the chance of the project being successful is 35 percent and of failing is 65 percent. Next, let us assume that the manager believes that, after utilizing the consultant's services, the chances of a vendor being successful will be either 60, 40, 20 or 5 percent, and that the likelihood of each potential event is equal.

To complete the analysis, there must be a payoff (measure of success) and a loss associated with failure. Although this may be difficult to estimate, an

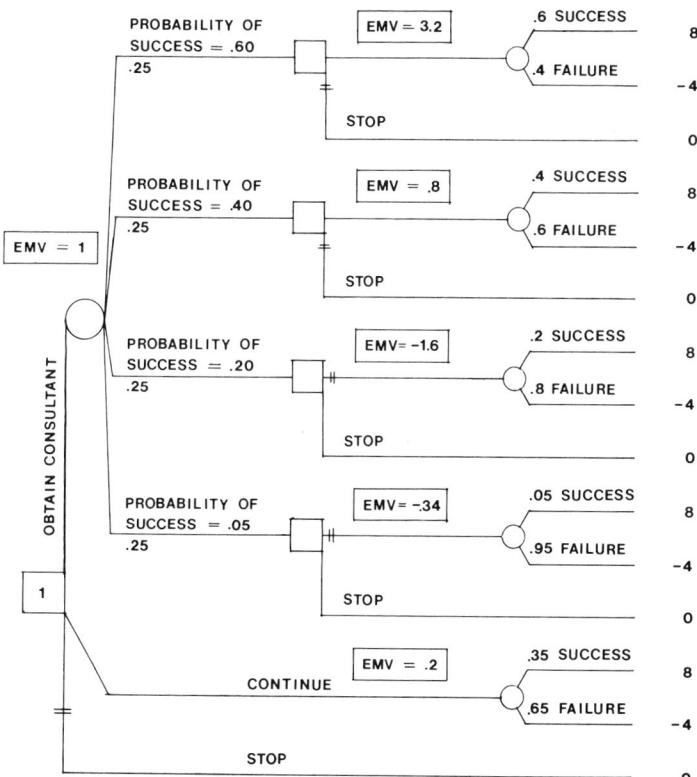

Fig. 67. EVSI for Cataloging Vendor Decision

information manager will probably have some clues as to the costs involved in failure—lost customers, lost production time, and other opportunity costs—and the benefits in terms of saved time, reduced errors, etc. In this example, we assume that the potential gain, measured in terms of productivity, is $8 million. The loss, measured in lost market potential, is $4 million. As you can see from the decision tree in Figure 67, our best alternative is to hire the consultant. The next-best alternative is to continue, so that the value of additional information is $800,000.

We have not determined the optimal decision strategy. To do so, we require the results of the consultant's report. However, we have outlined a technique for evaluating the worth of the consultant's report and a method for selecting the optimal decision strategy. In addition, we may wish to evaluate the efficiency of the sample information:

$$E = (EVSI/EVPI)(100)$$ Eq. 9.16

where the level of E measures our confidence in using the sample information. Put differently, it signifies the efficiency of sample information relative to perfect information. Thus, a low level of efficiency suggests the need for other types of information. The decision to pay for new information would require another EVSI analysis.

Using sample or additional information, the analyst can determine an optimal decision strategy by constructing a decision tree. We compute posterior probabilities in order to determine state-of-nature and indicator branch probabilities. Next, we work backward through the tree diagram and calculate expected values at the state-of-nature and indicator nodes, and establish the best decision branch for each decision juncture. By following this procedure, the analyst can establish the optimal decision strategy and its expected value.

Summary

The basic problem confronting the library manager is how to allocate resources, and the difficulty of this problem is compounded by risk and uncertainty. In certain situations, most notably those which involve a limited number of alternatives, where the payoff is relatively small and the time constraint is severe, intuition or instinct may be warranted. However, when decisions are complex and uncertainty is high, the decision process can benefit from an analytical approach. Use of models for determining an optimal decision strategy does preclude intuition or rule-of-thumb procedures; they can be factored into the analysis. Under an uncertain and risk-filled future, the decision theory approach enables managers to identify the constituent parts of choices and the best alternative.

In this chapter we reviewed the decision theory approach to analyzing alternatives. We introduced the concept of payoff tables, a decision analysis procedure designed to assist in solving problems with a limited number of alternatives. Next we discussed four criteria for making decisions under uncertainty, without using probabilities. Without probability estimates of each outcome, we are restricted in our ability to formulate optimal rules for information managers. However, even *with* probability estimates, we must be careful and utilize estimates which are meaningful, or the analysis will yield misleading results.

After we explored the use of decision-making rules under uncertainty, we discussed two techniques, the expected monetary value and expected loss value, for solving decision problems under uncertainty, using probabilities. Finally, we reviewed methods for estimating the contribution of new information. The problems with which we illustrated basic concepts of decision theory were limited to one uncertain variable. In more realistic situations, the number of

Information Economics   213

actions and states of nature will be numerous and independent. Nonetheless, decision theory is a fairly reliable representation of the process of decision making and, consequently, supplies valuable guidelines for making choices.

Exercises

1. Assume you have been given the following payoff table:

	s1	s2	s3	s4
d1	12	13	14	16
d2	10	11	11	12
d3	20	15	11	8
d4	15	13	9	7

   Use the maximin and maximax decision rules to decide which course of action to take.

2. Suppose you are the marketing manager for an information network and you are trying to decide whether or not to introduce a new product. You are uncertain about both the potential market and the per unit cost of production. The net profit (expressed in thousands of dollars) depends upon these factors:

	Unit Cost		
	$2.00	$2.50	$3.00
High acceptance	20	15	5
Low acceptance	6	−3	−6

   You have the following probabilities: H(.65), L(.35), U2(.3), U2.5(.15), U3(.55).
   a. Given this information, what should you do?
   b. How much will you pay for perfect information?

3. The driver of a library bookmobile can take two alternative routes to the first destination. Route A is usually faster, but at times there are traffic jams which cause excessive delays. Route B is somewhat longer, but has fewer traffic problems. If there is a traffic jam on Route A, we want to take Route B; however, we do not know this in advance. The following payoff table shows the estimated travel times:

	Travel Time	
	A—Okay	A—Not Okay
Route A	30 mins.	50 mins.
Route B	35	38

   After several weeks (28 days), the driver finds that Route A is jammed 7 times. What is the optimal route to take in the future?

4. A library wants to know how many terminals to purchase for its automated circulation system. To simplify matters, let us assume that you feel that option A (which involves more terminals and, consequently, added costs: terminals, computer memory, telephone lines, etc.) would be highly "profitable" if use is high. You forecast that if use is high, option A will result in savings of $10,000, $6,000 if use is moderate, and a loss of $8,000 if use is low. Based on research, you estimate that P(H) = .35, P(M) = .4, and P(L) = .25. Use the expected monetary value criterion to recommend a decision to invest in option A.

Suggested Reading

Baumol, William J. *Economic Anaylsis and Operations Research.* 3rd ed. Englewood Cliffs, N.J.: Prentice-Hall, 1972.

Luce, R. D., and H. Raiffa. *Games and Decisions: Introduction and Critical Survey.* New York: Wiley, 1967.

Malinconico, S. Michael. "Decisions under Uncertainty." *Library Journal* 109:1 (November 15, 1984): 2129–2131.

———. "The Value of Perfect Information." *Library Journal* 110:4 (March 1, 1985): 63–65.

Schlaifer, R. *Analysis of Decisions under Uncertainty.* New York: McGraw-Hill, 1969.

10

COST-BENEFIT ANALYSIS

Project managers are responsible for allocating monies in such a way as to maximize the benefits of library expenditures. Cost-benefit analysis, using a systematic and quantitative approach, seeks to appraise and compare project costs and benefits. What distinguishes cost-benefit analysis from other forms of expenditure analysis, such as cost-effectiveness, is the attempt to estimate the costs and benefits which accrue to the society, as well as those that accrue to the individual. Rather than dwell on the differences between types of expenditure analysis, we shall outline some basic techniques for expenditure analysis. The cost-benefit approach is a useful device for focusing attention on alternative means for achieving various ends. Thus, the information manager must be able to express the objective and goals of the library. When there are multiple goals, tradeoffs between goals have to be examined.

In terms of time-priced information services, the primary limitation of expenditure analysis is the difficulty of estimating and assessing project benefits. How can we place a value on story hours, reference service, public reading rooms, and the like? Since these goods have no counterpart in the private marketplace, they are not priced in terms of dollars and, therefore, cannot be precisely valued. Further complicating their measurement, many information services are public goods, the benefits of which are shared by the entire community. Briefly, if the value derived by one individual is shared by the community, that person has no way of assessing the communal value. Given the public nature of library services and the lack of prices, we are restricted in our ability to incorporate the different values that consumers place on a service.

Another limitation of cost-benefit analysis is the difficulty of accounting for such dynamic aspects as changes in prices and costs over time. One can attempt to incorporate such changes by using the probability theory discussed in Chapters 7 and 8. Finally, cost-benefit analysis cannot indicate new alternatives; it can only assist in selecting the best choice among those alternatives which have been listed.

The basic technique of cost-benefit analysis involves listing the decision or effectiveness criteria to be maximized, revealing any or all assumptions, identifying all feasible alternatives, identifying and measuring project cost and benefits, comparing the relative merits of each project, and choosing the best project. In effect, we are asking: What is the connection between library expenditures and benefits to the library consumer? A part of this question was addressed in our analysis of costs, or the way in which expenditures generate library services. Another portion was answered through an investigation of the production function, or how different services generate library consumption. Building on the microeconomic theory presented in the first portion of the text, cost-benefit analysis, a method which attempts to account for all costs and benefits over time, expands our ability to choose the optimal alternative.

Cost-Benefit Approach

The *cost-benefit* approach (or B/C ratio) examines the relationship between cost and output within the context of system objectives. (Measures of system performance should be chosen on the basis of their relationship to objectives.) The goal of a library program cannot be imprecise; however, an objective such as an increase or supplement of the education level of the community does not lend itself to analysis. Thus, goals, when possible, should be stated in terms of observable and quantifiable measures, such as increased use of certain categories of materials, increased use of the library by specific types of users, decreased number of directional questions, etc. In brief, goal statements must relate library processes to the user and to any specified missions which may have been delegated to the library by an entity to which it is responsible. Objectives, to be of any real value to those charged with the management of libraries, must be specific. A set of priorities must be designed to implement the goals. Otherwise, ambiguity will surround the issues of performance measures and resource allocation.

We have indicated that there is no ideal technique for linking collection content, staff, etc. to library use or utility. Yet, library policies need to be analyzed and weighed. Will the library function as a product-service evaluation center? Will the library function as a job skills center? These and other service options need to be decided before the library can reasonably choose between effective resource-allocation alternatives: quality and quantity of staff; types of equipment; size, design, and location of facilities; types and quantity of materials and circulation policy. Each of these decisions will have an impact on the ability of the library to reach its objectives. Further, it is within the context of service objectives that use can be interpreted and tradeoffs evaluated.

Production theory showed us that the impact of a change in the level or quality of an input depends upon the production function, the level of activity, and prices. Thus, when we evaluate new projects we can investigate them in terms of the way in which new procedures or policies influence the supply of library services. Some of the aspects of library service which affect the supply curve are accuracy, timeliness, response time, breadth and depth of the collection, level and composition of staff, hours of service, delivery technique, facilities, and so on. The cost-benefit technique, by providing guidelines for evaluating the effect of library projects, enhances our ability to make choices.

Basic Decision Criteria

The four key decision criteria that may be used for comparing alternative library projects are to (1) maximize benefits for a given cost, (2) minimize costs for a given level of benefits, (3) maximize the ratio of benefits over costs, and (4) maximize net benefit. For most library applications, the net benefit approach is the most useful; all of the other criteria suffer from various problems. The attempt to maximize benefits for a given cost, or minimizing cost for a fixed level of benefits, neglects the effect of incremental changes in costs or benefits. Maximizing the ratio of benefits to costs is sensitive to small changes in costs and therefore can give misleading results. Moreover, evaluating projects in terms of B/C ratios has the disadvantage that we must determine whether to treat a project's impacts as costs or negative benefits. The B/C measure depends on how these questions are resolved. As we shall see, the maximization of total net benefits criteria does not depend upon how these problems are resolved.

Imagine that you are given a fixed revenue to spend on reference services, and your problem is how best to allocate a given sum between several projects. If the projects are divisible—that is, their scale can be altered in small increments—we maximize net contribution by equating benefits and costs at the margin. Even though you have a fixed budget, the amount that can be allocated to any given project is variable. In other words, the net benefit from the last dollar of expenditure should equal one dollar. (Observe the similarity between this allocation and the allocation of income between inputs.)

Unfortunately, not all library projects are divisible into small increments. For example, you are faced with making a choice between several security systems for your library. Each one may allow for some divisibility, but they will not be as divisible as buying books or hiring staff. Instead, you are faced with a choice similar to the roadbuilder or courier who must connect either points A and B or A and C: there are no marginal adjustments.

Again, suppose you have been given a fixed budget of $600,000 to allocate to several nondivisible (lumpy) information service alternatives. Given Table 21, your objective is to select that combination of projects which yields the

Table 21
PROJECT COSTS AND BENEFITS

Project	Costs	Benefits	Net Benefits	B/C	B/C Rank
A	100	200	100	2.00	2
B	90	110	20	1.22	4
C	50	110	60	2.20	1
D	150	180	30	1.20	5
E	300	410	110	1.36	3
F	70	80	10	1.14	6
G	300	280	−20	0.93	7

highest net benefit within the budget constraint. To determine the best package, we must try various combinations that add up to our allotment. The data in Table 21 indicate that projects A, C, D, and E, with a net benefit of $300,000 are the optimal combination.

To avoid this method of choosing the best package, we may be tempted to base our selections on the absolute net benefit rank of projects. But, given lumpy projects and a fixed budget, ranking projects in this manner is meaningless because different costs are involved. Maximizing the ratio of benefits to costs avoids this difficulty; however, the results can be misleading. Total net benefit may be lower if we use this approach. In our example, ranking by the B/C ratio calls for the inclusion of project B instead of D, resulting in a net benefit of $290,000. Perhaps more important, ranking by a benefit-cost ratio involves the problem of whether or not to treat certain costs and benefits in the numerator or the denominator of the ratio. (The maximization of total net benefits does not depend upon how these problems are resolved.) Finally, had we been given a variable budget, the net benefit approach recommends project acceptance when the net benefit is greater than zero.

Multiperiod Projects

When we evaluate the net contribution of long-term projects, we must account for the fact that costs and benefits do not accrue immediately, but over the life of the project. Expenditures for plant and equipment yield costs and benefits which accrue in the future. A book or record purchased with current monies will yield benefits until the item has worn out, whereas expenditures for utilities and current salaries yield immediate benefits. To determine the net benefit of long-term projects, we must be able to compare costs and benefits that occur in different time periods. They must be translated into a *term* which accounts for the fact that costs and benefits that occur in the future have a different value.

The reason why the delivery of library services *next year* has less value to you *today* is because of their delayed availability; future use is "marked down" in value. To calculate the discounted value, we use a measure, known as the interest rate, which reflects the rate of substitution between current and deferred library services. To compute the present value of costs and benefits, we must select a discount rate which reflects the time value of money. Thus, the discount rate places less weight on an effect the further in the future it will occur. This process permits us to calculate the value of future library services in terms of their current value. In other words, we wish to reduce the streams of costs and benefits to a single number which captures the economic value of the project in terms of current opportunities. Without this single measure, we would not be able to compare information services with different life spans; we would, so to speak, be in a position of trying to compare apples and oranges. Thus, the object of aggregation is to determine the costs and benefits of projects in terms of present value.

The technique for determining the time-adjusted value of project impacts is known as the present-value rule and is determined by the following equation:

$$PV = \sum_{t=0}^{n} At / (1+r)^t \qquad \text{Eq. 10.1}$$

where r is the discount rate, n is the number of time periods until a benefit or cost is realized, and At is the net change in project effect, benefits-costs, in time period t. In general, lower interest rates, or a lower relative opportunity cost of time, result in a higher present value of all projects. However, lower interest rates favor long-term projects and higher rates favor short-term projects. Keeping these factors in mind, once the analyst has chosen the discount rate, the present-value method is used to compute the net benefits of information services with variable life spans.

Benefits of Library Service
Definition and Measurement

Libraries perform a variety of activities which yield benefits to both the users of the library and the community at large. The key activities of library service are selection of documents, physical and intellectual access, user assistance, cultural programming, facilities, and equipment. Identifying the activities of a library may appear relatively simple, but defining and measuring the benefits of these operations is more complex.

How do we measure the impact of library services on a goal such as a literate public? And how does one determine the value of a literate public? Yet library managers are forced to incorporate such judgments into resource-allocation decisions. By making choices, we implicitly weigh the value of different service options. Expenditure evaluation provides us with an explicit technique for investigating the library's goals, the methods used to achieve them, and the costs and benefits of library programs. Our concern will not be to measure the absolute value of library services to the community. Rather, our goal will be to suggest methods for estimating the relative value of alternative service options. The source of the manager's problem is limited funds. Some means must be established for measuring the success and value of library operations. According to John H. Wilson, Jr.:

> The search for a definition of cost-benefits may prove as unrewarding as the search of 19th century economists for "utility." But until we can better define and trace the uses and effects of information—its value, price, utility, whatever we want to call them—the idea of benefit, whether measured in dollars, or other units, is at least forcing us to search out the purposes that information serves in our society.[1]

Economic benefits are typically separated into several categories: those which can be measured in monetary units; others which can be measured in terms of some common denominator, such as the impact of higher library materials budgets versus higher librarian salaries on information service use; effects which can be quantified, but not compared, in terms of a common denominator, such as the capability of improving health and reducing crime; and those effects which are nonquantifiable.

Cost-benefit analysis generally relies on prices as a first approximation of value. Thus, benefits of library services would be expressed as the price consumers would be willing to pay for information services. Internally, the benefits of projects which lead to improved production techniques would be measured in terms of the price of labor or capital. Similarly, costs are measured by the prices libraries pay for factors of production. In both cases, we have a measure of what society is willing to sacrifice in order to receive library services.

When the market does not provide prices, surrogate or proxy values must be found. For example, the value of library use may be expressed in terms of the time it takes the user to get to the library, or increased money income. Internally, projects intended to improve employee skills or morale could be measured in terms of changes in the rate of absenteeism, the ability of employees to handle new tasks, the level of compliments vs. complaints.

Effects which cannot be evaluated in terms of market value must be measured. For example, how can we determine if our objective of increasing literacy among children is meeting with success? While we may not be able to place a monetary value on the benefits of these projects, we may be able to devise a measure which signals project success. Thus, within the library, measures such as use, attendance at programs, questions asked, and voters registered may serve as indicators of project benefits.

Cost-Benefit Analysis   221

Estimating the Benefits of Library Projects

Ideally, all benefits and costs are compared in terms of a common financial denominator, which simplifies the process of comparing alternatives. However, the benefits and value derived from information services are not readily convertible in money terms. The outputs of libraries are heterogeneous and difficult to measure, and many of the benefits are intangible. Some effects cannot be quantified, such as the impact of libraries on the preservation of the principles of a democratic society, such as free speech and intellectual freedom.

This does not mean, however, that the benefit of library services cannot be captured by economic analysis, and to make such an argument is to fail to recognize the economic nature of library service production. Like all other production, the generation of library service is aimed at the satisfaction of human values or desires. Libraries are economic entities in that they use resources to satisfy these human wants. Still, the most difficult part of an economic evaluation of public library service is the measurement of benefits. Assuming that it is not feasible to derive dollar values for tangible or intangible benefits, the analyst must devise a surrogate measure of consumer satisfaction. When we cannot evaluate benefits, we can use the cost-effectiveness approach (e.g., maximize the desired effect at least cost).

The value or impact of a project may manifest itself in time and materials saved, ability to reduce inventory, increased utilization of assets, improved customer relations, lower error rates, cost avoidance or reduction, and changes in return on investment in research and development projects. Increased utilization of assets may occur because of increased capability to locate, reserve, and deliver items, thereby maximizing the use of library resource capacity. The ability to reduce inventory may be a result of increases in the speed with which the library can respond to changes in demand. Increased return on investment, or higher profits to the company, can be estimated on the basis of the value of information in decision making. The ability of a project to achieve any one of these results must be measured in terms of system objectives. Reducing inventory will rarely be an objective unto itself; rather, it will be related to ability to provide service. In the final analysis, some measure of value must be utilized—use, dollars, time, and so on.

Information managers, as do all service managers, face the problem of devising a technique for measuring the value of library production. One criticism of measures of library use is that they do not address the question of value: "These measures say little about effectiveness of these activities, since they ignore such vital questions as: how useful is the book to the person who takes it out; how pertinent is the reference service; how adequate is the cataloging?"[2] Yet, it seems reasonable to assume that if people return to the library and use its services, they are deriving value. If use in the aggregate were to decrease (unless the objective was in fact to decrease use of a particular service), it would appear reasonable to assume that the "value" of the service had diminished. Increases in use, attendance, voters registered, school visits—all suggest that consumers are deriving value from the service. Of course, with a fixed budget, at some point diminishing returns will set in (it is here that limits on use may be applicable).

We have suggested that measures of library use would appear to be acceptable indices of the minimum level of benefits obtained from library services. Yet several key problems exist. We have already identified the general problem of measuring value, and a related problem is weighing the value by type of use and type of user. Each type of use may generate different levels of value, and the question of how use is distributed may affect the net value of a project. In effect, when we value each use in an equivalent manner, we implicitly ignore the distributional consequences of decisions. While we cannot ignore the distribution of benefits, one technique for dealing with this is to weight benefits according to the mission of the library. More will be said on this topic later in the chapter.

If we assume, as it concerns library benefits, that use is a crude measure of benefits, increased use (normally considered a performance measure) would mean an increase in benefits. Maximization of use implies use in the aggregate sense. We do not mean to suggest that when patrons check out more books, or ask more questions, they are better off than if they had checked out fewer books or asked fewer questions; more information is not necessarily better. Rather, we want to maximize use in the aggregate. Actual use of information by an individual and the public follows the law of diminishing returns; but this only applies to a particular subject and a particular individual. Society as a whole gains when more people are informed. Assuming that the library wishes to maximize its use, the manager will have several methods of achieving this goal and measuring its achievement. The next few sections suggest several methods for evaluating the benefits of library projects.

Applications

Security Systems

In this section, we illustrate techniques for evaluating and estimating the benefits and costs of increased library security.[3] A variety of means exists for reducing theft of library materials, but each of these methods involves the expenditure of library monies. Our goal is to choose the alternative which maximizes the net benefit of our efforts to reduce theft. To this end, we will make certain assumptions about the value of library materials over time, about the percentage of books that are missing, and those which are actually lost due to theft, the proportion of stolen items which will be replaced, the effectiveness

Cost-Benefit Analysis   223

of each security alternative, and the life span of the project. Having made these assumptions, and evaluated costs and benefits, we will determine the optimal approach to increasing security. Essentially, we are following the same analytical procedures we introduced in Part 1 of this text. We make assumptions about the behavior of some aspect of library operations, indicate the costs and benefits of alternatives, and devise a method for choosing the optimal alternative.

We will evaluate two alternative solutions to our objective of increasing security: use of a guard, or installation of an electronic security system. The cost of either approach must be weighed against the benefits. While it is relatively easy to estimate the cost of either security system, estimating benefits is considerably more difficult. To obtain some notion of the value of a security system, it is necessary to estimate the number and value of items which are lost due to theft, and the reduction in the rate of loss. Then we can compare the value of reduced loss with the cost of alternative security systems.

One method for estimating losses due to theft is to take a random sample of items in the library, to search library records to determine the number of items which are presumed lost, and to make certain assumptions about the nature of library use.[4] Our first task will be to estimate how many items are lost in one year. We will assume that the loss rate for items in the library is related to their publication date. Consequently, we will separate our sample by publication date. Once we have determined the number of items lost (unaccounted for) in the sample in a one-year period, we estimate the total number of lost documents by first establishing the proportion of items lost for a given sample. To arrive at the estimated number of items lost in a specific class, we multiply the sample proportion of unaccounted for items by the total number of items within that class.[5]

For example, if we assume we have 100 books in our sample of items published in 1975 and that the number of items found to be missing is 2, then 2 percent of all items in that publication-date class would be our estimate of lost items. To determine the number of items missing in that class of library materials, we multiply .2 by the number of items in that class. Similar estimates would be made for all publication-date classes. Based on our hypothetical sample, we have determined that 2 percent of the collection will be missing in any given year, or that, in our collection of 100,000 documents (a constant for this example), that 2000 items will be missing. However, not all items that are reported missing can be presumed to be lost. Some will be found and still others will be paid for by users.[6] For the purposes of this example, we will assume that a search of the records of the sample items shows that 10 percent of them will be found or paid for by users. Thus, of the 2000 items reported missing, approximately 200 items will be found or paid for by users.

Now that we have devised a method for assessing the number of items which are lost due to theft, we must determine the opportunity cost of theft—e.g., the benefits of a security system. First, we note that not all of the books which were lost to theft will be replaced. We assume that of the estimated number of items lost to theft, some portion will not be demanded and, therefore, will not be replaced. Let us assume that of the 1800 items lost due to theft, only 600 would be replaced by the library. If the average cost of replacing library materials is $25, then the loss (cost) due to theft would be $15,000 per year.

Other costs include tracing lost items, the cost of interlibrary loans for items which were stolen, and the intangible benefit of lost local availability. Further, there is the cost to users of attempting to locate documents which are lost, plus time spent waiting for the receipt of interlibrary loans. While the cost of interlibrary loans and tracing lost items will be relatively easy to estimate, it is considerably more difficult to estimate user time costs. Nonetheless, if the annual cost of interlibrary loans due to theft is $1200, then the total annual cost incurred by the library due to theft is $16,200, plus any intangible benefits. Finally, we must note that no security system is 100 percent effective; therefore, we must make some adjustment to the cost of theft. Let us assume that all alternatives are 95 percent effective, implying that the total annual cost of not having a security system would be $15,390, plus intangible costs.

Having estimated the benefits of having a security system, we must evaluate our alternatives. The cost of a security guard service is dependent upon the number of hours the library is open and the hourly wage rate. Assume that the library is open 70 hours per week and that guard services can be acquired for $5 per hour. In that case, the annual cost of guard services would be $18,200, plus any inconvenience to the users caused by having their parcels checked. Given our assumption of 95 percent ability to detect theft, the security guard can be ruled out as an effective method of reducing theft. Even if the security guard were 100 percent effective, a library administrator, to choose the guard, would have to place a high value on intangible benefits and a relatively low value on the inconvenience of having patrons' parcels inspected.

Turning to the electronic security system, let us assume that outright purchase of such a system is less expensive than lease or rent options. The cost of such a system should be separated into one-time costs and annual operating costs. One-time costs include the initial purchase, the installation of equipment, and the cost and installation of detectors in items already owned by the library. Annual operating costs include yearly maintenance, as well as the cost of new detectors and their installation. Finally, the costs and benefits which accrue in future years must be discounted to the present, as follows:

$$PV = \sum_{t=0}^{n} B_t - C_t/(1+r)^t \qquad \text{Eq. 10.2}$$

where r is the discount or interest rate, n is the life of the project in years, Bt is the value of the benefits in period t, and Ct is the value of costs in period t. One could also compute the benefit-cost ratio simply by computing the present value of the stream of benefits and the stream of costs, and then divide the present value of benefits by that of costs. The benefit-cost ratio would indicate how much benefit is yielded for every dollar spent.

In our example, assume that the initial costs are $50,000 and that annual costs thereafter are $4000. The latter figure includes labor, materials, maintenance, and some estimate of inconvenience to users. Yearly benefits are $15,390 plus intangibles, which have been estimated to be worth $2500 per year, for a total of $17,890. Now let us assume that the interest rate is 8 percent and that the life span of the project is 10 years. In this instance, the present value of the project is

$$PV = \sum_{t=0}^{10} \frac{(-\$50,000)}{(1 + .08)^0} + \frac{(\$13,890)}{(1 + .08)^1} + \ldots \frac{(\$13,890)}{(1 + .08)^{10}} \quad \text{Eq. 10.3}$$

$$PV = -\$50,000 + \$93,203 = \$43,203 \quad \text{Eq. 10.4}$$

To determine whether or not the electronic security system warrants funding, the net benefits of all library programs would have to be evaluated and compared. Given the same amount of money, we would estimate the net value of other library projects, such as adding computer terminals or staff in the cataloging department. On the other hand, if we were to compare a security system to increased expenditure on library materials, we would have to convert security benefits into uses and make assumptions about the value of use over time.

One final word of caution. The merits of alternative security techniques depends on the assumptions we make concerning the rate of theft, the cost of replacement, the discount rate, and the rate of effectiveness of a security system in reducing theft. A reduction in the rate of effectiveness lowers the benefits; an increase in the cost of replacement increases benefits; changes in the discount rate affect the stream of costs and benefits.

Circulation of Library Materials

The steps used to calculate the net benefits of library use will illustrate the cost-benefit process: to state the objective of the project; to examine alternatives; to determine the relationship between costs and benefits; and to select a method for comparing projects. To accomplish this, we will make certain assumptions concerning how the method of circulating library materials affects use over time. We will discuss approaches for calculating net benefits and alternative techniques for selecting the optimal circulation system.

We will assume that the library has two alternatives for circulating materials: manual or automated techniques. To measure the effectiveness of either system, we must define the objectives of the library. Let's assume that the library administrator's objectives are to maximize circulation; to maximize materials' availability; to maximize inventory control; and to minimize user effort in the circulation function. Our criteria of effectiveness will be changes in use, changes in the time it takes for a person to receive an item, rate of loss, and time saved by users in borrowing items. Finally, we will assume that with increases in population, the library's current circulation, 50,000 per year, will also increase. Our estimates of the increase are that, with the manual system, use would increase to 100,000 in the 9th year whereas, with automated circulation, it would increase to 100,000 in the 4th year. Rather than assume that circulation would increase gradually, to simplify our analysis we have assumed that circulation would go from one level to the next in those years.

The library under investigation currently handles its circulation function manually, and we will only be interested in the annual operating costs of the manual system. We ignore historical fixed costs because they remain the same, regardless of our decision. In terms of opportunity cost, such costs do not reflect current opportunities. Previous fixed expenditures on the manual system of circulating library materials do not represent an alternative that we can avoid in the future by present decisions. Only the extra costs incurred should be included. (A different example will make this important concept easier to grasp.)

Assume you are in the process of determining whether or not to use a currently owned van or a commercial courier to ship materials. What cost should be included if you choose the library's van? Since the original price of the truck remains the same, regardless of your decision, the only costs to be considered include gas, insurance, added labor, and general depreciation.

On the other hand, when we set up a new circulation system, we will be required to examine development and installation costs, as well as costs arising from changes in circulation procedures. To analyze costs to both the user and the library accuately, one should disaggregate the activities in the circulation function, including supervision and training, checking out, discharging materials, renewals, reserves, circulation inquiries, overdues, fines, snags, interlibrary loans, and other basic circulation activities. In other words, our investigation should concentrate on the ways in which the automated system changes the operations of the library and the behavior of users.

Costs to the library will be for labor, equipment, and materials. Aside from installation and development costs of the automated system, circulation costs will either be fixed or related to the volume of circulation. Cost to the user will be expressed in terms of user effort. Rather than list costs for each activity at different levels of circulation analysis, we will simply list the total cost of the two systems over time, assuming different levels of circulation as in Table 22.

Observe that the cost of the automated system fluctuates over time. The reason for this is the initial cost of installation and training and because we assume that, at some point, major parts of the system will have to be replaced. Other possible reasons for changes in costs include improved computer tech-

Table 22
ALTERNATIVE CIRCULATION COSTS
(in thousands of dollars)

Manual System

Circulation Level	Y1	Y2	Y3	Y4	Y5	Y6	Y7	Y8	Y9	Y10
50,000	10	15	20	30	40	50	65	75	90	100
100,000	35	40	45	65	75	85	95	105	120	130

Automated System

	Y1	Y2	Y3	Y4	Y5	Y6	Y7	Y8	Y9	Y10
50,000	40	25	25	30	40	70	55	60	75	80
100,000	75	55	50	85	60	65	70	75	100	95

nology, which affects the productivity of the automated circulation system (the level and mix of staff needed to circulate materials), and changes in prices. For instance, a component of the computer may wear out, and when the library replaces this part, it finds that the new part costs more—but that it also increases the efficiency with which materials can be circulated. The net result may be an increased net benefit from that point onward.

Now let us turn to an examination of the benefits of the automated circulation system. Benefits can be expressed in terms of increased productivity (staff, patron, materials): in time saved, increased use, and reduced loss rate. Potential intangible benefits of the automated system include improved customer relations, increased use of all library services, improved information for planning, and greater responsiveness to changes in demand. For the purposes of this example, we have assumed that the tangible and intangible benefits of the automated circulation system result in increased use of the library. We base this prediction on the belief that the automated system will save consumers time and enhance the productivity of both the staff and the collection. That is, the library staff will be able to reduce circulation control effort per unit of output and, consequently, increase efforts (and perhaps productivity) devoted to information service, which we assume leads to increased use.

Having indicated that the net benefit of the automated system is 50,000 in circulation from year 4 to year 10, we must now attempt to value these uses in terms of dollars. For the sake of simplicity, we will assume that all uses will be valued equally. Since libraries do not charge fees for services, some proxy method must be found to measure benefits, and we have chosen to express benefits in terms of increased circulation. Thus, we must devise a technique for valuing 1 circulation. Newhouse and Alexander suggest that use of library materials provides the user and the non-user with some fraction of the value of ownership;[7] and value of use is directly related to the purchase price. The discount rate adjusts this value for time—that is, it accounts for the time-value of future use.

228   Applications and Extension of Theory

Table 23

NET GAIN IN USER EFFORT

(in thousands of dollars)

	Y1	Y2	Y3	Y4	Y5	Y6	Y7	Y8	Y9	Y10
User	−5	5	10	15	10	20	20	25	−5	10

An alternative way of measuring benefits would be to examine the time saved by users with an automated circulation system. Table 23 summarizes anticipated savings, based on hypothetical wage rates.

Our next step is to subtract these benefits from the yearly costs of automating circulation routines in the respective years. We have assumed that the library would install the automated system in year 1, so that, by year 4, circulation would be 100,000. In the fourth year, the library upgrades the system, so that it will be capable of handling the additional circulation-related activity. Our new stream of costs is depicted in Table 24.

In effect, we have compared the library and user costs of both systems. Using an 8 percent discount rate, we compute the net benefits in terms of reduced costs by taking the sum of the costs of a project in each year, divided by the discount factor $(1 + d)^t$. We assume that t is zero in the first year, implying that all costs occur at the beginning of the year:

Pv manual = (10/1) + (15/1.0800) + (20/1.1664)

+ (65/1.2597) + (75/1.3604) + (85/1.4693)

+ (95/1.5868) + (105/1.7138) + (120/1.8509)

+ (130/1.999)

= $456,613.00   Eq. 10.5

Similarly, we can show that the present-value cost of the automated circulation system is $372,362, for a net benefit of $456,613 − $373,960 = $82,653.

As with the security system example, the effectiveness of a particular circulation system depends on our assumptions. For example, we could have assumed that, over 10 years, circulation would have been different in each

Table 24

ALTERNATIVE CIRCULATION COSTS

(in thousands of dollars)

	Y1	Y2	Y3	Y4	Y5	Y6	Y7	Y8	Y9	Y10
Manual	10	15	20	65	75	85	95	105	120	130
Automated	45	20	15	70	70	45	50	50	105	85

year and different for each system. Then we could have analyzed the costs of either system at specified levels of circulation. In this instance, we would have used a breakeven chart to discover the circulation level at which one system becomes cost effective. With all of these approaches, one must be sure to include some measure of user benefits.

Finally, the analyst should compare the benefits and costs of changes in circulation procedures with alternative methods of meeting the library's objectives. Increased acquisitions, more open hours, better phone service, and additional outlets represent a few of these options. We select library service options on the basis of their net ability to contribute to the objective of the library. If we select use as our measure of contribution, we would add to each component of library input until the added cost of another dollar's worth of any input yielded an equal amount to use. If projects are lumpy, we would choose all feasible service options which maximized net benefit.

Multiple Objectives and Constraints

Up to this point, we have concentrated on the efficiency aspect of library service. Efficiency requires that an extra dollar allocated to a particular library function provide as many additional uses as an extra dollar allocated to some alternative service. Usually, however, library managers are confronted with multiple objectives. The library, like other public agencies, does not exist to pursue efficiency alone, nor simply to promote circulation.

Libraries have multiple objectives. They seek to promote and/or provide services which aid scholarship, intellectual freedom, a sense of cultural identity, formal and informal education, reference services, evaluation services, and a host of other information activities. These services are provided in varying degrees, depending on the community. Moreover, some attempt is made to provide these services within the context of other social goals: income redistribution and equal access to information.

When these goals—efficiency, promotion of social advancement, and promotion of citizenship—are in conflict, the problem of evaluating library policy is more complex. The degree of difficulty stems from the fact that the same mix of library activities does not usually maximize all objectives. From a practical standpoint, when goals are in conflict, the library must make explicit tradeoffs. In terms of efficiency, this implies that lower levels of output may be necessary in order to provide service to persons who require special programs.

To make rational judgments about tradeoffs between objectives, we require a common unit to measure output. However, because library goals are broader in scope than efficiency, because there is no service or price counterpart in the private sector, and because of the public nature of the service, library output is more difficult to translate into a common metric. One method of dealing

230   Applications and Extension of Theory

with this problem is to apply ethical or social weights to the various outputs of the library. For example, we could give greater weight to use of the library by low-income patrons or school-age children than use by middle-income patrons. In effect, we are attempting to take into account the distributional consequences of alternative service options.

Another approach that is used to assist us in resolving the dilemma of conflicting goals relies on choosing one primary objective, one decision criterion, and treating all other objectives as project constraints. For example, you might be in the process of selecting a new 16mm film projector, with costs expressed in dollars. The projector will contribute to the media program through increased use, quality of picture, ease of use, and lower levels of maintenance. Perhaps ease of use, a criterion, turns out to be the primary objective. In this case, all of the other measures of value would serve as constraints. Hence, any projector which maximized ease of use, but didn't meet a given level of picture quality, would be rejected. A final decision may involve an evaluation of tradeoffs between some of the constraints.

Similar tradeoffs can be established and evaluated for number and types of uses, such as exposure to documents, displays or ideas, circulation, attendance, visits, questions, and type of user. In the final analysis, to evaluate such choices requires that the library manager define objectives, maximize the effectiveness of library resources, and have some understanding of the role tradeoffs play in resource allocation.

Application: Library Location

Let us assume that a library system views additional facilities as one way of increasing library use. Furthermore, we will assume that the director has chosen three potential sites, all located within an area where the library wishes to expand services. With a fixed budget, site selection will be based on a variety of decisions. The criteria that are chosen reflect the library management team's assessment of how much a site will contribute to the new library's information service potential. We will use a simple scoring device to evaluate the different locations. Each criterion will be ranked on a scale of 1 to 4, with 4 indicating the highest potential for that criterion.

From experience, the library management team knows that the following criteria affect the success of a library facility: proximity to certain types of commercial sectors, median age, median income, number of housing units, population, proximity to schools, proximity to other libraries, the projected use rate after 15 years, and the benefit-cost ratio. Each of these criteria has been given a rank which indicates its relative impact on projected benefits. (See Table 25.)

In Table 26, the numbers next to the criteria (in parentheses) are the weights attached to each criterion. To evaluate each site, we take the sum of the weighted

Table 25
LIBRARY LOCATION BENEFITS

Proximity to Commercial Sectors
- No business center — 1
- Arterial street with businesses — 2
- Large shopping center — 3
- Community business center — 4

Median Age
- 45 or more — 1
- 35–40 — 2
- 25–35 — 3
- 10–25 — 4

Median Income
- $40,000 and above — 1
- 4,000–10,000 — 2
- 15,000–20,000 — 3
- 25,000–30,000 — 4

Number of Housing Units (within 5-mile radius)
- 1,500–3,000 — 1
- 3,001–4,500 — 2
- 4,501–6,000 — 3
- 6,001 or more — 4

Population
- 3,000–5,000 — 1
- 5,001–10,000 — 2
- 10,001–15,000 — 3
- 15,000–50,000 — 4

Projected Use Rate (per month) after 15 Years
- 65,000–75,000 — 1
- 75,001–85,000 — 2
- 85,000–100,000 — 3
- 100,000 and above — 4

Number of Libraries (within 5-mile radius)
- 1 — 4
- 2 — 3
- 3 — 2
- 4 — 1

Number of Schools (within 5-mile radius)
- 1 — 1
- 2 — 2
- 3 — 3
- 4 — 4

232 Applications and Extension of Theory

Table 26
BENEFIT EVALUATION FOR LIBRARY LOCATION

Criteria	Weights	Rank			
		Site A	Site B	Site C	Site D
Commercial	(25)	4	3	3	1
Age	(20)	3	2	4	2
Income	(15)	3	3	4	3
Housing	(10)	4	2	3	2
Population	(20)	3	3	3	3
Schools	(30)	4	3	4	3
Libraries	(10)	3	2	2	2
Use Rate	(15)	3	3	4	3
B/C	(10)	1	1	2	1
Total Score = Σ(Rank)(Weight)		510	405	525	355

rank-scores for a given site. For example, to evaluate site A, we take (4)(25) + (3)(20) + (3)(15) + (4)(10) + (4)(30) + (3)(10) + (3)(15) + (1)(10) = 510. The total score for each site would be evaluated in light of any additional constraints on the project.

To maximize community benefit with a fixed budget, assume that all of the sites have the same construction costs and long-run facility cost—personnel, materials, maintenance, and utilities: Then, regardless of how we value use, the site with the highest use would have the largest benefit-cost ratio. Note that our weights indicate that the team places greater emphasis on certain types of uses. For example, proximity to schools ensures a high educational use (for school projects and literacy), and we feel that this type of use has greater value than other types. Finally, a word about use rate. We have assumed that it is affected by the other factors we have listed. It is possible to set the distributional weights in such a manner as to offset the value of projected use rates. However, this implies a different primary objective.

Let us assume that the constraints on this project are zoning: the site must be legal for the branch size we have in mind, population growth must be above 3 percent, number of persons per household must be 2.5, and there must be a minimum number of low-income/elderly in the vicinity—5 percent of the population. For simplicity, we assume that each site meets the constraints. However, site C has a lower number of persons per household and a lower population growth rate than site A. Now it is up to the management team to decide how important these differences are in the site-location decision.

Tradeoff analysis can aid us in making decisions between alternative sites which do not meet constraints. We could evaluate the extent to which the overall "profitability" of a site offsets a constraint violation. In addition, we can examine the impact of altering the budget on final site selection, comparing monetary costs with investment potential.

The primary objective of this type of analysis is to illustrate the steps or phases one might go through in evaluating locations. To this end, we set down, in a logical framework, library objectives—that is, the critera which will be used to evaluate the project and any constraints. The purpose of such a framework is to assist managers in selecting projects which are consistent with library objectives.

Alternatives to Library Facility Expansion

As with our two other examples, the analyst should compare the benefits and costs of facility expansion with alternative approaches meeting library objectives. Both rural and urban libraries have several options in providing library service, besides buildings. If the goal were simply to maximize use, some libraries would find that closing a facility and allocating the monies to other services would yield a net increase. However, we might get a different set of users. Moreover, we are adding benefits to one set of users while imposing costs on another set of users. Although there is no rational technique for resolving this dilemma, alternative service options should be evaluated.

Rural libraries can provide service by bookmobiles, mail, on-line access to catalogs, on-line reference service, a toll-free number, an electronic bulletin board, and so on. To assess benefits, one would use the techniques we have suggested: time value, such as travel; value of items used, expressed as a percentage of market value and option value; willingness to pay; and the value of substitutes for library service, expressed as money spent by users to make up for the inconvenience of having service curtailed. The library could provide computer terminals to all potential users, or place a terminal with a staff member in a central location. Thus, a traditional library outlet could be closed and service in the particular district might actually be expanded. In an urban library setting, the closing of a branch becomes more complex. The number and concentration of users suggest that alternative delivery systems might not be cost effective or equitable. Nonetheless, depending on how use is measured, an urban library might find that an existing branch does not meet the objectives of the library or the wants of the community—so that, as with the rural library, the manager must examine alternatives to the current service mix.

Summary

Cost-benefit analysis and its variants provide a systematic method for analyzing choice among alternatives. To implement such a study, one must relate costs and benefits to organizational goals. Once the objectives have been defined, the analyst should list alternative techniques for meeting them. Next, project impacts will be examined. Finally, we must relate cost to effectiveness criteria.

Although the basic steps are relatively simple, the application of cost-benefit analysis is complex because of the difficulties of measuring costs and benefits. However, the cost-benefit approach takes us through a series of steps which allow us to use an analytical technique that is founded on the economic theory with which we investigated library consumption and production. Thus, its major contribution is creation of a framework or system for weighing the tradeoffs in information service expenditures.

Exercises

1. In terms of present value, describe how you might measure (a) the benefits and costs of a library item over time and (b) the costs and benefits of a person's use of a library.
2. Describe how you would estimate the benefits of library use in terms of travel time.
3. A library wants to compare the costs and benefits of mail order and bookmobile services. Assume that the costs of the two services have been ascertained. Suggest several ways for estimating the benefits of these services in terms of time and money saved by users.
4. Discuss how the use of standards ignores several key economic concepts employed in the cost-benefit approach.

References

1. John H. Wilson, Jr., "Costs, Budgeting and Economics of Information Processing," in *Information Science and Technology Annual Review,* vol. 7, ed. Carlos Cuadra and Anne Luke (Washington, D.C.: American Society for Information, 1972), p. 55.
2. Rosemary R. Du Mont and Paul F. Du Mont, "Measuring Library Effectiveness: A Review and an Assessment," in *Advances in Librarianship,* vol. 9, ed. Michael Harris (New York: Academic Press, 1979), p. 125.
3. Joseph P. Newhouse and Arthur J. Alexander, *An Economic Analysis of Public Library Services.* (Lexington, Mass.: Lexington Books, 1972); James Michalko and Toby Heditman, "Evaluating the Effectiveness of an Electronic Security System," *College and Research Libraries* 39:4 (July 1978): 263–267; and Michael Bommer and Bernard Ford, "A Cost-Benefit Analysis for Determining the Value of an Electronic Security System," *College and Research Libraries* 35 (July 1974): 270–279.
4. Bommer and Ford, "A Cost–Benefit Analysis," pp. 270–276.
5. Ibid., p. 275.
6. Ibid., p. 276.
7. Newhouse and Alexander, *An Economic Analysis,* pp. 9–10.

Suggested Reading

Braunstein, Yale M. "Cost and Benefits of Library Information: The User Point of View." In *Key Papers in the Economics of Information.* Ed. Donald W. King, Nancy A. Roderer, and Harold A. Olsen. White Plains, N.Y.: Knowledge Industry Publications, 1983. Pp. 348–356.

The Economics of Information. Ed. Jana Varlejs. Jefferson, N.C.: McFarland, 1982.

Getz, Malcolm. *Public Libraries: An Economic View.* Baltimore: Johns Hopkins Univ. Press, 1980.

Goddard, Haynes C. "A Study in the Theory and Measurement of Benefits and Costs of the Public Library." Ph.D. dissertation, Indiana University, 1970.

Griffiths, Jose-Marie. "The Value of Information and Related Systems, Products, and Services." In *Annual Review of Information Science and Technology,* vol. 17. Ed. Martha E. Williams. White Plains, N.Y.: Knowledge Industry Publications, 1982. Pp. 269–284.

Hu, Teh-wei, Bernard H. Booms, and Lynne Warfield Kaltreider. *A Benefit Cost Analysis of Alternative Library Systems.* Westport, Conn.: Greenwood Press, 1975.

McKean, Roland N. "The Nature of Cost-Benefit Analysis." In *Microeconomics: Selected Readings,* 4th ed. Ed. Edwin Mansfield. New York: Norton, 1982. Pp. 467–476.

Musgrave, Richard A., and Peggy B. Musgrave. *Public Finance in Theory and Practice.* New York: McGraw-Hill, 1980.

Prest, A. R., and Ralph Turvey. "Applications of Cost-Benefit Analysis." In *Microeconomics: Selected Readings,* 4th ed. Ed. Edwin Mansfield. New York: Norton, 1982. Pp. 477–495.

Raffel, Jeffrey A., and Robert Shisko. *Systematic Analysis of University Libraries: An Application of Cost-Benefit Analysis to the M.I.T. Libraries.* Cambridge, Mass.: M.I.T. Press, 1969.

11

PUBLIC LIBRARIES: COMMUNITY FINANCE

Classical economic theory details the conditions under which markets will efficiently allocate resources. On the supply side, firms employ resources in a manner consistent with the assumption of profit maximization. But how should libraries allocate resources? We suggested that library managers will utilize resources so as to maximize use, but are there particular uses which maximize social benefit? In the first portion of this chapter, we will review the economic rationale for public funding of libraries. The second part will discuss pricing and how it can be used to achieve library objectives.

Public finance theory describes the reasons why a society, through the auspices of its government, chooses to provide certain goods and services. The theory of government economy is both normative and positive, in that it not only details how the public sector functions but also develops the principles of *how* it should function. Traditionally, the primary mission of the public sector has been to correct sources of market failure. During the course of this chapter we will outline the major sources of market imperfections. In terms of public finance theory, we will be analyzing the contribution of libraries to the well-being of the society. Indirectly, we will be able to suggest the primary objectives of the library.

Having reviewed the economics of public finance, we shall examine the rationale for using fees to finance library services. Pricing theory will be discussed in the context of marketing library services. Marketing, the process of identifying and satisfying the wants and values of consumers, is concerned with the development, pricing, distribution, and promotion of goods, services, and ideas. When pricing goods and services, many sellers have traditionally focused on costs and the availability of resources, while neglecting the role pricing can play in building use. In contrast, the marketing approach to pricing places greater emphasis on the role of demand or the price-quantity relationship. In this chapter, we will define price, review basic pricing principles, and relate them to library policy.

Most libraries do not sell their products in dollar-denominated markets; instead, price is expressed in terms of time. Time prices are established through the intersection of supply and demand. They are affected by library policy, consumer preferences, the availability of substitutes, wages, and the ability of consumers to use the service. Because wage rates and ability vary, each individual faces a different price. Thus, even though libraries do not sell their services, consumption of these services is not without cost.

From the consumer's perspective, product design, place or channel of distribution, and the process of communicating details of library services affect the price of using a library's offerings. In other words, the price of library services takes into account how much effort the user must expend to hear about the services, to make decisions about the utility of a specific offering, and the length of time it takes to use the service. An additional factor that may affect price is the level of consumer effort spent establishing the price: price search.

Since the amount of time required to consume library services varies from one client to the next, the library administrator is in a position to affect the types of uses and users of a given service. Several key marketing concepts and the microeconomic model of consumer behavior will be used to investigate the pricing of library services. A basic understanding of how pricing affects library use will assist the library manager in establishing policies which are consistent with objectives.

Efficiency and Market Allocation

Economists employ the perfectly competitive model both for predictive purposes and to illustrate how firms and consumers in markets promote optimal resource allocation, thereby maximizing the welfare of society. The ability of the market automatically to attain efficiency in allocating goods and services rests upon certain conditions. Consumers maximize utility when the marginal benefit of the last dollar spent on any good is equal to that of alternative uses. Alternatively, utility is maximized when the marginal benefit is equal for all goods, and the marginal benefit of the last good purchased is equal to its price. On the supply side, producers will attain the highest value from their resources when the marginal revenue of the last unit sold is equal to its marginal cost in production. Thus, in a competitive market we found that the price which "clears" the market is equal to marginal cost and marginal benefit. What the consumer pays for a good is equal to the social cost of satisfying that particular want. Under these conditions, markets will automatically clear and promote maximum welfare for society.

In reality, to a lesser or greater degree, these conditions rarely prevail. Markets are subject to a variety of imperfections: production which is subject to decreasing costs may lead to natural monopolies; consumers and producers don't have perfect information; and the costs and benefits of economic activity are not always private. When the market fails to provide the community with maximum welfare, the government may intervene to provide corrective action in the form of legal regulation or provision of some goods and services. With the aim of investigating the contribution of the library to public welfare, the next few sections will define the major sources of market failure that tend to justify government action.

Externalities

The competitive microeconomic model assumes that producers and consumers incur all costs and receive all benefits directly associated with a particular economic endeavor. We also assumed that consumption of goods depends upon whether or not a person pays the market price. That is, those who pay for goods can consume them, and those who do not pay are excluded from consumption. In this sense, consumption of a private good is considered to be "rival." For a given level of production, consumption of goods such as food, automobiles, and clothes by one person reduces the quantity available for consumption by others. Consumption is "rival" because the market system must ration goods among competing users. In effect, each party of an exchange acquires all the values specified in a contract; but occasionally, third parties bear some uncompensated cost or enjoy an economic benefit for which they did not have to pay. For example, when a factory creates pollution, costs are imposed on people not directly involved in the activity. When a person gets immunized against communicable diseases, both the community and the individual receive benefits. The shared or *external* benefit is the equivalent of a reduction in potential for the spread of disease. However, because the benefit (or cost) is external, it is unlikely that it will influence consumption or production decisions. When making production decisions, the factory owner will not take into account costs associated with pollution; consequently, too much pollution and goods will be produced. On the other hand, from a social point of view, not receiving compensation for external benefits is likely to lead to underconsumption. These unintended costs and benefits of economic activity are termed *externalities*. In cases where the private and the external costs and benefits are equal, we have what is termed a *public good*. From an efficiency and equity point of view, when there is this divergence between the private and social cost-benefit equation, there will be either too much or too little economic activity.

Let us take a moment to examine externalities in terms of economic efficiency. In Figure 68, which depicts three different demand curves for library

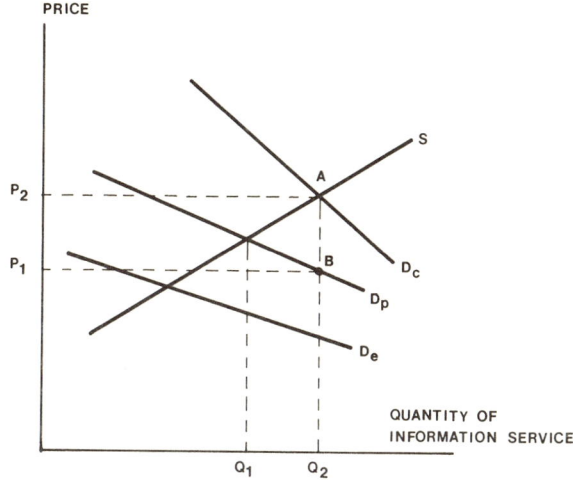

FIG. 68. Optimal Level of Information Service Output

service, Dp reflects the private evaluation of library benefits. The person who comes to the library and learns how to read, to write a résumé, to prevent crime, to prevent illness, etc., receives a private benefit. Such persons have increased their likelihood of getting a job and reduced the chance of becoming a victim of crime. However, in the process of consuming library services they have also conferred benefits on other members of the community. They have reduced the need for unemployment assistance, and they may prevent a crime involving other members of the community. Demand curve De reflects the vertical summation of the community resident's evaluations of these benefits. This follows because all consumers simultaneously receive benefits. Each person is assumed to offer a price equal to his or her marginal evaluation of the external benefit. Yet, unlike rival goods, all parties consume an equal amount and contribute to the cost of this shared consumption. In effect, the price available to cover the cost of library service equals the sum paid by each member of the community.

It is unrealistic to assume that we will be able to determine the preferences of each member of the community. Since people cannot be excluded from enjoying the benefits, they will not be inclined to reveal their willingness to pay (or, knowing they will have to pay, will purposefully underestimate value). Hence, society must devise a way for estimating the size of these benefits (or cost) and method of payment. For the moment, we will simply assume that consumers have revealed their preferences. Demand curve Dc illustrates the combined private and external benefits. Again, because the benefits and costs

240   Applications and Extension of Theory

are shared, the combined benefit is derived by vertically summing the two demand curves.

Private markets respond to demand curve Dp, and equilibrium output occurs at Q1. But from an efficiency point of view, not enough library service is being consumed. Consumers base their choice of how much library service to consume on their private costs and benefits. But if the society at large is also enjoying consumption benefits (De in Figure 68), the most efficient level of consumption should be higher than Q1. For consumption to occur at a higher level, society must find a method of lowering consumption costs. Since all members of the community are sharing in consumption benefits, the entire community should share the financial burden of consumption.

Given the demand-and-supply schedules in Figure 68, optimal output occurs at Q2. At this point, external social benefits have been internalized. For output to be expanded to the optimal level, society must devise a method of covering the cost differential between Dc and Dp: AB. This subsidy makes Dc the effective demand curve, and output is expanded to Q2. Consumers pay an effective price of P1, with the subsidy making up the difference. The size of the subsidy depends upon the extent to which a service exhibits external benefits. As we move from the pure private good to the pure social good, the size of the subsidy increases. The form of government intervention may not be a monetary subsidy to consumers, because production of external benefits may be directly subsidized. In both cases, however, society bears the cost of increased economic activity.

Externalities associated with information may also be analyzed from the supply side. Information firms, directly or indirectly, may be responsible for the introduction of a scientific discovery, the benefits of which have wide application. If the owners cannot receive full compensation for the social benefits, they will underproduce. In essence, once the discovery has been announced, it can be used by others without diminishing the amount of knowledge available to other producers. This follows because information is nondepletable. In most cases, information producers cannot go into the full range of activities in which knowledge has use. Since it is likely that the social benefits of knowledge will be greater than the private benefits, the market mechanism will not allocate the socially optimal amount of inputs to information/knowledge production.

To summarize, economic theory indicates that when there is a divergence between private and social costs and benefits, society must find mechanisms that create an incentive to production and/or consumption. Public finance theory suggests that information services in the public sector should place emphasis on products which generate significant externalities.

Library Service and Externalities

Library services which are linked with formal and informal education generate externalities. Both society and the individual benefit from the education process. Society reaps the benefits of having knowledge and skills disseminated to all of the members of the community. Skills which are taught in primary education are considered to be critical to the workings of an "advanced society"—reading, writing, and arithmetic. These and other subjects contribute to the ability of the members of the community to participate in the economic and political systems, thereby ensuring an orderly society.

Establishing a link between libraries and the external benefits of education would appear to be a simple task, but because we have no method for measuring the size of their contribution to the functioning of a democratic society (public benefit) in relation to increased wages (private benefits), the question of how to fund the service link is quite complex. Economic theory suggests that where the benefits are primarily private, exchanges should occur within the private sector; when the benefits are public in nature, a subsidy is required to induce an optimal rate of production and consumption. To the extent that we can establish a link between library service and positive external benefits, the case for relatively large public subsidies is strong.

Some economic researchers[1] have attempted to draw conclusions about library user attributes, library use, and the appropriate mix of library services and implicit public-private funding:

> Service to children encourages them to become more literate and to develop a greater appreciation of books and the printed word. Public-library services to students are an extension of their formal education. Making library services available at zero cost to these users encourages their use of the library and could be justified in the same way that free public education to children is justified.... When we turn our attention to adult users of the public library, the case becomes less strong.... Most public library use by adults is not wholly or even primarily frivolous, but it would be hard to argue that most adult use of the public library brings anything close to the external benefits to society conveyed by children's and students' use."[2]

Yet, the attempt to predict the level and composition of external benefits on the basis of user attributes has not been clearly established.[3] Without a method for determining the relationship between user, type of use, and the relative size of expected external benefits, economists are unable to determine the appropriate level of subsidization. Perhaps there is a link between adult use and children's use of the library which necessitates the joint provision of a variety of services for adults and children. Furthermore, the assumption that there are diminishing returns to the level of externality, generated with increases in age, ignores the cost to society of unemployment and forgone productivity.

A further investigation of the nature of library services will highlight their dual nature. Direct user assistance and physical access yield considerable private benefit. In the short run, aside from any direct benefit received, when a person is using a catalog, a particular item, or requests staff assistance, he or she diminishes the value of library service by causing others to incur waiting costs. In contrast, information, its collection and development, storage, and organization are nonrival in nature.[4] Once used, these services can be reused by others, and excluding consumption would be inefficient.

Information services which convey external benefits require public subsidy. However, our inability to measure the relative magnitudes of private and public benefits makes it difficult to determine the extent to which public subsidies are required. But even the user-assistance aspect of library service may be associated with benefits which are public in nature. Yet, because information, once produced, can be shared equally by all, regardless of whether or not they have paid for it, the user-assistance aspect of library service can be considered to be public in nature. Consequently, excluding people from using the service is inefficient. In this case, the market will fail to provide the service in an amount sufficient to maximize social welfare. Unlike public goods, however, where the private and social effects are equal, these goods convey private and social effects unequally. Because of the diffuse nature of library benefits, and because the size of externality depends more on the use to which the information will be put than on the service, our ability to distinquish between private and external library transactions is quite limited. Nonetheless, economic theory indicates that the primary role of the library is to supply services which convey significant externalities.

Decreasing Average Costs

To stay in business, a private firm must recover at least the average cost it incurs in providing a good. In the long run, at prices less than average costs, the firm will shut down. When production exhibits decreasing average costs, marginal costs will be less than average costs. However economic theory dictates that maximum community benefit is achieved when marginal cost is equal to price. Thus, if a private firm charges a price that is higher than the marginal social cost of production, the community will underconsume. In other words, a firm, subject to decreasing average costs, would charge a price which leads the community to treat a good as relatively scarcer than it is, and thus a social inefficiency occurs.

Natural monopolies can occur when production is subject to decreasing average costs. For example, once the capital investment (such as a library building or a bridge) has been undertaken, the cost of generating an additional unit of output decreases as more people use the service. Decreasing average costs are often associated with large-scale production and natural monopolies. Monopolists tend to produce less and charge more than a large number of competitors. Hence, to prevent monopolies and to ensure maximum social benefit, a subsidy is required to bring price down to the marginal cost. Based on the natural monopoly thesis, the degree to which library services should be subsidized depends on the extent to which the market economy fails to provide the optimal level of information.

Theoretically, a case can be made for decreasing costs in information-production dissemination.[5] Once an article or book has been published, the cost of additional copies is much less than the cost of the first few copies. Similarly, once a book, journal, film, or database has been produced, it can be used by more than one person. Thus, after the library incurs the cost of purchasing, classifying, processing, and storing the item, the per use cost decreases as output increases, until the item has worn out or queuing forms. The marginal cost of reading (use) is less than the average cost.

Empirically, the question remains: whether library service production is characterized by decreasing average costs. Research into the production function of library services is flawed by a lack of adequate output measures and by the nature of the studies. One cannot determine the value derived from a unit of output if significant externalities exist. Circulation statistics do not capture the full nature of library production. They are not capable of generating information concerning the quality or social value of services rendered by the library. In-house use of library materials by patrons and staff promotes economic efficiency; materials are used more intensively than if they were checked out. For example, noncirculating newspapers are read by many people in one day. If in-house use and reference services had increased during test periods, economies of scale would have been understated to an even greater degree. Hence, to have a more reliable picture of library production, we must take note of the difference in the product mix in different-size libraries and the quality of library output measures.[6]

White considers the question of natural monopoly and the need for library service by asking if "the community would be at the mercy of a monopolist who would charge excessively high prices for library services?"[7] He feels that this is not a likely prospect. Bookstores provide an alternative to some of the library's services. In the absence of public libraries, other types of libraries, including academic libraries, would provide a similar service for a modest fee. Rental libraries flourished in the 1930s, and the number of private information companies is growing. While White is correct in indicating that the natural monopoly argument for public finance of libraries is weak, his comments do not negate the decreasing average-cost argument for public finance of library services. First, economic efficiency is promoted when information is shared. Bookstores and other private information channels do not take full advantage of the decreasing cost properties of information. Second, libraries are meant to complement these services, not supplant them. Hence, the government has not chosen to grant monopoly privileges to libraries.

The degree to which library services should be subsidized depends on the extent to which information production is subject to a decreasing cost of production. Neither the theoretical nor empirical evidence provides us with adequate proof of decreasing costs in library services. A more accurate picture of the relationship between costs and output will require additional research into the number and types of transactions completed at libraries.

Income Distribution

Government not only intervenes to correct market failures, but also functions to ensure an equitable distribution of society's income and wealth. Each community, expressing its values through the political system, decides on methods for redistributing wealth and, in addition, how much and to whom it will redistribute its income. Economic theory is useful for suggesting effective methods for achieving income redistribution, but not the objective itself. Redistribution of income is a normative value, decided upon in the political arena. Finally, economics assists in the evaluation of the distribution consequences of political actions.

Libraries redistribute wealth by promoting equal opportunity for economic and social advancement. Wealth in relation to library services is represented by the value of services received. By providing free access to services which increase the social and economic skills of users, the library effectively increases the income of users. But public library service is not free; the costs of the library are borne by taxpayers. Thus, the distribution of benefits flows from the taxpayer to the user. We will analyze who pays for and who benefits from library services, and the degree to which the library redistributes wealth in accordance with commonly accepted goals of the community. Our aim is to investigate the cost-and-benefit incidence of library service. To this end, we will attempt to determine the proportion of income a particular economic segment of society contributes toward the support of the library. And we will compare the fraction of income paid with the benefits gained from library use.

Taxes range from regressive to proportional to progressive. Regressive taxes burden the poor, whereas progressive taxes shift the cost to higher-income groups. Public services which are intended to promote social equity are typically financed on the ability-to-pay basis. The ability-to-pay principle requires people of greater wealth to pay a greater share of the financial burden. In essence, benefits should accrue in greater proportion to need than to ability to pay. Another taxation principle is founded on the benefits-received principle. Here, financial support is based on the value a person places on the benefits received. For normal goods, as income rises, consumer valuation increases. If we assume that, as dollars are added, the value of another dollar diminishes, then, as income rises, people will be willing to pay more.[8] The implication of this philosophy of taxation for library services is that libraries should redistribute income toward the lower end of the income scale.

Library-use surveys have primarily concerned themselves with adult usage. The Gallup organization's study of library use among persons aged 18 and older indicated that 40 percent had used the library at least once in the past 12 months and that 25 percent claimed to have used the library at least once in the past 3 months.[9] Among both groups of library users the demographic pattern is similar: young, high level of education, and "higher" job status. An earlier survey, completed for the National Advisory Commission on Libraries, generated data consistent with the Gallup study.[10] An added finding of this survey was that a disproportionate number of users were white and had higher incomes.

Very few data exist on the demographic characteristics of juveniles who utilize library services. Surveys of adult usage of libraries provide some information concerning library use by children. Alexander and Newhouse's study revealed that use of the Beverly Hills Library was disproportionately concentrated among students.[11] Mills estimated that 64 percent of library users in Newark, New Jersey, were students.[12] A study of the Chicago Public Library revealed that approximately 42 percent of the population between the ages of 5 and 14 had library cards; that 57.8 percent of persons between ages 15 and 19 had library cards.[13] In her poll of metropolitan library users, Mary Lee Bundy found that 47.3 percent were students.[14] Data in a survey completed for the National Commission on Libraries suggest that 33 percent of the adults were using the library on behalf of their children.[15] Goddard states that "as much as 75 percent of public library circulation is accounted for by school-age children."[16] Evidence provided by the Gallup Poll suggests that a higher percentage of persons with a low job status and lower education level send their children to the library than use the library themselves.[17] However, the majority of juvenile library users come from middle-class families.

Although the evidence is sketchy, on the basis of these and other studies of library use one finds that, in the past, library users came from middle-income families with a high level of education. Given a changing demographic structure, these studies may no longer lead to valid conclusions about library users.

Our picture of the net incidence of library services would be incomplete without a discussion of "who pays." Typically, libraries are financed through a combination of sales and property taxes. Businesses usually shift the sales tax forward to the consumer, rather than backward to employees, to suppliers, and, ultimately, to profits. Because low-income groups use a relatively larger proportion of their income for consumption, it is generally accepted that sales taxes are regressive. That is, savings as a percentage of income rise with increases in income. Sales taxes are proportionately related to the amount one consumes, but regressive to income.

The incidence of the real estate property tax is less clear. The degree of tax incidence cannot be determined directly; its derivation depends on the assumptions concerning the direction in which a particular tax is shifted. Empirical studies of the property tax have led most economists to the conclusion that property taxes are regressive. Most of these studies assume that single-family residences are underassessed to a greater extent than multifamily units, that higher-value dwellings are underassessed to a greater extent than lower-value dwellings, and that renters, rather than landlords bear the property tax.[18] Based on these assumptions Goddard,[19] Levy,[20] and Weaver and Weaver[21] conclude that library funding is regressive. More recently, some economic theorists are inclined to believe that the incidence of property taxes is proportional or progressive.[22] Aaron[23] and Netzer[24] argue that renters do not bear the entire burden of property taxes, and that the value of housing rises proportionally with income. The newer view of property tax incidence suggests that it is proportional (neutral) or slightly progressive.[25]

To arrive at the net incidence of library services, one must compare use patterns with payment. Since library use patterns show that very few consumers come from the lowest income categories, Weaver and Weaver conclude that "the public library is not simply neutral in regard to the disadvantaged whom it serves poorly; it is an integral part of the burden resting on those least able to afford it."[26] In this context, White notes that even though Weaver and Weaver assumed the most regressive pattern, their conclusions are "robust enough to withstand even . . . alternative tax-incidence assumptions. . . ."[27] An implicit assumption of these studies is that the value of an individual's use is the same, regardless of income. This assumption is based in part on the willingness-to-pay criterion of value. However, this criterion is not valid where externalities are present.

The question of who pays for and who receives the benefit of library services has implications for the way in which libraries should be financed in the future. If current tax and use patterns are not consistent with commonly accepted notions of equity, another form of finance might correct the situation. However, "since neither the distribution of those who finance the library nor the distribution of those who benefit from library services is very carefully observed, no firm conclusions about the [current] distributional consequences can be made."[28] Further, the distribution of use neither negates the public nature of information and library services nor proves an inequity in the fiscal system. "Nonusers may gain option value . . . . Nonusers may gain disproportionately from other government sources . . . [and] in-library use has not been observed . . . . Is in-library use greater among low-income groups?"[29] At best, the studies which indicate that the net incidence of library services is regressive indicate society might achieve its redistribution objective through more progressive tax funding of library services.

Since the current use pattern of library service is a function of the cost of use, lowering the cost of library consumption would alter the net tax incidence of library services. To this end, we will discuss the pros and cons of fees for service. Having reviewed the opposing views, we will examine current fee-setting practices and pricing theory. The last portion of this chapter will be devoted to techniques of time pricing information services.

Fees for Public Library Services
Background

The argument for public subsidization of library services rests upon the notion that information is a public good; that education conveys substantial positive externalities; that access to cultural records has option value; that literacy promotes social order and economic efficiency; and that an informed citizenry is a necessary ingredient of a democratic society. The degree to which libraries in theory and in reality meet these criteria forms the foundation of "free" public libraries.

On the other hand, public-finance theory provides an equally convincing argument for the introduction of fees for library service. The belief that library services provide significant externalities does not necessarily imply free information services provided by publicly funded libraries. The presence of externalities dictates that the government should take a role in the provision of some goods and services. Yet, public provision does not mean the absence of fees. Rather, it means that the amount to be paid by the user is less than would be paid in the private market. The result is that while a case can be made for public finance of library services, there are instances in which charging fees might promote economic efficiency and equity.

The question of whether or not libraries should charge fees for information services has been widely debated. On one side of the debate are those who suggest that providing information on a willingness-to-pay basis, rather than on a need basis, would have a negative affect on the distribution of information.[30] On the other side, it is argued that fees are required to supplement the funding base of libraries and that charges should be levied for those services which do not generate significant positive externalities.[31] Bearing these different philosophies in mind, we shall review the issues surrounding the pricing of library services.

The debate centers on the questions we raised in the preceding sections of this chapter: What level of "free" information should be provided? What types of information should the library supply? To whom shall they be provided? And what method of financing should be employed? As we indicated, these questions are not easily resolved. In part, the question of how fees will affect use can be best addressed by examining how the library currently prices its services. We will discuss current dollar pricing, but not its effect. Instead, we will restrict ourselves to a theoretical investigation of the impact of alternative pricing policies. But first, we will review arguments for and against monetary fees for library services.

Opposing Views

The use of fees for public-sector services is considered justifiable when benefits are primarily private, where the costs of collecting fees are small in relation to the revenues generated by fees, where demand is highly elastic, and when fees result in unacceptable inequities.[32] Direct user charges differ from taxes in that a voluntary exchange occurs between the user and the supplier; taxes are involuntary in nature. Prices provide the market with resource-allocation signals, and under perfect competition they encourage equity and efficiency. In addition, user charges would provide libraries with additional sources of income.

Fees for service assist library managers with resource allocation. The kinds and the level of information services would be determined on the basis of community preferences reflected in the marketplace. Currently, society allocates revenue to the library. However, the fact that libraries do not receive their revenue directly from users creates a potential imbalance between supplier and consumer. Since the library's funding base is not directly linked to the wants or demand of users, the library does not have to meet the wants of the users to receive financing. In effect, financial support does not automatically increase or decrease with changes in demand. The lack of a direct relationship between libraries and funding sources poses a potential divergence between consumer wants, the level of funding, and the types of services provided. Introducing fees would make libraries more responsive to the demands of the community and would generate sufficient revenue to meet those wants. Information products would be supplied on the same basis as other commodities: services which met the economic litmus test would be produced.

The information generated by user charges enables the manager to perform cost-benefit analysis; therefore, long-run planning becomes more effective. User fees serve to allocate or ration library services. Economic theory dictates that a good should be provided up to the point where the marginal benefit of an additional unit equals the marginal cost. When price is below marginal cost, a condition of excess demand will prevail. A rationing system, based on market forces, would allocate resources efficiently. Additionally, since fees limit consumption to those who value the service, financial support is contributed in direct proportion to use, thereby promoting equity. Currently, time rations library demand. However, time does not ration demand with respect to benefit received; fees do. Ultimately, the net benefit of user charges depends upon the pricing scheme employed by the library and the elasticity of demand. Although little is known about the elasticity of demand for information in general or for specific user groups, the level of demand is usually very sensitive to the initial introduction of user charges. Once charges have been instituted, demand becomes less sensitive to additional price changes.[33]

If libraries exhibit the essential characteristics of public goods—relative efficiency in joint consumption and relative inefficiency in exclusion—economic theory suggests that library services would be more efficiently provided without fees. While it is possible to exclude people from using a library, exclusion is inefficient because one person's partaking in the consumption does not limit the benefits available to others. Casper[34] and Cooper[35] have stated that only the information aspect of library service can be classified as a pure public good. The format and timing of the service limit the degree of public-good quality. Moreover, only information of an educational nature generates significant externalities. While libraries are not entirely responsible for the format in which information is produced, they do select the types of materials and services to produce. Selection, maintenance, and organization of the human record are activities which convey benefits to the community at large.[36] But the provision of user assistance and physical access generates both private and public benefit.[37] Given the nature of information (nondepletion), once an item or service is supplied it is inefficient to exclude.

From our earlier discussion of externalities, we know that although we can identify types of users and measure units of service, our ability to measure and predict the size of externalities associated with library use is limited. Within this context, a basic level of library service should be provided to all users free of charge. For services which are tailored to an individual user's need, which are rival in nature, and which generate substantial transaction costs, prices could be charged. For example, books and library catalogs and items which can be used more than once would be free of charge, whereas customized bibliographies, which cannot be shared, would not be free of charge. In this way, the public-good qualities of the library would be preserved while efficiency and equity in resource allocation are promoted.

The ability of the library to respond to the wants of its clientele is limited by its ability to generate adequate funds. By providing an additional source of income, user charges would allow publicly funded libraries to invest in new technologies and offer a higher level of service. If libraries choose not to levy fees for these services, they may have to reallocate resources and/or limit the range or level of services they can offer. Private firms would enter the market, and those unable to pay would be effectively barred from the benefits of consumption. Fees would enable the library to expand its revenue base, without limiting existing services or users.

With respect to the generation of income, the advantage of user fees is that financial contribution depends on the amount of service consumed; both efficiency and equity are promoted. On the other hand, user charges discriminate against consumers who lack the means to pay.[38] This desire of librarians to provide equal access to information resources is at the center of the opposition to fees. Horn states that "access to information is a fundamental right of a citizen in a democratic society" and "having fees levied which discriminate against those unable to pay creates barriers that negate that right."[39] But proponents of fees suggest that the issue of dicrimination isn't clear. The poor and the disadvantaged are not the primary users of library services. Time prices do not serve the poor well.[40] Since all taxpayers currently pay for library services, only those who use the service benefit. Promoters of the no-fee argument implicitly assume that fees must be levied for all services and all users. User charges can be discriminatory and subsidy systems can be organized.

Vouchers or library stamps could be used to subsidize those who could not afford the service.[41] In this way, consumers of library services will use them in relation to net value received. The potential for competitive conditions is optimal for effective voucher systems: variety of tastes; individuals are well informed as to market conditions (quality, location, and cost of goods); many competing suppliers; quality of goods and services is easily measured; and the product or service is relatively inexpensive and purchased frequently. Vouchers could provide market signals to library managers: they place the citizen in an active role; provide those citizens who would normally not use a service with an incentive to use it; supply a mechanism for distributing library services to rural areas; and bring forth services which are in demand. In order to attract clients, libraries would have to increase marketing activities, which would reduce information search and other transaction costs.

Yet, voucher schemes for library service might be difficult to administer. They might result in social costs which outweigh any benefits to be gained from fees. The problem with voucher schemes lies in the ability to provide free services to students and children while providing pay-as-you-go services to others. A dual system of fees for some uses and users is difficult to manage. Separation of services is costly, and students and children could use adult services on behalf of their parents. Further, who shall establish voucher amounts, and on what basis shall the amount be set?

Another argument against fees is based on the notion that they represent a form of double taxation.[42] Advocates of this argument neglect essential components of public finance theory. Fees are charged to cover the marginal costs of operation; taxes are levied to support the fixed costs of the library. Yet, two-part tariffs usually are levied in cases where the private benefits can be identified. We have already indicated that the benefits of library use are intangible and difficult to measure.

Other objections to the introduction of user charges are that they would restrict the flow of information and encourage a shift to revenue-generating services, neglecting nonrevenue services which are vital to users of free services.[43] Yet, of necessity, libraries now limit the demand for and the flow of information. Time rations service to those who are willing to wait; consumers with information skills pay a lower price for service. Limited budgets restrict the ability of the library to provide adequate services.

With respect to the effect of fees on the allocation of resources, one must ask how the library currently allocates services. Does it emphasize services for adults or the affluent? The lack of fees does not eliminate the need to allocate resources. Instituting fees would simply add another element to the management equation. Reviewing the debate over the use of fees to finance library services, we find that, theoretically, they should be instituted for those services which generate significant private benefits and where the marginal cost of use is relatively high. On the other hand, some mechanism must be found to subsidize the use of library services by low-income people, children, and students. The administration of charges and subsidies might result in social costs which outweigh the benefits of both the fees and the service.

Current Pricing Policies

Librarians may oppose fees, but in practice they charge for some services. Several surveys have identified library services which have been subject to fees: interlibrary loans, photocopies, typewriter and book rentals, meeting-room use, special materials, and nonresident library cards.[44] While libraries have charged for a wide array of services, most service charges tend to be quite small and the portion of total revenues derived from fees has been small.

Substantial vendor charges are associated with specialized and computer-based reference. On-line services differ from traditional services. They are relatively expensive; transaction charges are identifiable and require a rationing mechanism; and given the individualized nature of the product, economies of scale may not be achieved. Like telephones, typewriters, and writing supplies, on-line reference searching is a service which, if provided freely, would lead to unacceptable costs. On-line reference searching shifts the boundaries between self-help and information-specialist–generated services. Further, given the cost of these services, if the patron were allowed sole discretion over their use, costs would increase rapidly. Fees allow the library to "pass on" a portion of the costs of on-line services. Similar reasoning applies to charges for photocopies and other services where the marginal cost of providing these services is not controlled by the librarian. DeWath found that libraries are more likely to charge for on-demand services,[45] but in general they do not attempt to recover the full costs. The usual practice is to "pass on" the direct vendor charges (a similar practice is used for interlibrary loans). Thus, libraries currently provide a two-tier service—one for which the patron exchanges time income for library services and the other for which the user exchanges money income. Fees do not limit the patron from using the library; patrons are charged for services which are associated with private benefits and which generate substantial marginal costs.

Fees for on-line searching are designed for clients who want a service they either prefer not to perform or cannot perform as efficiently for themselves. If they want the service, they pay; if not, they do the work themselves. The purpose is to provide a wanted service that could not otherwise be furnished. Yet, the same rationale cannot be used for trade between libraries. Interlibrary loan charges are based on the fact that the beneficiaries of the service lie outside the funding base. The institution of interlibrary loan fees provides libraries with a mechanism for coping with the impact of bibliographic utilities on demand for interlibrary loan services. As with other special services, fees may be appropriate. These services are additional; they go beyond those mandated by the local taxing authorities. Nevertheless, fees for interlibrary loans impede the free flow of information and run counter to the library profession's philosophy of sharing.[46] As Gell states: "It is imperative that librarians clearly distinguish between those activities which are fundamental to the library identity and those services that derive from it."[47] Should we focus our efforts on fulfilling the primary mission of education and information transfer? Can libraries justify, to any individual borrower, the reasons why he or she must pay for the privilege of interlibrary loan while monies are allocated to recreational materials which people can borrow for free?

Librarians have generally priced services for which significant transaction costs are generated by individual user requests. Services which are priced appear to generate a relatively large private benefit, and do not exclude the consumer from other library services. Those that do charge provide a basic level of service for free, and only "pass on" the marginal cost of production. Other libraries simply do not provide the service; most of them impose librarian-time rationing limits on use.

Review of the Role of Prices

Many factors stimulate a consumer to purchase goods and services: age, income, lifestyle, season, occupation, and education—to name just a few. One may analyze a consumer's decision to purchase by a variety of human behavior models. The basic contribution of economics to the study of consumer behavior lies in demand analysis. It provides us with an understanding of how consumers act in the marketplace and gives us a starting point for analyzing the pricing of library services.

We have stated that the basic problem of society is the allocation of scarce resources among its constituents so as to maximize community welfare. When each resource is employed in the function which contributes most efficiently to society, the objective of maximum welfare will be achieved. In a market economy, the price system is the mechanism which moves the economy toward this objective. Prices, serving as signals, indicate how resources should be used. That is, prices determine *what* will be produced, *how* goods and services will be produced, and *for whom*.

Prices affect spending behavior; given tastes and income, they influence what the consumer will buy and how much of each product he or she can purchase.

The consumer is the economic agent who purchases information to attain some personal objective. To make choices, the consumer relies on signals to match wants with ability. As it concerns libraries, wages, education, and age play an important role in determining library services consumption.[48] As the level of education increases, the productivity of library time increases; time spent locating materials is lowered, and the material itself can be converted into higher income. A person with a low level of education might be more inclined to use staff assistance to locate materials than to use the catalog. At some point, though, as income rises, the time price of library services becomes high relative to purchasing alternatives.[49]

A person's wage rate will affect the time of day that he or she may prefer to use the library. Income levels may also affect the level of telephone reference service that will be demanded. Age, insofar as it affects wages and the ability of a person to convert library services into income, will affect library use. Finally, the way in which the fee is set will affect library use. Just as at a smorgasbord, where there may be a flat fee for unlimited service, the result may be "overuse"—or heartburn or information overload, whichever may be the case. On the other hand, fees may be directly linked to the amount of service used: the number of items and amount of time. In this instance, users are more likely to limit consumption; and more time will be devoted to the process of selection.

Changes in prices lead consumers to convert their resources to alternative uses. Thus, changing elements of library service which affect use-time also affect incomes and spending behavior. Ultimately, the price-quantity relationship will be decided in the marketplace. Initially, however, the library manager will decide the price component of this equation. Therefore, it is essential that the library administrator have a basic understanding of pricing theory. To achieve this objective, we will discuss the meaning of price and basic pricing techniques.

The Pricing Decision

Pricing of services is usually based on the objectives of the firm, intuition, past experience, and economic analysis.[50] Traditional economic theory assumes that the firm's pricing objective is to maximize profit. In a competitive market, this objective produces the marginal cost pricing practice. However, in general, a firm with a number of products will have pricing policies that are likely to vary from this principle, and they will often be in conflict. For example, whether intended or not, a price which encourages use in one service may implicitly limit use of another service. With an understanding of the consequences of different pricing practices, the library manager will be better able to balance the tradeoffs between conflicting or constraining objectives. In the next few sections, we will review general guidelines for pricing, and then we will examine pricing within the context of time.

Pricing Guidelines

Because library pricing is an essential factor in achieving service goals, this section will introduce factors that should be considered when library prices are set. To determine and evaluate pricing alternatives, an organization must have a basic understanding of its costs, its demand, its competition, and its basic objectives.

The objectives of the library play a major role in its pricing structure. Some libraries stress a high rate of circulation and others do not. High-circulation libraries allow a greater number of materials to circulate. Also, a library may establish target rates of return or use for its offerings. Since price affects use, this can be used as a factor in achieving a specific target rate of return.

A common pricing goal is to recover a portion of the production cost. Library utilities may choose to use this form of pricing: fixed costs may be paid by state or federal agencies, and operating costs by users. Many libraries which charge for interlibrary loans or on-line searching seek to cover variable costs, often absorbing most fixed costs. Other examples of partial cost-recovery pricing include fees for lost library cards, room fees, and fees for reserves. Although the pricing objective may be to recover costs, the pricing method need not be related to production costs. Several pricing approaches or methods, such as demand, competition, or target rate-of-return pricing, can be used to achieve this objective. Nonetheless, with cost recovery as the goal, an organization must determine its costs and what portion will be recovered.

Market penetration or maximum participation pricing is often used in conjunction with the introduction of a new service. Mail order services may be used as a maximum participation pricing mechanism in large service areas with few fixed distribution sites. The two primary advantages of this pricing method are that low prices encourage many consumers to enter the market, thereby lowering per unit production costs as output increases. For example, low introductory prices often allow retail firms to test the nature of demand and quickly train employees in the use of new products. Libraries can also use market penetration or incentive pricing to study demand, obtain information on costs, and establish future pricing policy. However, adopting a low price may limit the size of subsequent price increases; it may suggest a low-quality product, and a low price may stimulate such high use that other programs must be curtailed. Finally, as the product goes through its lifecycle of introduction, growth, maturity and decline, different pricing strategies may be called for.

Once a new product has become established, low prices might lead to excess demand; so, to limit the market, a disincentive program could be established.

Raising the fee would ration demand, in accordance with economic principles, and would provide information on the elasticity of demand. Yet use of a market- limiting price structure ignores the cost function and poses the possibility of being in conflict with commonly accepted notions of equity. In other words, how does increasing the price affect users with low incomes?

Market equity pricing seeks to price services according to the economic nature of the good—private, public, or merit. Public goods, by definition, should be funded through community taxes, with no user charges.[51] The benefits associated with merit goods accrue to the individual but are perceived to spill over to the community at large. Hence, the pricing of meritorious goods would be set so as to recover a portion of costs. For example, a group of libraries, contracting for interlibrary borrowing services, could base charges on the assessed value of property or some other index of community wealth. Communities with greater wealth would pay more per unit of service. On the other end of the scale are goods whose benefits flow directly to the individual. In this instance, financing the service through direct user charges appears to be equitable. To achieve this type of pricing, one would have to able to predict value on the basis of type of use and user. We have indicated that our ability to measure and predict value of externalities is quite limited. One method of solving this problem might be to have fees for particular services and to subsidize low-income users, children, and students (an ever-growing and hard-to-define group).

Several library pricing objectives have been proposed: cost recovery, market penetration, market equity, and market limitation. We have listed these objectives separately, but, in practice, a library with a diverse set of offerings and clientele may be pursuing multiple and often conflicting pricing objectives. In response to these problems, the library manager will have to examine the tradeoffs between pricing objectives. To understand these tradeoffs, one must also be aware of the alternative pricing methods. Typically, alternative pricing practices are grouped according to the elements of market structure: cost, demand, and competition.[52]

Introduction to Pricing by Market Structure

Successful pricing requires that we consider not only our objectives but also the many interacting factors which influence economic decisions. To understand demand implies having knowledge of the factors which influence consumption decisions. The economic model of consumer choice uses prices, income, and preferences to analyze choice. The role of price in the purchaser's decision process is dependent upon the ability to substitute; on whether or not the product is used as an input in the consumer's production function, and if so at what level. In essence, when we set a price we need to consider the factors which affect price elasticity. It is also necessary to know the underlying causes of changes in costs and how costs vary with changes in the levels of activity. First, an understanding of cost assists the information manager in determining whether or not a service can be supplied "profitably" at any price—that is, determining the opportunity costs. Thus, ignoring price-quantity relationships can lead the library to incur costs for which it has not planned.

Consideration of both supply and demand provides a clearer picture of the importance of evaluating elasticity and cost. For example, a library has the option of allowing or not allowing reserves for its materials. Now assume that a particular material has an elastic demand curve, so that permitting reserves results in a large increase in quantity demanded. On the other hand, suppose that the library's supply curve is relatively inelastic. In this instance, the cost of handling reserves may increase but quantity supplied will not increase. As it concerns opportunity cost, the library has given up more of other services than may be warranted. Perhaps thinking in terms of dollars will help make this point clearer. A library has the option of selling a service at various prices, $4, $4.50, and so on. Each price results in a given volume of sales and variable costs. Fixed cost are constant for the relevant range of production, but only one price will lead to the highest level of "profit." Hence, knowing how costs vary with quantity provides the library with a basis for choosing between pricing alternatives.

Knowing your competition implies understanding its behavior. For libraries, this may simply mean knowing the competition's offerings and prices. Information of this sort allows the library to analyze how its services compare with those of its competitors. The relationship between the library's price structure and its competitors will depend upon its objectives.

Another factor in pricing is knowing your market. Are new products being developed that the library wishes to include in its product line? At what stage of its development will the library adopt the product? For example, if the product is new, there may be large start-up or development costs. When price is set, these costs should be spread over the life of the product. As the product is adopted by more consumers, economies of scale may be achieved, leading to lower variable costs, and more competitors will have entered the market. The range of possible prices will be limited by the increase in competition. When a service is started late in the development cycle, the library will be able to examine historical cost and demand data when setting its price. Also, demand may have stabilized, making cost-volume and price-volume relationships easier to estimate. Yet, this advantage may result in lost market share.

Another question to consider is whether or not a given product is a complement or substitute for other products currently offered. If it complements another service, a relatively low price will encourage use of both products whereas, if it is a substitute, the low price will reduce consumption of the alternative service.

Pricing by Market Structure

COST-BASED PRICING Cost-oriented pricing has its origin in a production or cost orientation, with little or no emphasis on demand factors. It is important for all organizations to know the composition and behavior of its costs. Profit-making firms cannot stay in business long if revenues do not cover average cost. That is, costs serve as the bottom line; they indicate whether or not a product can be sold for a profit at any price. But costs do not indicate how consumers will react to a particular price.

The most common methods of cost-based pricing include markup, cost-plus, and target rate of return. When setting up an on-line search service, a library might measure its fixed and variable cost. Then, based on an estimate of demand, it could mark up each search by an amount equal to indirect or overhead cost, divided by an estimate of demand. Yet, when a flat fee is used, fixed costs are spread out disproportionately over searches. That is, each user will pay the same flat fee, regardless of how long he or she uses the service. One way to avoid this problem would be to add a percentage surcharge rather than a flat fee.[53] For example, suppose that two people use a database service, and that person A incurs a $10 time-charge and person B incurs a $20 time-charge. If a $2 flat-fee is charged to each search, person A will pay $12 and person B will pay $22. However, if a 10 percent surcharge is levied, person A will pay $11 and person B will pay $22. Hence, the percentage surcharge is more equitable than the flat fee pricing technique. Similarly, a percentage surcharge approach could be used to price information network services. An alternative method of covering fixed cost would be an annual fee based on use, plus a per use charge. Annual fees based on use and percentage surcharges are cost-based pricing methods which also consider demand.

Opportunity cost pricing reflects the use or income forgone by not following an alternative course of action. When setting loan and use policies for a particular product, a library would analyze the impact on other types of uses. A loan policy for one type of material that led to high transaction costs for the library might reduce the quality of other services.

Although cost-based pricing is popular, this method of pricing, by ignoring the buyers' response to price, does not consider the eventual affect of price on volume of use and, consequently, on revenues and costs. Another limitation of this pricing technique is the difficulty associated with allocating overhead costs to different products. A large proportion of information-center costs may go toward administration, which is difficult to apportion among a varied product line. Also, one must beware of the differences between current costs and historical costs. "Thus costs for decision making should be prospective rather than retrospective."[54]

Libraries offer a wide variety of services which may serve as complements or substitutes for others. Lowering the price of some items may increase demand for other products. Introduction by the library or its competitors of services which complement existing services can lead to increased use of the existing product line. But pricing with an emphasis on cost may lead the library to ignore these relationships. Nonetheless, it is important for the library to understand the behavior of production costs so that it can evaluate the effect of changes in its rate of production and its prices on costs. The two key elements of price that we have discussed are average and marginal costs of production. However, there are several disadvantages to using either of these costs to set prices for information services.

The problem with average-cost pricing is that the price may be too high from a social welfare point of view.[55] When the fixed costs of the service are very high, MC may be less than AC, and too little of the product will be consumed. From previous discussions of efficiency, we know that price should be equal to marginal cost. Thus, only when marginal cost is equal to average cost is total cost recovery consistent with the maximization of social benefit. In this instance, partial cost recovery becomes socially optimal; fixed costs are subsidized. One might find this type of pricing in library networks where the fixed cost, if funded by the state, and marginal cost pricing is used to cover variable cost. In situations where the marginal cost is zero, the service will be marketed at a zero price, with fixed costs covered by subsidies. Other pricing techniques which take into account the revenue and equity problems posed by high fixed-cost services are flat access charges, plus fees related to use. For example, a library might allow free browsing and in-house use, with a flat fee for limited borrowing privileges, and added charges for additional services. An alternative to cost-based pricing is based on demand.

DEMAND-BASED PRICING Demand-oriented pricing looks to the consumer as the basis for setting price. Price is set in relation to the price-quantity or price-value relationship. The former is expressed in terms of elasticity; the latter is concerned with structuring the price in accordance with the wants of the customer. Pricing according to the consumer's wants implies charging for (what the producer perceives) the utility the product provides, rather than the cost to the supplier.

A common form of demand-based pricing is price discrimination, where a product is sold at more than one price, depending on customer, time, place, or product version. For price discrimination to work, a firm must be able to segment the market by intensity of demand, there must be strict limits on the resale of the product by one market segment to another, a lack of competition, and the cost of administering the policy should not exceed added revenues. Utilities rely on this type of pricing by segmenting the market into commercial and residential users; academic libraries segment users into faculty, students, and off-campus users. Libraries could have discriminatory annual membership fees for individuals, families, businesses, students, low-income people, etc.

However, when it is used to recover all costs, price discrimination in publicly funded libraries raises questions of who will pay more or less than marginal cost. Typically, this is decided on the basis of price elasticity of demand. An example of product version pricing would be allowing reserves on only on certain types of materials. Another method of segmenting the market is to separate the intensity of demand by the timing of use, more commonly referred to as peak-load pricing.

PEAK-LOAD PRICING Peak-load pricing is a special form of discriminatory pricing. Many public utilities employ this type of pricing mechanism to cope with variable demand rates. For example, demand for information might be greater during evening than during daytime hours. Peak-load pricing may also vary by season. How might an information manager price a service with a variable demand rate? We will examine this question in the context of information databases, such as a cataloging network.

Peak-load pricing comes into play in information databases when, due to limits on the capacity of storage and communication facilities, the variability in demand affects response time. Regional library utilities, such as cataloging databases, may find that demand varies by time zone. If the information utility is based in the Midwest, demand would vary according to the time each part of the country starts and finishes its workday. One response to rationing demand would be to assign times of day to different libraries, or to could charge higher prices at peak-use time periods.

In Figure 69 we show two demand curves: Dp, peak demand; and Dop, off-peak demand. The marginal cost curve, MC, is drawn on the assumption that marginal operating cost is constant until the capacity of the utility is exceeded. At this point, the supply curve is totally inelastic; response time is infinite. To ration demand in this case, we have two prices and two different use rates, where P1 is the peak price, OA the peak use, Po the off- peak price, and OG the off-peak use.

Peak-load pricing is often employed to segment use by intensity of demand. Use is often restricted by rental fees, limits on the number of items used, and limits on the number of use-days. Once popularity has subsided, item restrictions are removed.

COMPETITION-BASED PRICING Competition-oriented pricing implies basing price decisions in relation to what other suppliers are charging. Price is not based on cost or demand. Going-rate, imitative, or competition-based pricing does not mean that all producers will charge the same price. One rationale for imitating one's competitors is that when costs are difficult to measure, the organization can rely on the collective wisdom of the industry. An example of competition-based pricing in libraries would be setting loan policy in relation to the policy employed by the majority of other libraries. However, setting

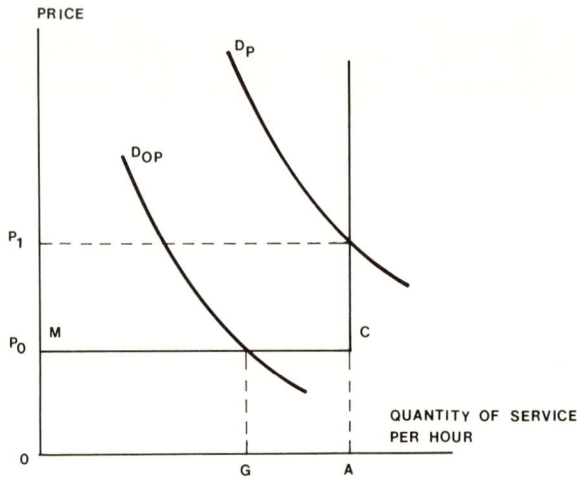

Fig. 69. Peak-Load Pricing

price in this manner overlooks elasticity of demand, the likelihood of competitive entry, and the nature of a library's product line.

Elements of Time-Priced Library Services

Prices serve as guideposts for making purchase decisions, and consumers use them to match their wants with limits on income. Likewise, firms use prices as a criterion in input allocation. Within the context of dollar-denominated exchanges, price is normally thought of as the amount of money one expends to acquire goods and services. Actually, price has several components: quantity of money, quantity and quality of the item in question. In terms of library service, these elements of price can be interpreted as quantity of time, materials, information, and quality of staff, materials, etc. From this perspective, we may ask, what are the elements of library service that affect the exchange process? All aspects of library service which affect the level of effort required of the user to hear about and use the service for the purpose of satisfying a want or need may be thought of as its price: open hours, location, skill level of staff, loan policy, reserve policy, and so on.

We are now in a position to discuss the meaning of price within the context of library service. Traditionally, consumers are quoted a money price for a specified quantity of a good or service. For example, when the price of a gallon of gasoline is quoted as $1.25 per gallon, the consumer sacrifices that amount and the seller provides a gallon of gasoline. Similarly, the library can set limits on the use of its goods and services. An administrator may charge a dollar amount for a specified level of service or may place time limits on the exchange. For instance, a library may allow an unlimited number of items to be borrowed for a specified period of time, such as one hour, one day, one week, or one month.

However, an alternative pricing strategy would be to set limits on the number of items that can be borrowed. Thus, a second method for pricing library services is to change the quantity of goods and services offered for use. A third method of pricing is to alter the quality of the service provided by the library. For example, reference services may be supplied by people with a variety of skill levels. Given a fixed quantity of service, when the skill level is raised, the price has decreased because the buyer actually receives more library service. When we decrease the skill level without changing the quantity, price has increased.

One may also affect the price by changing the time and place of the exchange of goods and services. Location and distribution decisions are often treated separately from price, but since they affect the cost of consuming library services we will treat them as a pricing strategy. Hence, a major pricing issue is how to distribute library facilities, staff, and materials over a given service region. Several location alternatives are possible: a large central library with smaller fixed sites, many fixed sites with no central location, and few fixed sites with bookmobiles. If the library chooses to have one central location, the distribution of materials may occur at the fixed sites and through bookmobiles, mail, phone, interactive video, and on-line catalogs that are available off-site. Depending upon the particular combination of location and distribution policy, the price of library services will vary. For example, if the library has one central location and only offers on-site exchanges, the library in effect transfers the delivery cost to the consumer. Thus, location and distribution affect the time expended by the consumer in bridging distance, as well as the time the patron has for using the service. These different methods of marketing recognize both the costs of selling and the preferences of consumers.

Price is the amount of time the consumer exchanges for the services offered by the library. The amount of time used in this process is affected by the nature of supply and demand. On the supply side, the library affects price through its marketing policies. Demand is affected by income, wages, preferences, and abilities. Finally, because price affects the quantity of use and the type of user, pricing decisions play an important role in marketing library services. To predict changes in use, we must be able to ascertain, from the consumers' perspective, the costs and benefits of alternative pricing practices. The theoretical concepts presented in the first part of the text will be used to analyze pricing and consumption choices.

Applications

Signs and Displays

Library use time is affected by the ability of consumers to locate library materials. Devices which increase the productivity of the user's time reduce the cost of library use. On the assumption that the wage rate has remained constant, an increase in the productivity of consumption time implies that the relative prices of time-intensive library services would fall, shifting consumption toward them. Microeconomic theory suggests that, regardless of whether or not a particular item or subject is being sought, any device which serves to assist the patron in locating preferred materials will lower time prices and increase use.

Libraries organize nonfiction materials by the Dewey or Library of Congress (LC) cataloging system. To assist patrons in locating items, the library could place Dewey or LC numbers/letters on the ends of shelves. Similar types of signs are often found in retail outlets; aisles are numbered and a central index is placed in one or more locations. Signage of this type assumes prior knowledge of the organization system or prior location of desired items in a catalog. As a result, all other types of users and uses incur higher time costs. These users will attempt to substitute away from using the signs and toward less time-intensive location devices: catalogs or staff. Hence, staff will be used more often for both catalog and location assistance.

An alternative signage technique would combine the number/letter combination with the appropriate subject. For example, signs might read 650.14–Résumé Books, or, in the case of open periodical stacks, title and class numbers for the range of serials in particular stacks. These signs serve to guide consumers to a set of materials which they find of interest. They also lower the price of the information search and increase the probability that consumers will find desired items. Given scarce space to place signs, signs of this sort should be created for subjects which are frequently requested.

Displays serve a similar purpose. They can be used to indicate new books, types of books, or recommended books. Books can be stored face out or spine out. As with signs which only indicate number-location, spine-out storage of materials only serves a purpose for those consumers who know in advance which item they are seeking. Since displays assist all other types of users in making choices, use or circulation should increase. Moreover, if we assume that the benefits of increased productivity of use time rise as we move down the education scale, externalities have been increased.

Reserve Systems

The reserve policy of the library affects the degree to which a person can be assured that he or she will eventually receive a particular item. Typically, reserves for library materials allow consumers to be assured that they will receive an item, but not when. In the case of popular items, this may cause "unnecessary" delays; once the delay exceeds an individual's original estimate of time price he or she will seek a substitute but may still remain in the queue. For certain types of materials, the library may have a reserve system which permits the consumer to indicate the day or time of day the consumer will be allowed to use an item. This type of booking system is commonly used for library equipment such as 16mm film projectors, microcomputers, and meeting rooms. In this instance, the level of uncertainty is reduced to zero.

A reserve system for library materials lowers the number of trips the consumer must make to the library to locate a desired item. Allowing reserves shifts a portion of the cost of wait time to the library. That is, the library must process the reserve, set up a system of "snagging" the item as it is returned, and notify the consumer that the item is available for use. Reserve policy, then, can be used as a form of library pricing.

A library may use reserves as a form of segmenting different versions of the same product. For example, reserves could be allowed for educational videos but not for entertainment-related videos. In a formal sense, this pricing technique takes into account the level of externalities. Further, this policy, through higher waiting time prices, may also serve a peak-load pricing objective. Items with low loan periods, such as those in reserve materials in undergraduate libraries and videos, will circulate more rapidly without reserves. The reason for this is that the time cost of processing reserves will usually be considerably longer than the loan period; as a result, total wait time increases.

A market disincentive objective suggests that the library would set up a fee-based reserve for materials in high use. In general, fees would limit reserves to those who value the use of an item regardless of the wait. Depending on the size of the fee, it might limit low-income users. On the other hand, a market incentive objective would permit unlimited "free" reserves on all types of materials.

Open Hours

Like all resources, time is scarce; and its value can be expressed in terms of forgone wages. To the extent that library use is related to production-investment and not consumption, the price of library use is less than the forgone wage. As wages increase, the price of goods relative to time decreases, resulting in the substitution of goods for time.[56] The higher relative value of time causes an increase in demand for goods which reduce forgone wages and wait, travel, and use time, such as calculators, microwave ovens, video-tape players, automatic tellers, prepared foods, 24-hour shopping, mail order, and food delivery services. Recognition of the value of time permits the library to implement pricing according to its service objectives.

Open hours, in terms of the cost of time, can have a significant affect on forgone wages. While it is true that the traditional workday for some people no longer follows the 9–5 Monday through Friday pattern, most people are working during the daytime hours. Therefore, those hours are costly in terms of forgone wages. Recognizing this fact, many retail establishments have added to, or altered, their operating hours: 24-hour supermarkets, automated tellers, and drive-up services.

Economic analysis suggests that a lower cost of library use will lead to an increase in the quantity demanded. To the extent that a change in library open hours accomplishes this objective, an increase in use will occur. Under our assumption that weekday daytime hours represent the highest value of time, the cost of library use will be greatest during these hours for persons who are currently employed, seeking employment, in school, or involved in household production. Low-cost alternatives to weekday daytime open hours include evening and weekend hours.[57] During these times, the opportunity cost of time in terms of forgone wages is lower.

Knowing that consumers have different time costs, we can go one step further and investigate the impact of changes in open hours on various consumer groups. Market segmentation, the division of consumers into groups with similar traits, permits us to analyze the impact of changes in economic variables on the process of choice.

The opportunity cost of library use time is highest for both the most and the least educated.[58] For high-income users, purchasing information services represents a less time-intensive alternative to library service. The implication for low-income or undereducated persons is that the yield (in terms of the present value of expected wages) per unit of effort in the library is relatively small. Also, the poor spend a greater amount of time on producing life-maintenance commodities; consequently less time-intensive entertainment alternatives appear to be less costly than library use. Hence, a change in open hours which lowers time costs should lead to increased use by these two groups.

For school-age children, time costs in terms of other alternatives are lower during evening and weekend hours. Parents are able to drive children to the library, achieving an economy of scale in both transportation and in family time. For one- parent families, weekend hours probably represent the lowest cost of time; thus, library consumption should increase for this consumer segment. Other options to lowering the cost of library use time include phone reference, phone renewals, and 24-hour access to on-line catalogs. Viewed as time-saving mechanisms, or factors affecting convenience, these service options lower the price and permit the user to consume or work more. In the case of normal goods, the net effect of a price reduction is an increase in consumption of that good.

Library Loan Period

A decision to change the length of a library's loan period involves examining the tradeoff between the period of time an individual may have the item against availability. A number of pioneering economic studies of libraries have shown that reducing the loan period increases the use of library materials.[59] Using economic analysis, we will show why, in general, a decrease in the loan period would increase use and an increase in the loan period would reduce use. Note that, as with any change in price, the end result depends upon the original price and the attributes of the item in question.

In terms of availability, a long loan period is convenient for one individual but is inconvenient for other individuals. The reason for this is quite simple: the longer an individual gets to keep an item, the longer all other patrons will have to wait for that item. In other words, what holds true for a part of a system does not necessarily hold true for the whole system. Knowing this rule—the fallacy of composition—should help alleviate some of the confusion surrounding prices expressed in terms of availability. If we increase the loan period and fewer persons use the library, availability, for those users willing to pay the higher price, may have increased. On the other hand, general availability has decreased. Of course, not all library items are equally desired, so that, for a given loan period, patrons will have to wait longer for items which are popular.

The reader will note that, for any given loan period, there is an inverse relationship between item popularity and item availability.[60] Demand analysis will help to show that this must be the case. Each item (title) or group of items (subject) will have its own demand curve. For any given number of copies, the more individuals who seek an item, given a fixed loan period, the higher its price will be, expressed as lower availability. Recall that the market demand curve was derived by adding the quantity demanded at each possible price for each consumer in the marketplace. Thus, if there are more consumers in the market for a particular item, the quantity demanded will be higher at each price. Hence, for any given number of copies and loan period, there is a direct relationship between an item's popularity and its price, however, there is an inverse relationship between an item's popularity and its availability.

Similar reasoning shows that, apart from the number of copies, loan period and availability for a given level of popularity are inversely related and that, for any given level of availability, popularity and loan period are also inversely related.[61] The important point to remember is that price and quantity are inversely related. The final result of efforts to reduce price on use (quantity demanded) depends upon the nature of the demand for an item and its supply.

Taking into account our previous discussions of the elements of library time price and elasticity, we will examine the question of how circulation policy affects quantity demanded. Loan period affects two elements of the price of library use: travel time and delay time. When the loan period is decreased, a library consumer will have to make more trips to the library, but, given limited renewals, delay time will be decreased. As we continually lower the loan period, the inconvenience of using the library (cost) begins to outweigh increased availability (benefits). Another aspect of the constraint on the consumer is his or her ability to process information. Generally, the less time a person has to use an item, the lower the value. Consequently, there comes a point where reducing the loan period interferes with use. An alternative to lowering the loan period is to increase the number of copies.

To summarize, the way in which loan period affects library use depends upon the relative value of time, the nature of the use of the materials being sought, the consumer's production function, and available substitutes.

In general, a longer loan period leads to a higher price and lower quantity demanded. Yet, the result of lowering the loan period is not as apparent. When we first change our circulation policy, current library consumers will be the first people to be aware of the change. Frequent users will be more aware of this change than infrequent users. As time passes, and availability increases, there will be an increase in quantity demanded by current users. In addition, the lower price will attract newcomers to the market. If all other variables are held constant, the full impact of a decrease in the loan period depends upon elasticity. The long-term result will exhibit a slightly lower level of availability than the period immediately preceding the reduction, but higher than the initial level of availability. However, quantity demanded will be higher in the long run than in both the original time period and the period just preceding the change in price.

Let us review the factors at work in our analysis of loan period. As the price of library services decreases, or as availability increases, the library user is able to increase the quantity consumed and, from consumer-preference theory, attain a higher level of utility. In general, lowering the loan period leads to a decrease in delay time. Delay time is measured in terms of the value of information to the user. However, travel time may have increased. Travel time, like queue time, is measured in terms of forgone wages. To the extent that information is for production, the value is somewhat less than the wage rate. For the individual, given a specific loan period, the net result depends upon the value of information and the value of time. As we move down the income and loan scale, a lower loan period leads to greater use. However, as it concerns level of education, the impact of a lower loan period on use depends more on the ability to process an item within the loan period. Quantity demanded for items of greater value—value being determined by the user and the situation—should increase faster than other types of information. The implication is that (given consideration of the rule of diminishing returns) loan period should be set in relation to demand.

Summary

The argument for public subsidization of libraries rests upon the notion that information is a public good, that education conveys substantial positive externalities, that access to cultural records has option value, and that literacy promotes equity. Within the context of public finance theory, we analyzed the degree to which libraries support these public-sector functions. By building and preserving a record of society, the library conveys considerable social benefit. However, because these services have public good properties, they will not be traded by competitive markets. Moreover, even those aspects of library service which primarily benefit the user generate spillovers to the community. We suggested that library production is subject to decreasing costs. To cover fixed costs, a firm would have to charge prices above the marginal cost of use.

On the other hand, we found that the library generates significant private benefits and it does not redistribute income from richer to poorer taxpayers. Although we can enforce fees and measure use, we are unable to measure the level of information provided or the relative magnitude of externalities. Thus, even though charging for some services might promote economic efficiency and equity, the cost of administering prices may outweigh the benefits.

With that in mind, we reviewed pricing guidelines: cost, demand, and competition; pricing by objective; and pricing by market structure. Finally, using the time price approach to analyzing price, we explored several approaches to lowering the price of information services. The objective is to diminish the transaction costs associated with information services, thereby increasing use and the level of positive externalities.

Exercises

1. Two consultants have completed a cost-benefit study of library services. One of the consultants estimated the benefit-cost ratio to be 2.0 and the other estimated it to be .85. Within the context of public goods, discuss the factors which make this disparity possible.
2. Use indifference curves to depict the loan period application.
3. List factors which affect the price of library services.
4. When fees are set according to cost, what is ignored? Describe what you expect to happen if each member of a network of libraries charged for interlibrary loans according to cost.
5. If a consumer's time is not a factor of production, which income group will benefit from a time price such as waiting in line for service?
6. In terms of use and availability, examine the impact of introducing fees for service in libraries.

268   Applications and Extension of Theory

7. How do portable (miniature) tape-playing machines affect the price of listening to tapes? Which elements of price have been affected?
8. How can a large urban library offset the inequality of service arising from inequalities of tax resources in surrounding localities?
9. Use microeconomics to analyze the following question: Have you seen any good (video) books lately?
10. What will be the effect on use of devices, such as fascimile transmission of information, which shorten the time between the request for materials and delivery?
11. In terms of price and quantity, describe the effect of telephone reference service. What elements of price have been changed?
12. How might the price of use differ between having many smaller libraries in convenient locations and having just one central large library?

References

1. Haynes C. Goddard, "An Economic Analysis of Library Benefits," *Library Quarterly* 41:3 (July 1971): 244–255; Richard Pfister and Jerome W. Milliman, *Economic Aspects of Library Service in Indiana,* Institute for Applied Urban Economics, Graduate School of Business, Indiana University (Indiana Library Studies, Report No. 7), (Bloomington: Indiana University Press, 1970); Lawrence J. White, *The Public Library in the 1980's: The Problems of Choice* (Lexington, Mass.: Lexington Books, 1983).

2. White, *The Public Library in the 1980's,* p. 131.

3. Mancur Olsen, "Information as a Public Good," in *Economics of Information Dissemination: A Symposium,* ed. Robert S. Taylor (Frontiers of Librarianship, No. 16) (Syracuse: School of Library Science, Syracuse University); Brenda Dervin et al., *The Development of Strategies for Dealing with the Information Needs of Urban Residents: Phase II—Information Practicioner Study,* vol. 1 (Seattle: School of Communication, University of Washington, 1977); Douglas Zweizig, "The Informing Function of Adult Services in Public Libraries," *Reference Quarterly* 18:3 (Spring 1979): 240–244; K. J. Arrow, "Economic Welfare and the Allocation of Resources for Invention," in *Economics of Information and Knowledge,* ed. D. M. Lamberton (Baltimore: Penguin, 1971), pp. 141–159.

4. Nancy DeWath, "Demand for Public Library Services: A Time Allocation Approach to User Fees" (Ph.D. dissertation, University of California, Berkeley, 1979); Michael D. Cooper, "Charging Users for Library Service," *Information Processing and Management* 14:6 (1978): 419–417; Cheryl A. Casper, "Subsidies for Library Services," in *Encyclopedia of Library and Information Science,* vol. 29, ed. Allen Kent, Harold Lancour, and Jay E. Daily (New York: Marcel Dekker, 1980), pp. 221–228.

5. Olsen, "Information as a Public Good."

6. DeWath, "Demand for Public Library Services," p. 62.

7. White, *The Public Library in the 1980's,* p. 129.

8. Richard A. Musgrave and Peggy B. Musgrave, *Public Finance in Theory and Practice,* 3rd ed. (New York: McGraw-Hill, 1980), p. 239.

9. Gallup Organization, *The Role of Libraries in America* (Princeton, N.J.: Gallup, 1975).

10. *Libraries at Large,* ed. Douglas M. Knight and E. Shepley Nourse (New York: Bowker, 1969), Chap. 2.

11. Joseph P. Newhouse and Arthur J. Alexander, *An Economic Analysis of Public Library Services* (Lexington, Mass.: Lexington Books, 1972), p. 58.

12. F. L. Mills, "Trends in Juvenile and Young Adult Use and Services," in *The Medium Size Library: Its Status and Future,* ed. Leon Carnovsky and Howard Winger (Chicago: University of Chicago Press, 1963).

13. Lowell A. Martin, *Library Response to Urban Change* (Chicago: American Library Association, 1969).

14. *Metropolitan Library Users: A Report of a Survey of Adult Library Use in the Maryland-Baltimore-Washington Metropolitan Area,* ed. Mary Lee Bundy (College Park: University of Maryland Press, 1968).

15. *Libraries at Large,* p. 78.

16. Goddard, "Economic Analysis of Library Benefits," p. 246.

17. Gallup Organization, *The Role of Libraries in America.*

18. Dick Netzer, *Economics of Property Tax* (Washington, D.C.: Brookings Institution, 1966).

19. Haynes C. Goddard, "A Study in the Theory and Measurement of Benefits and Costs in the Public Library (A Theoretical and Econometric Analysis with Special Reference to Indiana Public Libraries)" (Ph.D. dissertation, Indiana University, 1970).

20. Frank Levy, Arnold J. Meltsner, and Aaron Wildavsky, *Urban Outcomes: Schools, Street, and Libraries* (Berkeley: University of California Press, 1974).

21. Frederick Stirton Weaver and Serena Arpene Weaver, "For Public Libraries the Poor Pay More," *Library Journal* 104:3 (February 1, 1979): 352-355.

22. Henry J. Aaron, *Who Pays the Property Tax? A New View* (Washington, D.C.: Brookings Institution, 1975); Dick Netzer, "The Incidence of the Property Tax Revisited," *National Tax Journal* 26:4 (December 1973): 515-535.

23. Aaron, *Who Pays the Property Tax?*

24. Netzer, "The Incidence of the Property Tax Revisited."

25. Aaron, *Who Pays the Property Tax?;* DeWath, "Demand for Public Library Services."

26. Weaver and Weaver, "For Public Libraries the Poor Pay More," *Library Journal,* p. 355.

27. White, *The Public Library in the 1980's,* p. 63.

28. Malcolm Getz, *Public Libraries: An Economic View* (Baltimore: Johns Hopkins University Press, 1980), p. 101.

29. Ibid.

30. Fay M. Blake, "Let My People Know—Access to Information in a Postindustrial Society," *Wilson Library Journal* 52 (1978): 392-399; Fay M. Blake and Edith L. Perlmutter, "The Rush to User Fees: Alternative Proposals," *Library Journal* 102:17 (October 1, 1977): 2005-2008; R. Stoakley, "Comment: Why Should Users Pay Twice?" *Library Association Record* 79:4 (April 1977): 170, 185; "Presidential Timbre: The 79th Annual Conference of the California Library Association (Shank on Fees)," *Library Journal* 103:5 (March 1, 1978): 520-521.

31. White, *The Public Library in the 1980's;* Olsen, "Information as a Public Good"; Richard DeGennaro, "Pay Libraries and User Charges," *Library Journal* 100:4 (February 15, 1975): 363–367; R. M. Dougherty, "Editorial: User Fees," *Journal of Academic Librarianship* 3:6 (January 1978): 319.

32. J. F. Due and A. F. Friedlaender, *Government Finance: Economics of the Public Sector,* 6th ed. (Homewood, Ill.: Irwin, 1977).

33. Steven H. Hanke, "Demand for Water under Dynamic Conditions," *Water Resources Research* 6:5 (October 1979): 1253–1260; O. Firshein and R. K. Summit, "Online Search in the Public Library: Results of a Three Year Study," in *ASIS Proceedings, 40th Annual Meeting* (White Plains, N.Y.: Knowledge Industry Publication, 1979), pp. E10–F6 (Microfiche No. 3); Michael D. Cooper and Nancy A. DeWath, "The Effect of User Fees on the Cost of On-Line Searching in Libraries," *Journal of Library Automation* 10:4 (December 1977): 304–319.

34. Casper, "Subsidies for Library Services."

35. Cooper, "Charging Users for Library Service."

36. DeWath, "Demand for Public Library Services."

37. Ibid.; Olsen, "Information as a Public Good."

38. Blake, "Let My People Know."

39. Zoia Horn, "Charging for Computer-Based Reference Services: Some Issues on Intellectual Freedom," in *Charging for Computer-Based Reference Services* (Proceedings of a Program Organized by the Machine Assisted Reference Section [MARS] of the Reference and Adult Services Division at the American Library Association conference, Detroit, June 19, 1977), ed. Peter G. Watson (Chicago: American Library Association, 1978) p. 17.

40. DeWath, "Demand for Public Library Services."

41. A. Clayton and E. Bishop, "Potential Effects of Fee-for-Service and Automation upon Library Staff and Library Users," in *ASIS Proceedings, 40th Annual Meeting* (White Plains, N.Y.: Knowledge Industry Publications, 1977), pp. F5–F13 (Microfiche No. 2); Olsen, "Information as a Public Good"; P. G. Zurkowski, "Information Control and Marketplace Feasibility," in *Information Systems and Networks, 11th Annual Symposium* (March 27–29, 1974), ed. J. Sherrod (Westport, Conn.: Greenwood Press, 1975), pp. 195–200; Bruce P. Schauer, "Utility and Economics of Information: A Survey of the Public Library Industry," in *Encyclopedia of Library and Information Science,* vol. 32, ed. Allen Kent, Harold Lancour, and Jay E. Daily (New York: Marcel Dekker, 1981), pp. 319–341.

42. John Berry, "Double Taxation" (editorial), *Library Journal* 101:20 (November 15, 1976): p. 2321; Thomas J. Waldhardt and Trudi Bellardo, "User Fees in Publicly Funded Libraries," in *Advances in Librarianship,* vol. 9. ed. Michael H. Harris (New York: Academic Press, 1979), p. 48.

43. Blake, "Let My People Know"; Blake and Perlmutter, "The Rush to User Fees."

44. Haynes McMullen, "Historical Perspective of User Fees in Libraries," paper presented at the Reference and Adult Services Division, Machine-Assisted Reference Services Discussion Group Program: "Charging for Computer-Based Reference Services," American Library Association Annual Meeting, Detroit, June 17–23, 1977 (Cassette No. ALA 77/11); Nancy DeWath, "Summary of Survey Results" (Report of the California Library Association ad hoc Committee on Fee Charging), *California*

Library Association Newsletter 21:3 (March 1979): 5; Collin Clark, "Charge for Service, the California Practice," *News Notes of California Libraries* 72:2 (1977): 17–20; Mary Jo Lynch, "Confusion Twice Compounded: Report of a PLA Survey on Fees Currently Charged in Public Libraries," *Public Libraries* 17:3 (Fall 1978): 11–13; P. Atherton and R. W. Christian, "Financial Considerations," in *Librarians and Online Services* (White Plains, N.Y.: Knowledge Industry Publications, 1977), pp. 55–71; R. J. Penner, "The Practice of Charging Users for Information Services: A State of the Art Report," *Journal of the American Society for Information Science* 21 (1970): 67–74; J. Wanger, C. Cuadra, and M. Fishburn, *Impact of On-Line Retrieval Services: A Survey of Users, 1974-1975* (Santa Monica: System Development Corp., 1976).

45. Michael D. Cooper and Nancy A. DeWath, "The Effect of User Fees on the cost of On-Line Searching in Libraries," *Journal of Library Automation* 10:4 (December 1977): 304–319.

46. Ann E. Prentice, *Public Library Finance* (Chicago: American Library Association, 1977).

47. Marilyn K. Gell, "User Fees II: The Library Response," *Library Journal* 104:2 (January 15, 1979): 172.

48. DeWath, "Demand for Public Library Services."

49. Ibid.

50. Harriet W. Zais, "Economic Modeling: An Aid to the Pricing of Information Services," *Journal of American Society for Information Services* 28:2 (March 1977): 89–95; Rom Markin, *Marketing: Strategy and Management,* 2nd ed. (New York: Wiley, 1982), Chaps. 15 and 16.

51. John L. Crompton and Sharon Bonk, "Pricing Objective for Public Library Services," *Public Library Quarterly* 2:1 (Spring 1980): 5–21.

52. Zais, "Economic Modeling."

53. Helen Drinan, "Financial Management of On-line Services—A How-to Guide," *Online* 3 (October 1979): 14–21.

54. Zais, "Economic Modeling," *Journal of American Society for Information Science,* p. 92.

55. Musgrave and Musgrave, *Public Library Finance in Theory and Practice,* p. 744.

56. DeWath, "Demand for Public Library Services."

57. Frank Hennessy, "A Defense of Opening the Public Library on Sunday," *Library Journal* 110:8 (May 1, 1985): 25–26.

58. DeWath, "Demand for Public Library Services."

59. Newhouse and Alexander, *Economic Analysis of Public Library Services;* Michael K. Buckland, *Book Availability and the Library User* (New York: Pergamon, 1975), Chaps. 5–9; Michael Buckland and Anthony Hindle, "Loan Policies, Duplication and Availability," in *Planning Library Services: Proceedings of a Research Seminar,* ed. A. G. Mackenzie and I. M. Stuart (University of Lancaster Library Occasional Papers, No. 3), (Lancaster, England: University Library, 1969).

60. Buckland, *Book Availability and the Library User,* Chap. 5.

61. Ibid.

INDEX

Prepared by Answers Unlimited, Inc.

A priori probability, 207
Aaron, Henry J., 246
Addition rule, 158
Alexander, Arthur J., 227, 245
Alternative-use costs, 108–9
Average, 154
Average cost, 113–14
   decreasing, and library service production, 242–44
   and marginal cost, 115
Average cost curves, 113–14
Average cost function, long run, 121–23
Average cost pricing, 257
Average product curves, 88–90

B/C ratio, 216–18
Benefit curves, 126–30
Benefit maximization, 127–30
Benefits
   defined, 20
   of library service, 219–22
   See also Externalities
Breakeven analysis, 163–67
Breakeven point, 164
Budget lines
   and income changes, 26–27
   as objective constraints, 22–24
   and price changes, 24–25
Bundy, Mary Lee, 245

Capital, defined, 9
Cardinal utility method, 29
Caspar, Cheryl A., 249
Centrality, measures of, 154
Chance, 156
Chebychev's theorem, 168–70
Chen, Ching-chih, 178
Circulation and inventory correlation, inventory model for, 178–82
Circulation systems, and cost-benefit analysis, 225–29
Collection adequacy, inventory model for, 170–73
Compensation, potential for, 14
Competition, and equilibrium, 126–30
Competition-based pricing, 254, 259–60
Competitive model, 237–39
Complementary goods, 59–61
Composite-goods approach, to consumer equilibrium, 37
Conditional probability, 159
Confidence interval, 171
Consumer behavior and demand, theory of. *See* Consumption theory
Consumer budget-allocation model, 20
Consumer choice, theory of. *See* Consumption theory
Consumer demand curve, 58–59

273

274   Index

Consumer equilibrium, theory of
  and consumer preferences, 34–37
  and the income-consumption curve, 49–52
Consumer preference, 27–33
Consumer preference model
  applied to library materials, 37–39
  development of, 31–37
Consumer preference time model
  applied to learning and library use, 43–45
  development of, 39–43
Consumption theory, 7–9
Contractual costs, and the demand curve, 64
Cooper, Michael D., 249
Corner equilibrium, 36–37
Correlation analysis, 178
Cost
  average. *See* Average cost
  and consumption theory, 8
  defined, 20
  economic concept of, 108–10
  long run, of library production, 119–25
  marginal, 114–16
  monetary, 108–9
  measurements of, 8
  opportunity, 108–9
  and supply of library services, 108–10
  total, 10, 112–13
  total fixed, 110–11
  transaction, and the demand curve, 64
Cost analysis, 107–31
Cost-based pricing, 257–58
Cost-benefit analysis, 215–34
Cost curves
  average. *See* Average cost curves
  long run, 121
  shifts in the position of, 123–25
  short run, 121
  total, 110–11
  total product, 112–13
  total variable, 112–13
Cost modeling, 107–31
Criterion of least squares, 175
Cross elasticity, 70–71

Decision rule, formulation of, 172
Decision theory, 196–212
Decision tree analysis, 207–10
Decision trees, 201–4, 206–10

Delivery policy, and market price, 138–40
Demand, 134
  changes in, in equilibrium analysis, 140–45
  defined, 11, 48
  income elasticity of, 69
  individual, 48–76
  law of, 9, 48
  market, 11, 48–76
  price elasticity of, 65–68
  seasonal variations in, 144–45
  theory of, 5, 7
Demand-based pricing, 254, 257–59
Demand curve, 53–55
  consumer, 58–59
  market, 11, 61–62
  and the price-consumption curve, 59
  and supply of library services, 126–30
Demand function, and consumption theory, 9
Dependent variable, 173–74
DeWath, Nancy, 251
Diminishing marginal returns, law of, 90–92, 98–99
Diminishing marginal utility, law of, 29
Disequilibrium, 147–48
Disincentive pricing, 255–56
Dispersion, measures of, 154–55
Displays, as a time-priced library service, 262
Distribution-free statistics, 180–82
Distribution theory, 7
Dynamic theory, 4

Economic order quantity, inventory model for, 182–86
Economic theory, 4, 5–6
Economics
  defined, 6–7
  information, 196–212
  welfare, 13
  See also Macroeconomics; Microeconomics
Economies of scale, 99–103, 122
Efficiency
  economic. *See* Pareto optimality criterion
  and public finance theory, 237–47
Elasticity, 49. *See also* Cross elasticity; Income elasticity; Price elasticity

Engel curve, 51–52
Entrepreneurship, 9
EOQ. *See* Economic order quantity
Equilibrium, 134–36
  consumer, 34–37, 49–52
  corner, 36–37
  general, 7, 11–12
  library, and supply of library services, 125–30
Equilibrium analysis, 11–12, 134–48. *See also* Partial equilibrium analysis
Error level, acceptable, 172
EVPI. *See* Expected value of perfect information
EVSI. *See* Expected value of sample information
Expectations, and the demand curve, 63–65
Expected monetary value, 204–6
Expected opportunity loss, 206
Expected value of perfect information, 207–10
Expected value of sample information, 210–12
Experiment, 156
Explicit costs. *See* Monetary costs
External benefits, 238
External economies, and changes in demand, 143
Externalities
  defined, 238
  and library service, 240–42
  and public finance theory, 238–40

Facility expansion, decision theory and, 201–4
Fallacy of composition rule, 265
Fees
  and library services, 236–37
  and public library services, 247–52
Firm, theory of the, 9–10
  and library production, 79–104
Fixed costs, total, 110–11
Frequency distribution
  defined, 154
  and standard deviation, 168
Function, 8
Functions, library, and library production, 81–82
Future use prediction, inventory model for, 173–78

Gell, Marilyn K., 252
General equilibrium. *See* Equilibrium
Goddard, Haynes C., 245, 246

Horn, Zoia, 249
Hours of service, as a time-priced library service, 263–64
Hurwicz's rule, 198, 200
Hypothesis testing, 171–73

Implicit costs. *See* Alternative-use costs
Imput price change, and library production, 124–25
Incentive pricing, 254
Income, and the demand curve, 63–65
Income change
  and consumption decisions, 49–53
  effect of, on budget lines, 26–27
  and the time-allocation model, 43
Income-consumption curve, 49–50, 52–53
Income distribution, and public finance theory, 244–47
Income effect, 56–58
Income elasticity of demand, 69
Independent variable, 174
Indifference curves
  and consumer preferences, 29–31
  and the marginal rate of substitution, 31–34
Indifference maps, 30–31, 33–34
Inferior goods, 50
Information economics, 196–212
Information search technique, and equilibrium analysis, 145–47
Inputs, 9
Internal economies, 143
Inventory and circulation correlation, inventory model for, 178–82
Inventory control, and changes in supply, 136–38
Inventory models, 167–87
Investment activities, and consumption theory, 41
Isocost lines, 116–19
Isoquants
  basic properties of, 95
  defined, 85
  economies of scale, 99–101
  and library production, 85–86, 92–98, 116–19
  properties of, 85–86

276   Index

Joint probability, 158

Labor, 9
Land, 9
Learning curves, and budget lines, 43–45
Least squares, criterion of, 175
Leisure activities, and consumption theory, 41
Level of error, acceptable, 172
Level of significance, 171
Levy, Frank, 246
Library production, long run, and supply of library services
Library production model, 86–104
Library service benefits, 219–22
Library stamps, and subsidization of library service, 250
Library usage, and income distribution, 245
Loan period, as a time-priced library service, 265–66
Long run, 86

Macroeconomics, 4, 6
Marginal cost, 114–16
Marginal product curves, 88–90
Marginal rate of substitution
  and consumer preferences, 31–34
  and isoquants, 96–99
  and library production, 98–99
Marginal utility, 29
Market, multidimensional. *See* Multidimensional market
Market allocation, and public finance theory, 237–47
Market demand, 11, 62–65
Market demand curve, 11, 61–62
Market equity pricing, 255
Market penetration pricing, 254
Market price, and delivery policy, 138–40
Market supply curve, 11
Marketing, of library services, 237
Markets
  imperfections of, 238
  organization of, 11
Markov process, 177
Maximax, 198
Maximax decision criterion, 199–200

Maximin, 198
Maximin decision criterion, 198–99
Maximum participation pricing, 254
Maximum popularity, 154
McGrath, William E., 181
Mean, 154
Median, 154
Microeconomics, 3, 4, 6
Mills, F.L., 245
Minimax, 198
Minimax regret, 198
Minimax regret rule, 201, 206
Minimin, 198
Mode, 154
Models, 7, 14–15
  competitive, 237–39
  consumer budget allocation, 20
  consumer preference, 31–39
  cost, 107–31
  inventory, 167–87
  library production, 86–104
  queuing, 186–93
  time allocation, 70–74
Monetary costs, 108–9
Monopolies, natural, 242–43
Monte Carlo simulation methodology, 190
Morse, Philip M., 176, 177, 178
MRS. *See* Marginal rate of substitution
Multichannel queuing models, 189
Multidimensional market, consumer preferences in, 36–37
Multiperiod projects, cost-benefit analysis and, 218–19
Multiple copy decisions, inventory model for, 167–70
Multiple objectives/constraints, in cost-benefit analysis, 229–33

Natural monopolies, 242–43
Netzer, Dick, 246
Newhouse, Joseph P., 227, 245
Nonparametric statistics, 180–82
Normal goods, defined, 49–50
Normative analysis, 12

Objective probability, 155–56
One-tailed test of a hypothesis, 172–73
Open hours, as a time-priced library service, 263–64
Opportunity cost pricing, 257

Index 277

Opportunity costs, 108-9
Opportunity loss, expected, 206
Optimum output, short run, and cost of library production, 116
Ordinal utility method, 29
Outcomes, defined, 156

Pareto optimality criterion, 13-14
Partial cost-recovery pricing, 254
Partial equilibrium analysis, 7, 11-12
Payoff tables, use of, in decision theory, 197-98
Peak-load pricing, 259
Percentage surcharge pricing, 257
Population, and the demand curve, 63-65
Positive analysis, 12
Posterior probability, 208
Potential for compensation, 14
Preference
  consumer. *See* Consumer preference
  and the demand curve, 63-65
Present-value rule, 219
Price, as an economic factor, 4-5, 252-53
Price changes
  and budget lines, 24-25
  and library service choices, 53-58
  and the time-allocation model, 43
  and wages and library use, 72
Price-consumption curve, 54-55
  and the demand curve, 59
  and price elasticity, 66-67
Price determination, in equilibrium analysis, 135-36
Price discrimination, 258-59
Price elasticity, 65-69
Price of related goods, and the demand curve, 63-65
Price-ratio concept, 24
Price takers, 11
Price theory, 7
Pricing
  decision making in, 253-55
  guidelines for, 254-55
  of library services, 237, 251-52
  by market structure, 255-60
Pricing objectives, 255
Probability
  a priori, 207
  conditional, 159
  defined, 155-56
  joint, 158
  measurements of, 156-57
  objective, 155-56
  posterior, 208
  rules of, 157-61
  subjective, 155-56
  unconditional, 157-58
Probability theory, 155-61
  and decision making under uncertainty, 204-6
  and queuing models, 187-93
Product curves
  and library production, 88-90
  total, 88-90, 100-1
Production
  decision making in, 163-93
  household, and library economies, 141-43
  long run, and supply of library services, 116-25
  short run, 110-16, 164
  with multiple variable inputs, 92-98
Production costs, short run, and supply of library services, 110-16
Production functions
  defined, 84
  and library production, 83-98
  shifts in, 103-4
  and the theory of the firm, 10
Public finance theory, 236-67
Public good, 238

Quantitative methodology, 153-61
Quantity determination, in equilibrium analysis, 135-36
Queuing models, 186-93
Queuing theory, 186

Real income, defined, 56
Regression analysis, 173-78
Reserve systems, as a time-priced library service, 262-63
Resources, and consumption theory, 7-8
Revenue allocation, inventory model for, 170-86

Sample space, 156
Sampling, 156, 171-73
Scale, returns to
  determinants of, 101-3
  and library production, 99-101

278 Index

Scale of plant, 110, 120
Seasons, and the demand curve, 63–65
Security systems, and cost-benefit analysis, 222–25
Short run, 86
Signage, as a time-priced library service, 262
Significance level, 171
Simulation method queuing, 189–93
Site selection, and cost-benefit analysis, 229–33
Spearman's formula, 181–82
Standard deviation, 155, 167–68
States of nature, 197
Static theory, 4
Statistical analysis, 153–61
Storage, library, use of breakeven analysis in, 164–67
Subjective probability, 155–56
Subsidization
   and consumption, 52–53
   of library service, 236–67
   and voucher/stamp use, 250
Substitute goods, and individual demand, 59–61
Substitution effect, 55–58
Supply
   changes in, in equilibrium analysis, 136–40
   defined, 11, 134
   theory of, 5, 7
   and theory of the firm, 10
Supply curve
   market, 11
   and supply of library services, 130–31

Target rate-of-return pricing, 254
Taste shifts, and changes in demand, 140–41
Taxes
   and income distribution, 244–46
   real estate property, 245–46
   sales, 245
Technology
   defined, 10
   and the demand curve, 63–65
   and shifts in the production function, 103–4

Time
   as a budget constraint, 39–43
   as a medium of exchange, 21
   and inputs, 86
   value of, 39–40
Time-adjusted value, 219
Time-allocation model, 70–74
Time price, 71–74
Time-priced library services, 260–61
Total cost
   short run behavior of, 112–13
   and the theory of the firm, 10
Total cost curves, short run, 110–11
Total fixed costs, 110–11
Total product cost curves, 112–13
Total product curves
   and economies of scale, 100–1
   and library production, 88–90
Total utility, 29
Total variable cost, 110–11
Total variable cost curves, 112–13
Trade environment, defined, 21
Transaction costs, and the demand curve, 64
Transivity, rule of, 27, 31
Tree diagrams. *See* Decision trees

Uncertainty, 198–201, 204–6
Unconditional probability, 157–58
Utility
   and consumer preferences, 8, 28–29
   defined, 8, 28
   total, 29

Variable costs, total, 110–11
Variance, measures of, 154–55
Vouchers, and subsidization of library service, 250

Waiting-line models, 186–93
Waiting-line theory, 186
Wealth, 13
Weaver, Frederick Stirton, 246
Weaver, Serena Arpene, 246
Welfare, 13
Welfare criteria, 13
Welfare economics, 7
White, Lawrence J., 243, 246
Wilson, John H., Jr., 220

Zero net benefit, 130